ALMA
MAHLER
Muse to Genius

By Karen Monson
Alban Berg
Alma Mahler, Muse to Genius

ALMA MAHLER

Muse to Genius

KAREN MONSON

COLLINS
8 Grafton Street, London W1
1984

William Collins Sons & Co Ltd
London · Glasgow · Sydney · Auckland
Toronto · Johannesburg

First published in Great Britain 1984
© Karen Monson 1983

Monson, Karen
Alma Mahler: Muse to Genius
1. Mahler, Alma
I. Title
943.6'04'0924   DB98.M/

ISBN 0 00 216315 2

Books and articles quoted or cited in the text under the usual fair use allowances
are acknowledged in the notes and bibliography. I am grateful for permission to
use more extensive quotations from the following sources:

The Alma Mahler-Werfel Collection, University of Pennsylvania Library, cour-
tesy of Lady Isolde Radzinowicz, executrix.
Letters of Paul Kammerer, courtesy of Jessica Place.
Letters and poems of Oskar Kokoschka, courtesy of Olda Kokoschka.
Letters of Alexander von Zemlinsky, courtesy of Louise Zemlinsky.
My Life, by Oskar Kokoschka. Translated by David Britt. © 1974 by Thames
and Hudson, Ltd., London. Reprinted with permission of Macmillan Publishing

For Nora and David

Play to allure the gods.
— Jakob Emil Schindler
to the young Alma

❧

Jeder Mensch weiss Alles.

❧ ACKNOWLEDGMENTS ❧

MY GRATITUDE goes first to Anna Mahler and her husband, Albrecht Joseph, to Lady Isolde Radzinowicz, Lyman W. Riley, and the other kind and patient persons at the library of the University of Pennsylvania in Philadelphia. Thanks also to Robert Cornfield, my agent, and to Anita McClellan, my wise editor at Houghton Mifflin Company. Through this book, I met Kathe Berl, and I consider myself lucky to count her as a friend. Anna Marie Maier-Graefe, Luise Rainer, Anatole Fistoulari, Georg Solti, Leonard Bernstein, and Ernst Krenek were among the many individuals who were generous with their time and memories of Alma. In addition, for their cooperation and permission to quote from sources that are close and dear to them, I express deep appreciation to Louise Zemlinsky, Jessica Place, Hugh Iltis, and Olda Kokoschka.

The dedication is to Nora, who is not yet old enough to read, or even to know what a book is, but who will surely know soon. And to David, without whose support and encouragement the book certainly would not have been written.

•CONTENTS•

Illustrations *xii*
Preface *xv*

•ILLUSTRATIONS•

The photographs, unless otherwise credited, were provided through the courtesy of the University of Pennsylvania Library, Alma Mahler-Werfel Collection.

FOLLOWING PAGE 92

Anna, Alma, and Grete Schindler
The statue of Jacob Emil Schindler
Alma and Grete Schindler
Alma Schindler in her youth
Arnold Schoenberg (Used by permission of Belmont Music Publishers, Los Angeles, California)
Gustav Mahler
Alma around the time of her marriage to Gustav Mahler
Anna Schindler Moll
Carl Moll (Courtesy of Bild-Archiv der Österreichische Nationalbibliothek, Vienna)
Gustav and Maria Mahler
Alma Schindler Mahler
Alban Berg (Courtesy of the Portrait Collection, Austrian National Library)
Ossip Gabrilowitsch (The Bettmann Archive, Inc.)
Richard Strauss and family (The Bettmann Archive, Inc.)

FOLLOWING PAGE 188

Alma Mahler as drawn by Oskar Kokoschka (Private collection, Chicago; photograph by Michael J. Pado)

Paul Kammerer (Courtesy Hugh H. Iltis; photograph by Claudia Lipke)

Alma Mahler (Private collection)

Oskar Kokoschka (Courtesy of Bild-Archiv der Österreichische Nationalbibliothek, Vienna)

The young Anna Mahler (Courtesy of Bild-Archiv der Österreichische Nationalbibliothek, Vienna)

Die Windsbraut, Kokoschka, 1914 (Öffentliche Kunstsammlung, Kunstmuseum Basel)

Walter Gropius (The Bettmann Archive, Inc.)

Manon Gropius

Alma with Franz Werfel (Private collection)

Alban Berg and Franz Werfel

Alma in the countryside

Franz, Alma, and Manon in 1920

Johannes Hollnsteiner (Courtesy of Bild-Archiv der Österreichische Nationalbibliothek, Vienna)

Alma's mansion in Vienna

Following page 284

Alma and Franz Werfel (Private collection)

Bruno Walter (Courtesy of the New York Philharmonic; photograph by Fred Fehl)

Anna Schindler Moll

Thornton Wilder (The Bettmann Archive, Inc.)

Erich Maria Remarque (The Bettmann Archive, Inc.)

Franz Werfel in 1945

Anna Mahler (Courtesy of the *Los Angeles Times*)

Alma and Franz Werfel in California

Alma's New York apartment (Private collection)

Alma's New York apartment (Private collection)

Alma Mahler Werfel, about 1960

Alma and Anna Mahler, about 1960

A portrait of Alma by her friend Kathe Berl (Courtesy of the artist)

ON PAGE 324

Photograph by Manuel Rocca

⚜ PREFACE ⚜

"MY MOTHER ALMA was a legend, and legends are very hard to destroy."

This was Anna Mahler's warning to me as I began work on this biography. Gustav Mahler's daughter was right: Alma did become a legend, through her own efforts, the efforts of friends, and through some misguided attempts of people who would have discredited her and made her responsible for events that were not her doing, not even part of her life.

Far from wanting to destroy Alma's legend, my goal has been to give some insight into the life and the mind of a woman who lived one of the most remarkable lives of our century. In her eighty-five years, Alma lived through two world wars and changes in civilization of a magnitude that had not been seen before — perhaps we should hope they will not be seen again.

"The most beautiful girl in Vienna," she married Gustav Mahler, the composer and conductor who held the most powerful position in the world of music in 1902, when she was twenty-two. After Mahler's death she married Walter Gropius, and stayed his wife throughout the years when he was founding the Bauhaus and revolutionizing the world of design. When she was fifty, she married Franz Werfel, author of *The Song of Bernadette, The 40 Days of Musa Dagh, Jacobowsky & the Colonel,* and much more. Alma was united in love, sexually or not, with Alexander von Zemlinsky, her music teacher and the only mentor ever recognized by Arnold Schoenberg; with Ossip Gabrilowitsch, pianist and conductor; with Gerhart Hauptmann, the dramatist; and, most importantly, with the artist Oskar Kokoschka, who called her a "wild brat" on her seventieth birthday and wanted the love they shared to be immortalized for future generations.

The daughter of a celebrated Viennese landscape painter, Alma grew up privileged, with a taste for luxury but not always with the money to support her tastes. Over the years, she accumulated country houses, a dwelling of landmark stature on a Venetian canal, and a mansion in Vienna. She might have become an important composer; had she been born a century later, she could have been a conductor. As it was, she devoted her life to men whom she considered to be geniuses. She was a popular hostess, but salons were never the most important part of her life. A friend who loved her said that every young girl should have had the chance to take lessons from Alma in the art of soothing the male ego. She knew how to make friends, lovers, and husbands feel important, as if they were the only ones in her life, as if they had forever to court her to prove their commitment and their worth.

Women like Alma do not exist in the society of the 1980s. For that reason, it has been difficult for me to come to know and understand her, despite the amazing amount of material and a number of generously offered memories. Legend or no, Alma was not an angel; "Heaven was not her domain," her daughter says. Alma's fascism and her anti-Semitism are impossible either to overlook or explain. She married two Jews. She could live, she said, "neither with them nor without them."

Another cause of the difficulty has been the unreliability of the printed sources. Two of the books that appeared un-

der Alma's name — *Mein Leben* and *And the Bridge Is
Love* — are purportedly autobiographies. There is no doubt
that Alma did not write them herself, but there remains the
question of how much work she actually did on either, or
indeed how interested or aware of them she was in her late
years. Her earliest book of reminiscences, *Gustav Mahler,*
is, according to Anna, the best representation of her mother's attitudes. If one considers, however, that the volume was
supposedly compiled at a time when Alma and Franz Werfel
were moving into exile, one has to wonder how much Alma
had to do with what finally appeared in print.

The researcher has to make allowances for lapses in dates
and in minor details. Alma was an old lady when her so-
called autobiographies were published, and, age aside, no
one could have remembered perfectly situations that involved so many people, so many places, so many emotions.
Alma took much of her information from matchbooks and
coasters collected from the various inns and hotels where
she stopped on her numerous journeys. She burned the letters she wrote to her husbands and lovers; what remains in
the archives of the library at the University of Pennsylvania
in Philadelphia are their letters to her. All of these have been
transcribed on a typewriter. Alma never typed, so I have
laboriously spot-checked the transcriptions against originals
available in the collection. Though they seemed to be reliable, some have undoubtedly been edited.

I have made every effort to avoid information and situations obviously separated from what is or could have been
fact. I have avoided anecdotes seemingly recounted with the
faulty wisdom of hindsight. There have been times, however, when I have resorted to the most unscholarly criterion:
my own belief that there must have been some accuracy simply because Alma could not possibly have made up the story
or situation and got away with it. Her meeting and early

alliance with Walter Gropius is a case in point. Much as some of what the young architect is said to have done seems out of character with the distinguished and, indeed, regal man we have come to know through the decades, I could not imagine Alma's having manufactured the tale out of her imagination.

Unless otherwise noted, the translations are my own.

KAREN MONSON
Phoenix, Arizona

ALMA
MAHLER
Muse to Genius

1

Alma Maria Schindler

WHEN ALMA MARIA SCHINDLER was born, on August 31, 1879, her parents had no proper bed for her to sleep in. She was laid on their finest, softest linens in an open bureau drawer. After only a few days, Hans Makart, the artist who had previously shared a studio with the baby's father, brought her a wooden cradle with a down cushion and covers of pink satin. Alma kept the cradle with her for the rest of her life, using it finally to hold her favorite books and music.

Jakob Emil Schindler, Alma's father, was an artist and dreamer, the most celebrated Austrian landscape painter of the era, known for his detailed oils of the mountains and seascapes in the Hapsburg empire, gifted with an eye for recognizing views that would please wealthy nobility. He came from a Viennese family of industrialists in which every generation or two tended to produce an artist or a man of letters. His elders nurtured Emil's artistic interests at the expense of more practical issues, so the boy grew up encouraged to extend his imagination and his tastes for the finer things in life, caring nothing about finances or similar realities. When he began to study painting with Albert Zimmerman, he could not bring himself to hold on to pocket money long enough to have his shabby shoes resoled. In their studio, he and Makart gave parties attended only by the most beautiful and handsome young people in Vienna, and, now and then, by the composer and pianist Franz Liszt, who would play waltzes and dance music until dawn.[1]

Anna von Bergen went to Vienna from her native Hamburg to study music and drama in hope of being able to take part in that city's most lustrous operatic life. A triumph on a stage of Vienna would lead to a prosperous career not only in central and eastern Europe but across the Continent and into the Americas. Anna had a sweet soprano voice and a girlish charm that made her the delightful soubrette. Shortly after arriving in Vienna she found a role in an unpretentious presentation of a minor operetta. Her gaiety and prettiness caught the ever watchful eye of her leading man, Emil Schindler. With their marriage, Anna's musical aspirations and Emil's dalliances in the theater ended.

The match seemed to be a good one. For every extravagance or spree upon which Emil could embark, Anna would counter with wise and practical ideas. She ran their house with patient efficiency and good sense. Friends, relatives, students, and hangers-on visited more and more frequently as Emil's reputation as a landscape artist grew. The two most frequent visitors were Emil's white-haired patrician mother and Carl Moll, an aspiring artist with a facility for business who took a place as Emil's favored student and assistant. Both Carl and Grandmother Schindler enjoyed tending Alma. In turn the child grew especially fond of her paternal grandmother and thrived on the attention the older woman paid to her during the hours when Anna did the errands and chores that went along with running a household in which aspirations usually exceeded assets. The house, on the out-skirts of Vienna, was sparsely but comfortably furnished, more in the country style than in the typical velvet-and-fringe manner of Austrian cities.

By outward appearances Anna von Bergen Schindler was the most loyal and concerned of wives and mothers. When Alma was two, however, Anna bore a daughter who was not her husband's child, but, rather, that of a syphilitic fa-ther. Alma and her half sister Grete were close during their childhood, but they fell out of contact as young women. Grete married and had a son; only then did the severity of her mental impairment become evident. She was institution-alized indefinitely. Alma, suspecting the truth, challenged her mother to reveal the secret of Grete's father. Deemed "un-desirable" by the Nazi regime, Grete was put to death around 1940. Alma never concerned herself with her sibling's fate.

In 1881, the practical and disciplinary tasks of raising two little girls fell to Anna, but it was Emil who saw to it that fantasy and love surrounded Alma and Grete. While he ap-parently considered both daughters to be his own, it became increasingly evident that Alma was his favorite, his princess, even though he could never instill in her the adoration and appreciation of nature that had inspired him to paint works that in his lifetime were being called masterpieces.

As an adult Alma would always enjoy being in the coun-try with family and friends, but she could not love nature in its pure forms. Cities attracted her; the trials and responsi-bilities of rural life did not. Alma kept house pets — cats and dogs, particularly Irish setters — and she could appre-ciate a landscape's majesty, preferably from a well-trodden path or from the window of an automobile. Anything re-lated to vigorous exploration of the countryside or life in unimproved surroundings held no interest for her. She never tended a garden, and as an old woman she didn't even bother to pick up the citrus fruits or avocados that had fallen from the branches of the trees in her California yard.

As he extolled the virtues of the Viennese woods and meadows, Emil Schindler never denied his own tastes for luxury, tastes that made his wife's job of keeping the family within its budgets all the more difficult. Alma inherited his appreciation for beautiful and expensive objects, and he did his best to encourage her. Emil told stories about kings and princes in strange and wonderful places. He was a great teller of tales, and these were important parts of his daughters' education. To Alma's and Grete's delight, Emil and Anna had no belief in formal schooling, and had the children tutored at home.

Alma adored her father. In the early months of 1884, when Emil bought property that had once belonged to Prince Karl Liechtenstein in Plankenburg near Tulln (a town noted for its flower gardens), Alma felt like a princess in a castle bestowed upon her by a king. The area today is thought of as a suburb of Vienna, a simple one-hour trip from the center of the city. Before the turn of the century it was considered remote, out on the far side of the Vienna Woods. The house sat on a large parcel of land, had two stories and an onion turret, and must have looked magical to a five-year-old. Emil told his daughters about the ghost who was said to walk their woods by night, so Alma and Grete were afraid to be outdoors alone after dusk. But during the days the girls reveled in the freedom and the privacy of their new domain.

Their mother had been raised a Protestant; however, Alma and Grete were brought up in the Roman Catholic Church of their father. To the small altar that he found on his property, Emil affixed a statue of the Madonna, surrounded her with flowers, and honored the shrine with lighted candles. Alma was both attracted and repelled. She feared the aura of mystery that she seemed to feel there as the sun fell in the sky and the candles flickered. By daylight, like her father she was lured by the Madonna's serenity and beauty.

For Alma and Grete, the best time of the day was story hour with their father. When the girls were old enough to read, Emil told them the Faust legend and gave them a copy of Goethe's treatment of it. The book, he said, was very special, the most important legend of their heritage, a tale that would mean much to both of them throughout their lives. Anna could not imagine why her impressionable daughters should have to be exposed to such a complex and dreadful idea as the sale of a soul to the Devil, especially when the girls had to spend all their time in a lonely, isolated place. She took the book away and reprimanded her husband so strongly that Alma never forgot her parents' quarrel. At the time, the argument served best to pique the girls' curiosity. Securing another copy of Goethe's *Faust* became one of Alma's primary missions.

Alma was not quite ten in 1889 when the Crown Prince Rudolf expressed interest in the paintings that Emil Schindler might produce as results of a visit to the Adriatic coast. The family journeyed to the area between the Dalmatians and Spizza almost immediately, taking Carl Moll as assistant to both Emil and Anna. Moll was so much a member of the Schindler family that he could help tend the children and perform practical duties as well as artistic ones. As it turned out, Carl's assistance was especially necessary. In Corfu, bands of youngsters who resented foreigners taunted Alma and Grete whenever either ventured out of the house that the Schindlers had rented for a prolonged stay and rest. This first extensive trip away from home instilled in Alma a lifelong love of travel, but she was happiest when she could stay in the cottage playing the piano her parents had rented for the duration of their visit. During this time Alma began to realize how devoted to music she might become.

In the summer of 1892, the Schindlers' debts had been paid off to an extent at which it became possible for them to plan something that had previously been unthinkable: a pleasure trip. They went to the North Sea island of Sylt, again with Moll in attendance. They rented a modest house from which they could all go to the beach or take walks on mountain paths.

Schindler had not been well, but he managed to spend some time painting while Anna and Carl tended to the chores. On the ninth of August, Alma and Grete, twelve and ten respectively, announced to their elders that they were going into town for lunch. Permission was granted, since Anna wanted the girls to undertake the kind of outing impossible for them in their sequestered Austrian home. The young ladies sat at table feeling very mature when Carl burst into the restaurant. Obviously upset, he ordered Alma and Grete to come with him at once. Even before he told them, Alma reported later, she knew her father was dead.

Anna and Carl protected the children from the corpse by shutting them into a room near the one in which Emil had been laid before the trip back to Vienna. Alma would not be locked out; while her mother and their devoted family friend made funeral arrangements, she stealthily made her way into the chamber, where she knew she would find her father. He had always seemed so large and grand in her eyes. Suddenly he looked small and fragile. The same contradictions between life and death would strike her less than twenty years later, when her husband Gustav Mahler died.

In spite of her youth and the sheltered life she had led, Alma knew then, as she stared at her dead father, how important Emil Schindler had been and would always be to her. Her father was buried in Vienna. Shortly thereafter, a memorial statue was erected in his honor in the city park, not far from the statues of Schubert, Mozart, and Johann Strauss, pivotal figures of the city's great musical heritage. With its full beard and flowing cloak, the statue makes Schindler look both formidable and fanciful, like someone who might sit in judgment of his peers or tell stories to children and paint landscapes filled with fairies and elves and goblins. Throughout her life, Alma sent postcards of the statue to friends, often with a message saying how well the monument captured her father's nature.

After Emil's death, Alma paid more concentrated attention to music, working at the piano with a seriousness that transcended the childlike fascination of her earlier years. She ignored the operas and operettas her mother loved so and went to the works of her late father's favorite, Robert Schumann. She thought she played them for Emil. Unconcerned with the desires of her tutor, unburdened with strict assignments from any school, Alma could spend her free hours reading music and deciphering the basic principles of the art. She became an excellent sight-reader and honed her talent for improvisation. Only once was she persuaded to appear in a students' piano recital. She left with the promise that she would never do such a thing again, and was thereafter loath to play anything for anyone but herself.

Alma was allowed to study counterpoint with the blind organist Josef Labor, who introduced her to a great deal of the literature, as well as the operas of Richard Wagner, of which she was to remain almost irrationally fond. She played and sang through every Wagner opera, doing no good for what could have become a fine mezzo-soprano voice but gaining an intimate knowledge of the music and the sagas.

When she was about fifteen, Alma was sent to school. She had daydreamed, now and then, of how exciting it would be to attend class with other girls her own age, to wear attractive clothes, and be trained in the various tasks of life that would prepare her for marriage. The realities of the school were not like her dreams: her enrollment lasted only a matter of months.

Alma was convinced that she could do very well for herself at home on her own. The influence of her father's former student, Carl Moll, had come into full dominance, however. Alma resented the attention her mother was paying to the man who had formerly been only a helper, second to her father. During adolescence, Alma spent most of her time alone. Contemporaries recalled parties in Vienna. Whenever the princess Alma Schindler walked into the room, she was the center of attention, not only by virtue of her beauty, which seemed to grow with the years, but by virtue of the aura that seemed to surround her and with which she charmingly commanded respect. When Alma was reminded of these parties decades later, she would cringe, recalling how awkward and ugly she had felt, wearing dresses that Anna had sewn at home, not the store-bought gowns richer and luckier girls had been able to wear. No, no, there were many prettier and more desirable girls in Vienna than she.

Alma had become particularly aware of a disability that seemed to her insurmountable, and unfair. What had seemed to be a simple case of childhood measles had left her with diminished hearing. At first the affliction was hardly noticeable, but in adolescence it worsened to a point at which it affected almost every part of Alma's life. As is often the case, her aural sensitivity to music remained unaffected. She taught herself to compensate in social situations by paying rapt attention to the person who happened to be nearest to her — usually one of the male persuasion — making him feel as if he were the only other one in the world. The habit was flattering to those who received the attention, but it taxed Alma, who found herself doting on individuals who interested her not in the least. She felt awkward and avoided parties and gatherings where she might have risked revealing her handicap.

❧

Max Burckhard, the critic, author, scholar, and producer who was then director of Vienna's Burgtheater, was quite as eccentric as he was intelligent and talented. But, as a friend of Emil Schindler, he had the will and the empathy to realize that Alma needed a mentor in the aftermath of her father's death. Burckhard appeared at the Schindler house and presented himself as Alma's guide. He encouraged her to read and made her a devoted follower of Friedrich Nietzsche at a time when Alma barely fathomed the implications of that writer's words. Burckhard sent her tickets for plays at the Burgtheater and talked to her about the dramas and their performances, teaching her to distinguish between the works and their staged re-creations. He introduced her to the poetry of Richard Dehmel and Rainer Maria Rilke. One Christmas when Alma was about seventeen, two of Burckhard's servants arrived at the Schindlers' front door carrying laundry baskets full of books for Alma, most of them in fine classic editions.

Burckhard, then forty-two, was struck by the beauty of the young woman to whom his friendship meant so much, but there is nothing to indicate that there was any romantic link between the two. Alma innocently loved and appreciated the great and famous man of the theater, and always recalled how much she gained from the attention he had lavished upon her.

In 1897, Anna Schindler married Carl Moll. Her new stepfather was a familiar part of her life, but Alma still could not understand why her mother had taken Carl in her father's stead. Her response to Moll mixed love and resentment. He, for his part, reacted to Alma and Grete as if they were his own daughters, though there is much to suggest that Alma was his favorite until political circumstances estranged them decades later.

Anna and Carl Moll had a daughter, Maria, and the family packed and moved from the house Alma had thought of as her castle, into a dwelling at No. 6 Theresianumgasse, where they were closer to Vienna's centers of commerce and culture. More and more, Carl concentrated on making his living dealing in art rather than creating it. It was primarily in his capacity as a businessman that he was working in the parlor of his new house when Gustav Klimt entered Alma's life. The thirty-five-year-old artist was, with Moll, a founding member of the Secession, a group organized for the purpose of breaking with Vienna's tradition-bound Imperial Academy of the visual arts. The renegades took as their motto "To the Age Its Art, to Art Its Freedom," and elected Klimt their president. In 1899, with funds donated by the industrialist Karl Wittgenstein, father of the philosopher Ludwig, Josef Olbrich designed a palace-museum with a gold cupola of intertwining foliage (dubbed immediately "the gilded cabbage") on high-priced land in Vienna's central Karlsplatz, where the Secessionists showed their work. Ironically, the rebels were so popular that they quickly found themselves defining the mainstream, and in 1900 they were invited to be a part of the Paris International Exhibition. Even now, though, the City of Vienna treats the Secession Museum as a palace of the wayward, not listing its shows or activities on the calendars informing tourists of the area's pastimes and attractions.

Klimt had come into prominence and won the coveted Emperor's Prize in 1890 with his painting of the soon-to-be replaced Burgtheater, Burckhard's realm, showing its huge crystal chandelier and four horseshoe balconies. The commission to Klimt and his partner Franz Matsch had made clear that the painting should not show just the stage with actors on it. Klimt chose to paint the view from the performers' space, suspecting, correctly, that the theatergoers would vie to be included in his audience. Among those chosen to be portrayed were the surgeon Theodor Billroth, the city's future mayor Karl Lueger, and the actress who was also the Emperor's mistress, Katherina Schratt.[2]

To these and any number of other Viennese, it was important to be portrayed as part of the old era. They wanted to belong to the world in which the beautiful young Sisi won the heart of the beloved Emperor Franz Josef and became Empress Elizabeth, painted by Franz Xaver Winterhalter in a gold-embroidered dress made of layers and layers of the best, most fragile silk, and with diamond stars in her long brown hair. They wanted to see the men looking handsome in their expensive and well-tailored uniforms, stepping forward with polite smiles and bows to request the pleasure of the next waltz by Johann Strauss with a perfectly coiffured, lavishly jeweled young lady who was trained to swing gracefully across the highly polished dance floors of sparkling, candlelit ballrooms.

The standards of feminine beauty in Vienna were high and much discussed, second only to those of the women in nearby Budapest. The Hungarian women were elegant, the Viennese women sweet and poised. The Viennese women, moreover, could tell themselves that their city was the center of European culture, the envy of many Parisians and Londoners, and, in many ways, they were right.

But no one could ignore the signals of change, particularly the ones who had climbed up Vienna's many-runged social ladder in the times of those gold-embossed skirts, walls, and coaches. They were the ones who had lined up to be portrayed by Klimt as patrons of the Burgtheater. They were

also the ones who felt most strongly the emotion that still
pervades the city — an unrelenting hold on the old, even
when the new is not only unavoidable but firmly ensconced.
The old friendly nineteenth century would soon become the
unknown twentieth. On the new Ringstrasse, the boulevard
that gave a classically constructed circumference to the ancient middle city, this end-of-century fear met with some
more rational anxieties. The era of the Hapsburg regime
seemed to be coming to an end, and throughout Europe political unrest was becoming more the rule than the excep-
tion. As was inevitable in conservative, even reactionary Vienna, the intellectuals' instincts led them to radical stances.
Somewhat surprisingly, the artists were among the last to
break the historic molds, probably for the reason that this
heritage was the one of which the Viennese could be the
proudest, in which they could claim a tradition so rich that
in some areas it is still almost overwhelming. In music alone,
the city claims intimate associations with Mozart, Beethoven, Schubert, Brahms, Bruckner, families of Strausses,
and many others. The Opera, the concert hall known as the
Musikverein, and any number of other theaters and audito-
riums were crucial parts of Viennese life, and there was
hardly a person, rich or poor, who did not know what was
being presented on a given evening, its prospective worth,
and its social implications. Cultural gossip in Vienna was
quite as important and pervasive as political speculation, and
it was a mainstay even of the all-male café society. Every
man in Vienna had his favorite café, one where he was
known by name, and where his order and his newspaper
were brought without request. The neighborhood café was
not just an indulgence. During housing shortages, people
lived in these informal restaurants, waiting to hear of rooms
that might be available. For the affluent, cafés were places
to hear the pulse of the city.

When groups of young men talked about young women, Alma Schindler's name frequently was mentioned. She was not particularly beautiful by standards reflected in high-fashion drawings or photographs of the time. Her legs were shapely, but they were almost always hidden by long voluminous skirts. Her waist looked small only because it was cinched by a corset; in fact, her figure was sturdy. Her chin was imposing, but she never recognized that fact and complained when the same feature appeared on her daughter and granddaughter. She did have luxurious long brown hair. And Alma's best features were her eyes, radiant and blue, giving her an aura and poise that her companions found both riveting and challenging.

Alma had lessons in painting and drawing. She excelled especially in sculpture and even won some accolades for the small clay forms created in the classes she attended in the park known as the Prater. It was no surprise, given her heritage, that she had a deeper and more cultivated understanding of the visual arts than many of her contemporaries, or that she took the opportunity to learn from the many artists who gathered in the Moll home, even though she was ever more involved with music. In the early days of the Secession, Alma was intrigued by the plans and the lofty speeches meant to challenge the retrospective tastes of the Viennese art world, and she sat in on the meetings, trying to involve herself with the group's goals.

Klimt was enamored of Alma, so lovely and interested and articulate did she seem. Probably for the first time in her life, the young woman found herself sexually attracted to a man. The two kissed, which Anna Moll read all about when she looked into her daughter's diary. The concerned mother at once went about putting an end to future improprieties. Anna knew, as almost everyone in Vienna did, of Klimt's bohemian life and his bad reputation. He lived with a society dressmaker named Emilie Floege in a most nontraditional manner, without the benefits of matrimony. He wore flowing robes, and created scandals not only through his art and way of living but also through his very appearance. Worse, he seemed to enjoy being the object of gossip and ridicule. Like her mother, Alma would have known that Klimt was not the most dependable of suitors, but she was drawn to him both physically and artistically. Against her mother's strongest convictions, she did not discourage Klimt from following her and the family on a trip to Italy. Several times Alma managed to escape in order to be alone with her beau; on other occasions, the two flirted across the plazas of Venice. Although Alma made avowals of love and promised to leave everything and run away with Gustav, she made no serious commitment. When the artist continued his chase in Vienna, she distanced herself, and her passion cooled. Shortly thereafter Klimt perfected his best-known ornamental style of painting, in which the female subjects appear inaccessible, even abstracted. Alma, who came to own one of his early landscapes, did not like the decorative style, but the two remained friends until the artist's death.

In the fall of 1897, Alma had begun to study composition with Alexander von Zemlinsky, a musician whose works are now being rediscovered after years of neglect. Recognized as one of the foremost pedagogues of his era, Zemlinsky was the only mentor named by Arnold Schoenberg, the great and pivotal composer of the twentieth century, and he exerted direct influence on the music of Alban Berg, Anton von Webern, Ernst Krenek, Egon Wellesz, and a number of other members of the "new" generation of Viennese composers. Eight years older than Alma, Zemlinsky had received early encouragement from Johannes Brahms, whose work the young composer held in the highest esteem. With this imprimatur, Zemlinsky had the necessary credentials to join Viennese musical circles, where he was treated with great respect, despite his youth.

Alma was drawn both to Zemlinsky himself and to the people who surrounded him. Normally the teacher went to the Molls' house to give Alma her lessons, but occasionally she went to his studio, where she met her fellow students, among them the young Schoenberg, who was already the teacher's favorite. At first, Alma was put off by Arnold, so shabby and unpressed did he look. His music defied tradition strongly and, it was to turn out, imaginatively and intelligently. As their social circles closed and crossed over the next few years, Alma and Arnold built a friendship that would last for more than half a century.[3]

Alma's early lessons with Alex were based on the traditional aspects of the craft of musical composition, but they marked Alma's introduction to the innovative controversial group of Viennese who were to become known as the New Viennese School of composers — as opposed to the Old Viennese School of Haydn, Mozart, and Beethoven. The period of study and its intensity heightened Alma's dedication to music. She was less and less interested in Klimt and his colleagues, and she took her composition exercises very seriously. As one of the very few female members of Zemlinsky's class, she wanted to prove that her gender was not a liability. More than that, she appreciated the intellectual challenge, and began to realize that she could accomplish more than had been requested of her previously. Zemlinsky made her rework sonata movements and songs, and he warned her not to try to move ahead too quickly. He told her, quite sternly, which of her ideas seemed to be feasible, and which were too high-minded for her level. Alma's talent was significant; her energy was greater. In the last years of the nineteenth century, after her mother's marriage to Moll, Alma composed more than one hundred songs (most of which were destroyed in the world wars), several instrumental pieces, and the beginnings of an opera. At the time, Zemlinsky found opera to be beyond her capabilities, but she filled her days with music, playing it on the piano, writing it, studying it, and going out to hear it performed.

After the premiere of Zemlinsky's opera *Es war einmal* ("Once upon a Time") on January 22, 1900, at the Vienna Court Opera, Alma went out with some other members of her class to celebrate with their teacher. They wanted to drink a toast, but the company — mostly young, outspoken, and contentious — could not agree on an object to whom or to which they would all raise their glasses. Alma and Zemlinsky looked at each other, remembered the evening's remarkable performance, and said in unison, "To Gustav Mahler." The great maestro, the Director of the Vienna Court Opera, had been the conductor of the evening.

At this moment, Alma realized that she and Alex had more in common than their hours of lessons. To some, their liaison was strange, even inexplicable. She was privileged, imposing, and queenly (in spite of her height and weight, later recorded at five feet three inches and one hundred forty pounds), whereas Alex was attractive only by virtue of his mind and talent. Alma wondered whether he might not have been received more warmly by the populace had he been better looking. She once described him as "a hideous gnome. Short, chinless, toothless, always with the coffeehouse smell on him, unwashed."[4] He was hardly the kind of young man who might have been romantically associated with one of Vienna's finest young women.

Alma's description of an early encounter with Alex is romantic and melodramatic in the extreme: "He played *Tristan* [Richard Wagner's opera *Tristan und Isolde* in piano reduction] for me, I leaned on the piano, my knees buckled, we sank into each other's arms . . . I was too much of a coward to take the [pen]ultimate step. I believed in a virginal purity in need of preservation. It was not merely a trait of the period, it was a trait of mine. My old-fashioned upbringing and my mother's daily sermons had strapped me into a mental chastity belt. Zemlinsky and I embraced, that was all. I am still glad we did not go farther. That time was probably the happiest, most carefree of my life." [5]

Alma apparently did nothing to discourage Alex's love and devotion. Zemlinsky put her picture on the desk where he did his composition even before they began to discard the formal *Sie* for the familiar *du*. Their lives revolved around music; they spoke of the art and its practitioners, played four-hand piano music together, and reported to each other on concerts and operas one might have seen and the other missed. They rarely went to the same places and almost never were seen in public together. Alma was aware of the Viennese penchant for gossip and protective of her honor. Zemlinsky's early letters to her suggest that Alma acted aloof in his presence, as when he wrote, "My respect for you [the formal *Sie*] has become strong, and also so deep and so basic that, I must say, I can never expect it to change . . . I can no longer be as I was . . . Of course, you must be totally free. But believe me, I shall ever be grateful for those few happy hours that you have given me, and you will *never* hear from me anything that you don't want to hear." [6]

Not much later, when they were addressing each other with *du,* he wrote, "Nobody is like you! How can I thank you? . . . But promise me, love, that you will tell me when you want me no more. And that will happen—*must* happen . . . Do you know what I want the most? . . . I want you to write me a little song! Only for me! I will keep it with me´forever." [7]

Their passion grew for nearly two years, interrupted only by the Molls' summer excursions to St. Gilgen on the Wolfgangsee, the once quaint town near Salzburg where Wolf-gang Amadeus Mozart's mother was born. The letters Alex wrote to Alma during those summers when she was away are especially revealing of their relation. Sprinkled among loving notes filled with the pangs of loneliness and longing are carefully contrived communications using *Sie,* typical of those that might go from teacher to student. These were intended to be seen by Anna and Carl Moll, to remind them that the two young people were continuing their lessons and their work, and to tell them that the two musicians were on good terms with one another, all in the causes of art and pedagogy, of course.

Alex was hoping to be invited to visit the Molls in their summer home. In the formal letters he addressed musical matters both general and specific, reminding Alma that she must always have the essential direction of her music in her mind, and suggesting specific changes in her exercises that might help fill what he heard as the voids. These letters must have been written with the greatest care, for they give hardly a hint of anything more than a friendly working relation between teacher and student.

In the private letters, Alex berated himself for his physical unattractiveness. He felt unworthy of Alma's love, although he had concluded that he would not live without her. He knew he loved her more than she loved him, and he felt this might always be the case. But he would accept inequity if he were allowed to build a life with her. Alma had reservations, and he wrote, "Still, you believe that you have to be awakened by a Great Love. That is not at all true . . . But I must say to you: Nobody loves anyone more than I love you! That is the most important thing in my life." [8]

Numerous passionate letters followed, written not only when Alma and Alex were separated by many miles, but also when they were in the same city, within hours of their last meeting or their next one. Sometimes he lectured her, as when he wrote that she did not have the "sensibility, the unconditional devotion" necessary to apply herself to her work. He thought she would never have the discipline to become self-sufficient; she could not bring herself to put the money she might earn from one project into the completion of the next one, and would let herself spend any proceeds on baubles.

Alma had not thought seriously of having to get a job. Neither did she intend to devote herself, as her mother had done, to making and tending a house. Alma had thought of trying to be a conductor, although this was utterly unheard of for a woman at the time. Otherwise, she thought that she might be able to be a composer or a pianist. She never really pursued a career. Jealous of a rich doctor who was courting Alma one summer in St. Gilgen, Alex chided both her and Anna Moll for looking first to see whether or not a man was rich, then to see how good-looking he was, and then, finally, noticing what might be remarkable or outstanding about him. Alex knew he would have lost on the first two counts, "but I am a man and not a slave," he wrote.[9] Alma accused him of treating her like a plaything.

Alex wove a special motif just for Alma into one of his ballet scores. She, in turn, sent him the song that he had asked for, written especially for him. He would not be able to show this gift to any of his friends, lest their true feelings be revealed. The teacher told his beloved student that she had a flair for the dramatic in her music, but he continued to caution her not to take on too much, and to limit herself to projects for which she was prepared. Alma responded in similarly frank terms, telling him when he played some of his new music for her that she did not understand what she had heard. She used a tone of voice that told him that she understood perfectly, and did not like it.

Alma fretted and questioned Alex about whether he had had sexual relations with a woman with whom he had been associated in the months before they had met. He wondered why she would have to know such a thing, but he finally confessed yes, he had. "I want you so much! Your beautiful body: I'm mad to possess you!! But I know that what is, must be. You have probably never felt that desire." [10]

Alma taunted Alex: he loved music more than he loved her. She was merely being bitter, he responded. "I would be happy if you loved me more. You see, I don't believe in first loves. And perhaps because you do love me a bit, my music has come a little closer to you." [11] Several days later, Alma wrote to ask if he really loved her, or if he was just in love. He promised that he was both.

She could be most provoking. She nagged Alex to read the writings of Nietzsche, which she had learned under the tutelage of Burckhard. Finally, when Alex wrote that he was beginning to comply with her advice, he happened to spell the name incorrectly. Alma let him know at once that Nietzsche spelled his name with an *E*. With his characteristic good nature Alex responded, "I thank you for the interesting disclosures about Nietzsche's philosophy. Zemlinszsky [*sic*] uses the *sz!*" [12]

If Alma had purposely been trying to keep Alex unsure of himself, she was doing an excellent job. She told him that she would never marry. He wrote back that he wouldn't either. There had been some talk of announcing their engagement and planning a wedding. She developed what Alex called her "warm/cold" side. "I would be the mother of your children," she wrote to him, "but only if it were really sensible, and that it is not." [13] He offered her the option of switching from their loving relation back to a simpler friendship, but she said that such a thing was impossible for her. She wanted him to believe that she was in love with him, and that she might marry him, sooner or later. Nevertheless, she would not spend any significant periods of time alone with Alex, and he could conclude nothing other than that she did not trust him or want to be with him. He desperately wanted more from her. The tension mounted, and the end of their close friendship and the continuing music lessons came with startling speed.

2

The Most Beautiful Girl in Vienna

IN THE FALL OF 1901, when Alma was twenty-two, Carl
Moll moved his family into a house designed by Josef Hoffmann in the fashionable district of Vienna called the Hohe
Warte (the High Watch), with hills overlooking the center
of the city. The house was located on the spacious corner of
Wollergasse and Steinfeldgasse, and there, for a time, Alma
continued her lessons and her romance with Alex. She went
to the Opera and to concerts with friends, and lived the full
life that went along with her status in young Viennese society at the turn of the century.

From the new house, Alma frequently took walks around
the Ringstrasse, the recently built circular street where it was
fashionable to see and be seen. One afternoon, Alma ran
into Bertha and Emil Zuckerkandl, he an anatomist and she
a journalist, both friends of the Molls. Bertha's sister Sophie
was married to Paul Clemenceau, brother of the controversial Georges. The Clemenceaus were visiting from Paris,

where they had recently met Gustav Mahler. Bertha invited Alma to join them all for dinner that evening, when the Director of the Vienna Court Opera (now the Vienna State Opera) would be among the guests. Alma declined, as she had previously declined invitations that might have put her in the company of Gustav Mahler.

Her reasons were several. She felt, however irrationally, that such a meeting would be simple neither for him nor herself. She was convinced that she knew all she wanted to know about Mahler, and though she admired much of his work at the Opera, she cared nothing for what she knew of his personal life. Born in 1860, Gustav was the eldest surviving son of Bernhard Mahler, who had worked his way up from peddling with a horse and cart to owning a distillery in the Bohemian town of Kalischt, near Iglau. His childhood had been joyless, marked by the illness and death of several of his siblings, the exhaustion and sadness of his mother, and the driving sternness of his father, who read the prayer books of his Jewish faith and major works in French and German literature, then tried to impress the importance of somber diligence on his young son. Gustav never celebrated the freedom and irresponsibilities of youth.

Bernhard Mahler did everything in his power to promote his son as a piano virtuoso, and scorned the fact that the boy wanted to spend his time composing music of his own. Gustav's talent was such that he was acclaimed after his early piano recitals as a marvel, perhaps the successor to Liszt. Envisioning fame and fortune, Bernhard shipped Gustav to study in Prague, where he was boarded with a family named Gruenfeld. The change was more than the boy could tolerate, and in not many weeks he had fallen to the bottom rank of his class. In the Gruenfeld home, the eleven-year-old fell witness to an impassioned sexual encounter and concluded that the woman had been forced to undergo fearful pain and suffering. Gustav's imagination connected this with the plight of his own mother, and this impression influenced his sexual behavior throughout life.

Disappointed by what he saw as his son's failure, Bernhard brought the boy home and did not send him away again until he was enrolled simultaneously at the University and the Conservatory in Vienna. There the young man's studies proved successful and productive. In the summer of 1880, when he was twenty, Gustav embarked on a sequence of professional appointments that gave him impeccable credentials and ensured his future as a conductor. From the town of Hall he moved on to the theaters of Ljubljana, Olmuetz, Kassel, and some of the smaller opera houses of Vienna. In 1885, he joined the roster of the opera in Prague, where he began to present the music-dramas of Richard Wagner and soon succeeded Anton Seidl as the company's principal conductor. Between 1886 and 1888 he worked as an assistant to the great Arthur Nikisch in Leipzig. Thereafter, he was engaged as music director of the Royal Opera in Budapest, where he stayed for three seasons. In 1891, he began a six-year term in Hamburg, and the Vienna Court Opera was a logical next step. The musical authorities in the Austrian capital did not flinch at Mahler's youthfulness, or even at the rumors that the symphonies and songs he composed were very modern and difficult to listen to. Serious problems did arise, however, when Cosima Wagner, the widow of the composer, insisted that the directorship of the Vienna Opera not be given to a Jew. Mahler, who was already recognized as a great conductor of Wagner's works, bowed to her dictum and converted to Christianity. In 1897 he moved to Vienna and assumed what was then the most prestigious assignment in the music world.

Controversy inevitably surrounds a man in such a position. Alma heard Mahler conduct his own First Symphony on November 18, 1900, and agreed with those who found it too long and too far from accepted tradition. Alma also knew what people in Vienna were saying about the Director's reputation. He was sharing a small apartment with his sister Justine, "Justi," who was eight years his junior and who evidently had been enlisted as housekeeper and companion to make her brother behave. Mahler was said to have been intimate with a number of sopranos and mezzo-sopranos during his tenure in Hamburg, especially Anna von Mildenburg, whose friendship with the conductor was much publicized. He was also reported to be deeply in debt. He had not been in the best of health, and the gossip mills put him at death's door. It apparently did not bother the Viennese that they had branded Mahler as both a rake and a compulsive worker who ignored everything other than his music. Some said he was antisocial; it was well known that he shied away from strangers and should not be invited to gatherings in the company of people whom he did not already know. Alma did not doubt that, were she to accept an invitation to dine in Mahler's company, he would treat her rudely.

But when Bertha Zuckerkandl invited Alma a second time, the hostess could assure the young woman that, in addition to Mahler and the Clemenceaus, Burckhard and Klimt would also be joining them. Alma accepted, with qualms. Not accustomed to being on her own with people so much older than herself, she worried more than usual that her hearing impairment would make it hard for her to make polite conversation. Whether thoughtfully or impishly, Bertha seated Alma at the table between Burckhard and Klimt.

Since on the same day, November 7, 1901, Alex Zemlinsky had to conduct a concert with the violinist Jan Kubelik as soloist, Alma's absence from her home was not noticed by the man to whom she considered herself almost bethrothed. She dined with her two friends, while Mahler and Sophie Clemenceau carried on an amiable but relatively quiet talk on the opposite side of the table. Mahler repeatedly found himself distracted by the laughter and the congeniality of the trio sitting across from him. Feeling left out and wanting to have a share of the fun, he switched his attention and asked, in a voice that carried well beyond the table's width, whether he might possibly be allowed to join the revelry. Moments later, when another guest arrived from the Zemlinsky-Kubelik concert, Gustav and Alma agreed that they had no interest in performances of virtuosos who concentrated on technical feats; they did not want to hear about or discuss the evening's concert. Alma surely did not want to talk of Alex. She felt as if she were betraying him.

After dinner, when the company retired to the parlor, Gustav engaged Alma in conversation. What was beauty? Was Socrates beautiful? Alexander von Zemlinsky is beautiful, Alma answered, and went on to challenge her companion regarding Zemlinsky's recently completed ballet *Das goldene Herz,* the conception and development of which she had followed step by step. The score of the ballet had been submitted by its composer to the office of the Director of the Opera in Vienna, to no response. Gustav admitted that he had seen the score and found the plot of the ballet too absurd to deserve production. Alma replied that he could at least have responded to the composer's letter, even if his verdict on the music had to be negative. He knew she was correct and promised to write a letter the next day, whereupon Alma offered to explain the tale by Hugo von Hofmannsthal upon which the work was based. When Gustav accepted her offer, she countered with a challenge: she would explain *Das goldene Herz* only after he explained *Die Braut von Korea,* a ballet in the repertoire with an even more convoluted plot. Amused, Gustav invited Alma to show him some of the songs she had written. She accepted.

When the guests began to leave, Bertha and Sophie joined Alma and Gustav, who invited all three women to be his guests at the next morning's dress rehearsal of Jacques Offenbach's *The Tales of Hoffmann.* Gustav left on foot with Burckhard, while Alma arranged to take a taxi home. Later, unaware of Alma's liaison with Alex, Bertha remarked that she had spent a November evening entertaining Alma's past and present (Burckhard and Klimt) and her future (Mahler). When Alma left the Zuckerkandls' she felt unhappy and dissatisfied with herself, thinking she had talked too much and too loudly, and had given the company a bad impression. She feared Gustav would not like her, or, worse, would think her merely silly. "I must confess that I liked him enormously," she wrote in her diary. "To be sure, he's frightfully nervous. He bounded around the room like a wild beast. The man is pure oxygen; one gets burned when one comes close to him." [1]

Bertha and Sophie fetched Alma the next morning to go to the Opera, where Mahler was standing outside his office, waiting impatiently. He led them through the sumptuously appointed rooms and took Alma's coat but not the others'. The two older women carried on conversation with their host while Alma went off to the piano and let herself appear to be absorbed by the music that was lying there. After a few minutes of awkward talk, Gustav spoke to Alma: "Fräulein Schindler, how did you sleep?"

"Perfectly. Why not?"

"I didn't sleep the whole night." [2]

The rehearsal of *Hoffmann* suffered only one serious interruption, when the conductor sent the Giulietta, the renowned Mme. Gutheil-Schoeder, back to her dressing room to have the slits in the sides of her gown repaired in the name of what he considered to be simple decency. The next morning, a poem arrived at the Molls' house addressed to Alma but with no signature:

It happened overnight!
I never would have thought,
That counterpoint and the study of form
Would once again weigh on my heart.

But, in one night
They took power!
And all of the voices lead
Homophonically on a single track!

It happened overnight
— I was awake throughout—
So when there is a knock
My eyes fly instantly to the door!

I hear it: Word of honor!
It rings in my ears —
Like a cannon:
I look to the door—and wait! [3]

Alma thought she knew who had written the poem. She had given Gustav her word of honor that she would bring him some of her songs, and then he had confessed to her that he had been awake all night after they had met. When she showed the lyric to her mother, Anna was both baffled and worried. To be sure, it would have been unlikely for Alex to send such a present, but Anna felt it was impossible and stupid for her daughter to think that a man of Mahler's reputation would bother to write such a thing to a young and innocent girl.

Alma might have wondered whether she was the victim of a prank. Yet she did not doubt Gustav's concern for her. When he had left the Zuckerkandls' with Burckhard, he had asked a number of questions. Buckhard had put an end to the conversation by saying, "Those who are acquainted with Fraulein Schindler know what she is. Those who are not,

have no right to ask."⁴ Burckhard was feeling protective of
Alma, and a bit jealous.

On Thursday, November 11, Alma went to the Opera,
where Gustav was conducting, and found herself ever more
impressed by what this man accomplished in the theater. "It
was sacred to him," she wrote. "Perhaps *too* sacred."⁵ A
week later, she heard Gustav's friend and colleague from
Hamburg, Bruno Walter, conduct Gluck's *Orfeo ed Eurid-
ice*. Gustav was in the box permanently reserved for him
and his guests. Alma saw him at once; everyone knew where
the Director would be sitting when he was not on the Opera's podium. It took Mahler a bit longer to spot her, but
he stared and caught her glance. When Alma and her mother
left their seats for intermission, Gustav met them and invited
them into his office, where they would be able to escape the
throng that always gathered around him, and grew to almost unmanageable proportions when he happened to be
talking to a young woman.

In the office there began a rapport between Gustav and
Anna Moll that would remain strong, happy, and secure.
Mahler recognized in the older woman the same fortitude
and warmth that had characterized his grandmother and
might also have appeared in his mother, had she not borne
many children and become so worn early in life. Anna in
turn was able to understand Gustav's needs and his weaknesses, those parts of him generally overlooked or overshad-
owed by the power and the prestige attending him as a result of his professional rank. Gustav told Anna that walking
to the Hohe Warte was one of the things he most liked to
do, and she responded by inviting him to visit them. He
accepted without hesitation, picked up his oversized calendar, and suggested coming on Saturday. Alma had scheduled a counterpoint lesson for the same day, but she promised to change the time, and the appointment was duly noted.

Alma said little during the intermission conversation, but when walking out of the office she told Gustav she would like to conduct at the Opera. He said nothing would give him greater pleasure than to hand his baton over to her for an audition, perhaps even more. The spirits were high, and the three parted looking forward to their next meeting.

After *Orfeo*, Anna and Alma met Moll and Burckhard in a restaurant, where Anna was eager to recount her encounter with Director Mahler. The men, instead of being surprised or curious, were alarmed. Moll cited the musician's reputation as a *roué*. Burckhard, who had had some time to consider the situation, asked Alma what she would do if Gustav proposed marriage. Alma said that she would accept. Absolutely wrong, said her friend and mentor. It would never work. A girl with her beauty, heritage, and talent would be throwing her life away if she were to marry an old, degenerate, sickly Jew who was debt-ridden and wrote music that could not be listened to.

Preparations for a trip to Munich to conduct his Fourth Symphony made it impossible for Gustav to visit the Molls as planned. Alma, in those intervening days, was less concerned about Gustav than she was about Alex and the guilt she suffered at the prospect of betraying him. She wrote to her teacher to explain that her feelings about him and their future together were changing.

On Wednesday, November 27, a servant ran to Alma in great excitement, announcing the arrival on the Hohe Warte of Herr Director Gustav Mahler. Escorted to meet Alma in her music room, he immediately scrutinized the piles of books still lying on the floor, unshelved since the family's recent move. He saw the volumes of Burckhard's beloved Nietzsche and proposed that they be tossed into the fire. Alma said she would be glad to participate in the destruction but not until he convinced her of their worthlessness.

Embarrassed to find the young woman just over half his age being more rational and considerate than he, Mahler suggested a walk in the new snow. Putting on their coats they met Anna Moll, who warmly and insistently invited Mahler to stay for supper. There would be chicken paprika and Burckhard. Mahler admitted that neither prospect enchanted him, but he accepted the invitation.

The stroll had a new purpose: Gustav had to find a telephone where he could call his sister and tell her, for the first time in her life in Vienna, that he would not be home for dinner, the reason having nothing to do with pressing and unanticipated duties at the Opera. Alma remembered how, as they walked down the hill to Doebling, Gustav's shoes kept coming untied and how he repeatedly stopped to prop his foot on a wall or a stump, retie the laces, and walk on only to have them come untied a few steps later. When they finally reached a telephone, Gustav had no idea what his own number was and had to call the offices of the Opera for advice and assistance.

As the couple went back to the Molls' house Gustav nervously struck up the quick and awkward stride that had become his habit. Saying nothing for most of their climb, he finally burst forth with all that had been on his mind for three weeks. "It's not so simple to marry a person like me. I am free and must be free. I cannot be bound, or tied to one spot. My job at the Opera is simply from one day to the next." 6 Alma's mind flashed back to Burckhard's prediction that Mahler would propose marriage to her, but these were certainly not the words she might have anticipated, and she did not know what to say. The references to his needing freedom were quite reminiscent of what she had said to Zemlinsky, but she never would have expected such remarks from Mahler. They had spent only a few hours together, and she did not even know what to call him. Alma waited for a few minutes, silent, then responded by saying that she came from a family of artists, had herself been trained in the arts, and understood what he was saying. It would not be easy for anyone to be Mahler's wife. Alma did not agree to assume that role. Indeed, Gustav had not formally proposed to her.

Back at the Molls' large house, the couple went back upstairs to Alma's music room, where Gustav seemed happy and relaxed, kissed her, and began to discuss their wedding plans. Again Alma was at a loss for words, but she began to realize that she would marry this man, troublesome as their time together might be. Later, at dinner, they said nothing of their private conversations. The evening with Burckhard, Anna, Carl, and a young man who was also infatuated with Alma turned out to be exceedingly pleasant. Gustav was his most patient, articulate, and charming self. Anna was enchanted with her daughter's new friend, and even Carl had to reconsider some of his earlier objections as Gustav conversed easily and brilliantly at the table.

Alma's mind was reeling. She could not be fickle, could not bring herself to betray Alex; she was, if anything, too honest. The next morning all of Gustav's early songs arrived in a package addressed to her. She opened them only moments before Alex arrived for her composition lesson. The two agreed that the songs were unsatisfying, lacked continuity. Alex knew nothing of the recent events in Alma's life, but he had had Alma's letter warning him that something was amiss between them, so that morning he summoned all his goodwill and considerable musical acumen. Later Alma wrote to thank Gustav for the songs, addressing him as "Dear Herr Director" and saying that she looked forward to their next meeting; she asked him please to read what Maeterlinck had written about silence, and, saying that she shook his hand most warmly, signed off "with kind regards, Alma Maria Schindler."

In Alma's mind, many questions were as yet unasked and unanswered. Mahler visited the Hohe Warte again a few days later, and seemed to be most warm and fond. He told her he loved her, and they kissed before he played some of his own music on her piano.

When he returned to the question of marriage, Alma asked for more time to think. She did not mention Alex by name, but she told Gustav there was someone else who meant a great deal to her. Gustav accepted her need for time and even acknowledged his inconsiderateness in not having told her earlier that she should wait as long as she wanted before committing herself to him. Now, he said, he was still able to accept rejection; soon, it would be much harder, too late. Alma tried to think. She knew Alex appreciated the music she had written and seemed to respect it on its own terms but she was concerned that Gustav had shown only mild curiosity about her work on the first night of meeting, and had not seemed especially interested since then. What if Gustav were to dismiss her songs as worthless? What if the tide were to turn, and Alex would suddenly receive the recognition she felt he deserved, while Gustav would meet a decline in his status? Worst of all, what if she were to lose them both?

Gustav sent Alma tickets to a performance of *Hoffmann* at the Opera with a note informing her that he would leave for Berlin on the next Monday, and would like very much to see her again before his departure. He wanted Alma to answer immediately, but she did not. She still wanted to take the time granted her to make a decision. On the next morning, in another note, he made reference to "our favourites: Evchen — and Hans Sachs!"[7] characters from Wagner's *Die Meistersinger* with whom Gustav liked to compare Alma and himself — the older man in love with the lovely and much-desired young woman. The reference moved Alma greatly, reminding her that they shared a love for Wagner and his works, and also that Gustav was already recognized as the outstanding Wagner interpreter of the era. She also knew, however, that in the opera Sachs gives Eva over to Walther, a young handsome man who proved himself a Master Singer. Would Gustav reject her or hand her over to another?

Shortly before he was to leave, Gustav admitted to himself that there was no use waiting for Alma to issue him an invitation to visit her, so he walked to the Molls' house unannounced. Alma was glad to see him. They kissed and talked, and he told her he knew that his rival was Alex Zemlinsky. In the presence of this magnetic man Alma felt that her decision had already been made. She wanted Gustav. He left her with a promise to write from Berlin, and said he would conduct Mozart's *Die Zauberfloete* the next afternoon — Sunday — at the Opera especially for her, "during which we shall be together and united in the deepest sense of the word."[8] For this occasion he sent her his official pass to the box belonging to him as Director — the first time the pass was not to be at Justine's disposal. He also sent a score of his cantata *Das klagende Lied,* and either because it was a very youthful work or because her view of his music was beginning to soften, Alma immediately liked it. She no longer pretended to be confused or undecided, and wrote to him at greater length. He wanted to know everything about her and begged her to be both more curious and more responsive.

As he was on his way to Berlin, Gustav sent Alma a box of toffees and a letter asking her to write to him regularly, at the Palast Hotel. "For a moment your letter would make a strange room home, which now is only where you are . . . Write to me too about [*Zauberfloete*]. I can well understand how a work of that kind might not go down with you. You're still too much *yourself!* I was just the same for a long time with works you describe as 'naïve.' "[9]

Alma had arranged to meet Gustav's sister a few days hence. "How dearly I wish you two to get to know each other," Mahler wrote Alma. "Perhaps you will recognize in her many characteristics of mine — and at once feel more at home with them . . . she knows all and loves you already. We went straight home alone after dinner last night [after *Zauberfloete*] and talked till late about you and our future. She understands all about it and will be a true friend to us." [10] Just before his first rehearsal, he wondered in a letter to Alma, "What will it be like when you share everything with me and I with you, and when this vehement and consuming longing, which is mixed with such dread and anxiety, is assuaged, and when even in separation we know everything about each other, and can love each other and be inter-penetrated without a care?" [11] Two days later, "I find now (particularly since my thoughts have been bound up in you) that I am getting quite vulgarly ambitious in a way that is almost unworthy of a person like me! I should like now to have success, recognition, and all those other really quite meaningless things people talk of. I want to do you honour. I have always had ambition, but I have not coveted the honours my contemporaries can confer . . . In this, you must stand by me, my beloved." [12]

Alma met Justi Mahler at the Zuckerkandls', and she did see some of Gustav's traits in his sister. The two women planned to talk again at the Mahlers' apartment on the following Saturday. Gustav was relieved to hear that the pair had got on so well. He petitioned his sister's help, saying, "I beg of you really and truly to love Alma . . . Yet she's still so young and my courage continually fails me when I think of the difference in our ages. If you can, keep calm and consider, or at least help me to consider. It's no small matter, and the desire must not engender the thought." [13] He even asked Justi to join him on the second leg of his current tour, when he would go to Dresden to conduct his Second Symphony, so that brother and sister could freely and privately discuss their plans. Gustav was finding Alma's letters to him ever more reassuring as concerned her essential goodness and her honesty, but he still worried "whether a man who has reached the threshold of old age had the right to tie his extreme maturity to such youth and freshness, to chain spring to autumn, precluding summer? I know that I have much to give, but one cannot buy youth at any price. If Beethoven, Wagner and Goethe came to life again today, her young heart would kneel down before them and worship them. Flowers can only grow and bloom in the spring." [14]

When Alma went to visit Justi in the apartment on the Auenbruggergasse, she feared that Gustav's sister would turn against her, or discover what Alma thought of as her own heartlessness and incapacity to love Gustav as he deserved to be loved. At the end of the afternoon, Alma went home feeling she had been meanly scrutinized. Likely it was this paranoia that inspired her to write to Gustav, telling him about a young musician who had visited her and threatened to kill himself if she did not accept his love. Some of the sting of this message might have been lost, since Gustav responded with a justifiable complaint about Alma's quite illegible large and scrawling purple-penned handwriting. As he pleaded with her to write more slowly and carefully, he marveled that the postmen could decipher the names and addresses for delivery.

Friendship between Justine and Alma did not flower as Gustav had hoped, but for at least one important reason the sister never stood in the way of her brother's decision to marry. Justine was in love with the violinist Arnold Rosé, the concertmaster of the Vienna Philharmonic (and thus of the orchestra of the Opera). She had long denied herself marriage and a family out of what she felt to be her obligation to Gustav. At the age of thirty-three, Justi had begun to think she would never be able to have a home and life of her own, that she would be doomed to the fate of tending a brother who seemed quite unable to function without her. She dearly loved Gustav and the prestige attendant on being his hostess and companion, but his single-minded concentration on his work left her with long hours of loneliness. His lack of concern for the running of the household made her feel used and relegated to menial tasks. Furthermore, the rumors about the Mahlers' being in debt were true. Although his salary at the Opera should have left them plenty of funds, Gustav was unable to keep track of the money he spent and Justi could not manage the accounts.

Already, Alma's presence in his life seemed to have made Gustav more lighthearted and confident. He wrote to her on December 15:

> I have always dreamed and hoped, but never known till now, that you were my source of warmth and light. I should otherwise have given up dreaming that the happiness of being loved as I love could ever be mine. Every time a woman has crossed my path, I have been tortured afresh by having to recognize the gap between dreams of happiness and the sorry truth . . .
>
> I can never be free of the dread that this lovely dream may dissolve, and can hardly wait for the moment when your own mouth and breath will breathe into me the certainty and inmost consciousness that my life has reached port after storm . . .
>
> I want to pass the dessert over to you every time it is put in front of me, knowing your love of sweets and fruit . . . [Justi] is positively in love with you — I am not that any longer: there is no name that I know for what you have become to me, for that unique and deeply blissful oneness . . .
>
> Oh God, I am talking away today from sheer suspense and

longing for you, like Walther von Stolzing, and never give a
thought to the other half, to poor Hans Sachs, who yet de-
serves your love far more.[15]

Gustav could not believe that Alma would be his, just as
he could not forget the difference in their ages. But where,
at first, he had cast himself as the aging loser, Sachs, and
Alma as Eva, he was now thinking of himself as Walther,
the winner.

> What you have given me, my Alma! You have confessed to
> me so sweetly what you want to be to me. When I think of
> what I must and shall be to you, it puts me in a solemn
> mood . . .
> Never believe that you could be less dear to me, less be-
> loved, if you wished to speak differently. In the same way, I
> shall never weary of finding out and speaking your language,
> if you cannot follow me in mine . . .
> What I find so eternally lovable about you is that you are
> so genuine, so straightforward. Empty phrases are the last
> thing I'd expect of you! . . . We must share everything. The
> difficulty I find at present is not knowing where to begin.
> Everything is still unknown to you. You have no scale for
> measuring the worth or worthlessness things have for my life
> or for yours! (Oh, how delightful it is to think every single
> thing has its meaning for both of us, or neither.) . . .
> Carl [Moll] will be here soon. I have given him a rendez-
> vous here, and hope he stays on for the concert, so that a
> ray at least of my beloved sun will fall on me.[16]

Alma had gone from signing her letters to Gustav "Alma
Maria Schindler" to "Alma," then "Your Alma."

Gustav wrote, "When on Saturday I hold your beloved
hand in mine, I shall know that you give it to me for ever.
This too, like everything else between us, has come quite
suddenly." [17] He wanted a picture of her, and found himself

wishing that he had stolen one that she had shown him when they had last been together. In lieu of that, he instructed her to have a photograph taken, full face, so that she would appear to be looking straight at him.

As his travel drew to an end, Gustav wanted to be sure that Anna Moll knew about the place he would soon take in her family. "I must meet her from the first moment as her son . . . As you know, I did at first mean to speak to her myself — but that was before I, and still more you, had seen the whole truth. My idea was to consult her as the person who knew you best. But now that our minds are irrevocably made up, there is nothing I could say to her except: 'Give me what is mine — let me live and breathe,' for your love is as much a condition of my life as my pulse or heart." [18]

Alma made her break with Alex and was impressed by his poise under very awkward circumstances. To be sure, she had been gentle when she told Zemlinsky the bad news. It was certainly not that she had come to hate him, or even to love him less, but she had been won by another. The blow was made somewhat less devastating when Alex learned that the other man was Mahler, whom he idolized. Alma had come to look upon Alex very differently, however, and their meeting ended with her thinking how ugly and unkempt he was. She wrote to Gustav and duly reported having bid Alex farewell. She also told him about Burckhard's early prediction that a marriage between the two of them could never work. Further, she continued to include in her letters details of social occasions on which she had engaged in spirited flirtations with handsome young men. In Dresden, Gustav was anxious. He wanted Alma to know the music he was conducting there, his Second Symphony, which she had heard only in piano reduction. "And it is so important you should know it — for my Fourth will mean nothing to you. — It [the Fourth] again is all humour — 'naïve,' as you would say;

just what you can so far understand least in me — and what
in any case only the fewest of the few will ever understand
. . . But you, my Alma, you will be guided by love and it
will light your way into the most secret places. My love and
my longing, my hope and faith — a thousand thousand times
yours." [19]

Gustav sent that letter, then, after much thought, he wrote
another, harsher one. It was almost as if he wanted to push
Alma away, to give her cause to reject him. The letter and
its implied threats would affect their lives for years to come.

> It's with a somewhat heavy heart that I'm writing to you
> today, my beloved Alma, for I know I must hurt you and yet
> I can't do otherwise . . . Your conversation with Burck-
> hard — what do you mean by "personality"? Do you con-
> sider yourself a personality? You remember I once told you
> that every human being has something indefinably personal
> that cannot be attributed to either heredity or environment.
> It's this that somehow makes a person peculiarly what he or
> she is, and, in this sense, every human being is an individual.
> But what you and Burckhard mean is something quite differ-
> ent. A human being can only acquire the sort of personality
> you mean after a long experience of struggle and suffering
> and thanks to an inherent and powerfully developed dispo-
> sition. Such a personality is very rare. Besides, you couldn't
> possibly already be the sort of person who's found a rational
> ground for her existence within herself and who, in all cir-
> cumstances, maintains and develops her own individual and
> immutable nature and preserves it from all that's alien and
> negative, for everything in you is as yet unformed, unspoken
> and undeveloped. Although you're an adorable, infinitely
> adorable and enchanting young girl with an upright soul and
> a richly talented, frank and already self-assured person, you
> are still not a personality. That which you are to me, Alma,
> that which you could perhaps be or become — the dearest
> and most sublime object of my life, the loyal and courageous
> companion who understands and promotes me, my strong-

hold invulnerable to enemies from both within and without, my peace, my heaven in which I can constantly immerse myself, find myself again and rebuild myself — is so unutterably exalted and beautiful, so much and so great, in a word, my wife. But even this will not make you a personality in the sense in which the word is applied to those supreme beings who not only shape their own existence but also that of humanity and who alone deserve to be called personalities . . . Not one of the Burckhards, Zemlinskys, etc., is a *personality*. Each one of them has his own peculiarity — such as an eccentric address, illegible handwriting, etc. — which, because inwardly lacking self-confidence, he defends, by constantly remaining on his guard against his "nourishment" for fear of becoming unoriginal. A true personality . . . is like a robust organism that, with unconscious sureness, seeks out and digests the nourishment appropriate to it and vigorously rejects that which is unsuitable . . .

My Alma, look! Your entire youth, and therefore your entire life, have been constantly threatened, escorted, directed (while you always thought you were independent) and abused by these highly confused companions who spend their time groping around in the dark and on false trails, drowning out their inner beings with loud shouting and continually mistaking the shell for the nut. They've constantly flattered you, not because you enriched their lives with your own, but because you exchanged big-sounding words with them (genuine opposition makes them uncomfortable, for they only like the grandiloquent words . . .), because you all intoxicated each other with verbosity (you think yourselves "enlightened," but you merely drew your curtains so that you could worship your beloved gas light as though it were the sun) and because you're beautiful and attractive to men who, without realizing it, instinctively pay homage to charm. Just imagine if you were ugly, my Alma. You've become (and however harsh I should sound you'll nevertheless forgive me because of my real and already eternally inexhaustible love for you) vain about that which these people think they see in you and wish to see in you . . . but which, thank God

. . . is only the superficial part of you. Since these people also flatter each other all the time and instinctively oppose a superior being because he disconcerts them and makes demands on them that they cannot live up to, they find you, on account of your charms, an exceptionally attractive and, due to your lack of pertinent argument, a most *comfortable* opponent. Thus all of you have spent your time running around in circles and presuming to settle the affairs of humanity between you . . . And even you, my Almschi, are not completely without the *arrogance* that invariably inhabits people who regard their own insignificant and exceedingly limited thought processes as the sole task of intellectuals. Some of your remarks . . . such as that "we don't *agree* on several things, ideas, etc." prove it, as do many others! My little Alma, we must agree in *our love* and in our hearts! But in our ideas? My Alma! What are your ideas? . . . So here am I, poor fellow, who couldn't sleep at night for joy at having found her, her who, *from the start,* was intimately at one with him in everything, who, as a woman, belonged wholly to him and had become an integral part of him; who had even written to him that she felt she could do nothing better than embrace and enter into his world; who, through her faith in him, no longer searches but has become convinced that his creed is hers, because she loves him, etc., etc.

Again I wonder what this obsession is that has fixed itself in that little head I love so indescribably dearly, that you must be and remain yourself — and what will become of this obsession when once our passion is sated (and that will be very soon) and we have to begin, not merely residing, but living together and loving one another in companionship? This brings me to the point that is the real heart and core of all my anxieties, fears and misgivings, the real reason why every detail that points to it has acquired such significance: you write *"you* and *my music"* — *Forgive me, but this has to be discussed too!* In this matter, my Alma, it's absolutely imperative that we understand one another clearly at *once,* before we see each other again! Unfortunately, I have to begin with you and am, indeed, in the strange position of having, in a sense, to set my music against yours, of having to put it into the proper perspective and defend it against you, who don't really know it and in any case don't yet understand it . . . Believe me, this is the first time in my life that I'm talking about it to someone who doesn't have the right approach to it. Would it be possible for you, from now on, to regard *my* music as *yours?* I prefer not to discuss "your" music in detail just now . . . In general, however — how do you picture the married life of a husband and wife who are both composers? Have you any idea how ridiculous and, in time, how degrading for both of us such a peculiarly competitive relationship would inevitably become? What will happen if, just when you're "in the mood," you're obliged to attend to the house or to something I might happen to need, since, as you wrote, you ought to relieve me of the menial details of life? Don't misunderstand me and start imagining that I hold the bourgeois view of the relationship between husband and wife, which regards the latter as a sort of plaything for her husband and, at the same time, as his housekeeper . . . But one thing is certain and that is that you must become "what I need" if we are to be happy together, i.e., my wife, not my colleague. Would it mean the destruction of your life and would you feel you were having to forego an indispensable highlight of your existence if you were to give up *your* music in order to possess and also to be mine instead?

This point *must* be settled between us before we can even contemplate a union for life . . . You write, "I feel that I now have nothing better to do than to submerge myself in you, I play your songs, read your letters, etc." I understood and imbibed in this like a promise of eternal bliss. But the fact that, precisely during this period (which I've called our true *"Hoch-Zeit"* [meaning "marriage"; literally, "hightime"], your conscience should be bothering you because you're not working on theory or counterpoint is incomprehensible to me! . . .

Do you understand what I mean, Alma? I'm quite aware

that you must be happy with me in order to be able to make me happy, but the roles in this play, which could as easily turn out to be a comedy as a tragedy . . . must be correctly assigned. The role of "composer," the "worker's" world, falls to me — yours is that of the loving companion and understanding partner! Are you satisfied with it? I'm asking a great deal, a very great deal — and I can and may do so because I know what I have to give and will give in exchange . . .

How were you able to "make conversation" with my sister whose heart was wide open to you and who was only too anxious to give you the whole of it? Could you really spend a whole afternoon with her without talking lovingly of me and about me? Almschi, Almschi — it's all quite incomprehensible to me! What sort of conversations are these that can still come between us — what third party is still imminent?! What is this defiance, this pride? Toward me who trustingly gave my whole heart and, from the first moment, dedicated my whole life to you — (though I also know certain pretty, rich, cultivated, young, etc., girls and women). I beg you, Almschi, read my letter carefully. There must never be any question of a passing flirtation between us. Before we talk to each other again, things must be absolutely clear . . . You must renounce (as you wrote) all *superficiality,* all *convention,* all vanity and delusion . . . You must give yourself to me *unconditionally,* shape your future life, in every detail, entirely in accordance with my needs and desire nothing in return save my *love* . . .

And, Alma, I must have your answer to this letter before I come to see you on Saturday . . . Almschi, beloved, be strict with yourself — and (sweet and beautiful though I otherwise find it) don't be swayed by your love for me . . . Tell me everything you have to tell me quite ruthlessly and bear in mind that to part now would be infinitely preferable to a continued self-deception, for, as I know myself, that would end in disaster for both of us.[20]

her fanciful ideas of becoming a professional pianist or conductor, but she was convinced that in time she would compose works of great beauty. It did not occur to Alma that
she had been admitted to the company of the men whom
she thought of as her friends just because she was beautiful.
Her quick tongue and eager mind had worked to convince
both herself and her companions that she had something
substantial to offer. Much of the time, her ideas had been
quite as relevant and perceptive as those of her older, famous friends.

Alma's worst fear resurfaced: she would lose both Gustav
and Alex. As she made her way through Gustav's letter, she
knew that she was deeply in love with him, completely devoted to him. She wanted to tend and care for him. Gustav's
status, or daydreams of a life filled with luxury, did not
overwhelm her. Now, though, he seemed to be asking her
to give up her work, her self. In its stead, all he was offering
was something alien to her — his music.

Beyond this, wouldn't Gustav have denied what he called
"personality" to all women? Alma knew she was no vapid
untried teenager; she was a mature, self-reliant young
woman. Although she had always lived with her family and
felt that she would leave the Molls' home only when she
married, she had long been independent in mind and spirit.
Perhaps what she said was not as profound as she wanted it
to be, or had been led to believe, but at least her talk did
not center around gowns, beaux, and hairdressers. Hadn't
she allured Gustav with her conversation at their first meeting?

She would admit that she was young and still had much
to learn about the world, about her beloved music. Perhaps
she was vain, too, but surely not as much and not in the
same ways as the other girls whom she saw at parties. At
least she had worked at her lessons, devoted herself to her

3

Alma Schindler Mahler

WHAT MUST ALMA HAVE FELT as she read this long and extraordinary letter? That night she said in her diary it would be an eternal thorn in her side.

She knew the difference in their ages was causing Gustav great concern. The span between his forty-one years and her twenty-two seemed much greater at the turn of the century than it does today. Beyond that, Alma had to acknowledge her circle of friends and acquaintances as not what might have been considered normal for someone her age. Beautiful, privileged, and smart, she had come to accept the presence of men like Burckhard, Klimt, and Zemlinsky, as well as a number of less illustrious and opinionated people, as a matter of course. Her contemporaries might only have imagined how glamorous it would have been to be able to greet even one of these important figures of the culture.

Alma did believe, or she had let herself come to believe, that her musical talent was significant. She had dismissed art: she had made something of herself. Alex thought so, Burckhard thought so, but Gustav apparently did not.

Alma showed Gustav's long letter to her mother. Anna, much as she had come to love the man, advised her daughter to dismiss him. Alma's stepfather agreed, but by then it was too late. Alma had decided to answer Gustav at once, on the schedule he had proposed, agreeing to his stipulations.

Before he received her response, Gustav wrote again, just after he returned to Vienna. None of his strong words were taken back, but he said, ". . . you do understand, I know, how hard and implacably truthful I am where love is concerned. — And everything must be clear between us before we hold each other in our arms — for this afternoon I could never have enough control over myself to discuss with you what all the same must be decided between us." [1]

On the afternoon of December 21, 1901, Gustav visited Alma as soon as he finished his business at the Opera, and all was decided. He brought her the score of his Fourth Symphony and they played it together on the piano. He formally asked Anna Moll for permission to marry Alma. On December 23, Gustav and Justi Mahler were invited to the Molls' to celebrate the engagement — very quietly, since Gustav was reluctant to face friends and the press with explanations of his new status before he and Alma were accustomed to the idea. He sent his fiancée greetings on the eve of the last Christmas they would not spend together as man and wife, and on Christmas Day Alma visited the Mahlers in their apartment. Gustav rearranged his schedule to enable him to be able to visit the Hohe Warte almost daily, often staying until well after the trams and buses stopped running, so he had to make the long walk home in the cold and dark. Alma and Justi talked about wedding arrangements; Justi and Arnold Rosé would marry quickly after Alma and Gustav did.

On December 27, probably through the indiscretion of an unknown person, the Viennese newspapers announced that Director Gustav Mahler would soon wed Alma Schindler. The story was fabulous material during the otherwise fallow holiday season, and it was made much of. Alma received a barrage of flowers, gifts, notes, and good wishes. She enjoyed all of it, but Gustav was annoyed, resenting the distraction and interruptions in his daily routine. From that time on, whenever Alma attended the Opera, eyes and opera glasses were trained on her quite as much as on the stage. Lacking the peace they had wanted, the couple decided to marry in mid-February, 1902.

❧

Tension between them began at once. They barely knew one another, had never had the opportunity to relax together, and had not talked about the life they would build. Gustav went on with his work at the Opera, his composing (which, during the winter months, was limited primarily to retouching and orchestrating the music written during his summers in the country), and with his many concert appearances in other cities. Alma felt pressed and anxious about planning her wedding in barely six weeks. She was kept busy by friends who came to call with presents and bouquets, seeking explanations. Alma spent as much time alone with Gustav as possible, but he had become so anxious at the prospect of marriage and intimacy that he was often distraught. Alma believed he was not sexually sophisticated; the women who had previously figured in his life announced otherwise, though. Alma was more than likely a virgin. The two talked with fear of the moment when they would lie together.

Justi and Arnold would marry either on the same day or the next, so Alma could move into Justi's old room in the Mahler apartment. There was no thought of Gustav and Alma's sharing the same bedroom. Throughout their life together they had the luxury of space to give them both the privacy they wanted — a traditional pattern in their era. They shared a room only when traveling and finding themselves with no choice.

It was necessary for Alma to be presented to Gustav's circle of friends, so Justi had a dinner party on January 5, 1902. The guest list is not a matter of record. However, Gustav's friends in those days included Natalie Bauer-Lechner, the musicologist Guido Adler, the scientist Albert Spiegler and his wife Nina (Nanna), the poet and dramatist Siegfried Lipiner and his wife Clementine (Spiegler's sister), the archaeologist Fritz Loehr and his wife Uda, the artist Henriette Mankiewicz, and the conductor Bruno Walter. Of these, Alma became friendly only with Walter, a friendship lasting until Alma's death.

Those disapproving of Alma's engagement to Gustav called her a flirt, an opportunist, a girl unworthy of association with such a great man. Though Gustav's reputation was not unblemished, he had his title and the accompanying prestige to act as buffer. Maybe he had not always treated women as well as he should have, but, it was being said, he had totally lost his reason to Alma's beauty, youth, and greed. A man of such talent and import should not tie himself to a skirted tease. Alma knew what was being said behind her back. When she arrived at the Mahlers' for supper that evening, she had worked herself into a state of believing everyone there was against her, even the hostess and the host. As had been the case on the night she and Gustav had met and she had enchanted him with her openness and forthrightness, she felt intimidated and reacted strangely. This time, in Gustav's apartment, she answered what she felt were hostile questions and remarks virtually not at all, seeming tart and arrogant. When someone asked her what she thought of Gustav's music, her reply was that she did not know much of it but what she did know she did not care for.

The gathering was shocked. Only Gustav — trying either to dispel the blanket of tension or to let Alma know that he understood her feelings — laughed, then led his future bride into another room, where they embraced and sat calmly for a few minutes. With that, Gustav gave his guests more fodder for gossip. Alma began to imagine there was a conspiracy against her, and in some small way she was correct. Gustav himself had to wonder what he was getting into by marrying Alma, what kind of life he might be able to provide for this young woman. To make things worse, Anna von Mildenburg went around claiming to anyone who would listen that she had been led to believe in Hamburg that Gustav would marry *her*.

On January 5, only a few hours before the ill-fated dinner, Alma had written in her diary, "Now he's continually talking about preserving his art, but I can't do that. With Zemlinsky, it would have been possible, because I shared his feelings for his art — he's a genius. But Gustav is so poor, so frightfully poor. If only he knew how poor he is, he would hide his face in shame. And I'll always have to lie . . . to lie constantly, throughout my life — with him, that's just possible, but with Justi, that female! I have the feeling she's checking on me the whole time — but I must be free, absolutely free!"[2]

Alma could not lie any more than she could pretend to preserve her honor. She was committed to Gustav. She loved him and, more to the point, she knew how much he loved her. They went to bed together. In February, Alma suspected that she was pregnant, but nevertheless she and Gustav postponed their wedding until March 9, 1902.

❧

They were married in the morning, before crowds of curious people had time to gather around the ancient Karlskirche. Gustav walked to the church wearing galoshes against the rain, and Alma, Justi, and Anna Moll rode together in a car. Carl Moll and Arnold Rosé, who would become Gustav's brother-in-law the next day, were the witnesses. Spirits were not high at the small breakfast after the ceremony. Alma and Gustav began to prepare at once to depart for St. Petersburg, where he was to conduct three symphony concerts on the trip they called a honeymoon.

Mr. and Mrs. Mahler began married life with terrible head colds, but Gustav went ahead with his concerts. With his cousin Frank as their guide they toured the snow-covered city in an open troika. The couple heard Tchaikovsky's opera *Eugen Onegin* and they accepted a few of the numerous invitations to social gatherings. At these, French was the common language. Alma was uncomfortable; she spoke little, and, hearing the strange words pronounced with Russian accents, she understood less.

After three weeks, the Mahlers returned to Vienna to begin their life together in his old apartment, now increased from the original three rooms to six, including servants' quarters. Alma's first duty was to learn her husband's strict schedule, which hardly ever varied: he rose at seven (whereas she liked to sleep late); had his breakfast; worked on his own music; went to the Opera at nine; lunched at one; relaxed briefly; went for a long walk; took tea at five, and returned to the Opera, where he stayed well into the evening, even when he was not conducting. He came home for a late supper, spent some time reading, talking, or playing four-hand piano with Alma, then went to sleep. He could tolerate no break in the routine, even though he had made allowances during the months of their courtship.

Now that Alma was his wife, it was up to her to see that there was not a moment lost, never an interruption. Gustav's attendant telephoned from the Opera when the Director was ready to leave his office for lunch. As Gustav rang the bell on the street level of the building where they lived, his soup was brought to the table to be waiting for him by the time he had climbed to the fourth floor. Alma was expected to be at the Opera to meet him at the end of his day's work. When Gustav was conducting, she was in the Director's box throughout the performance. On the nights when they could go home before the final curtain fell, she would ask him to explain what was to happen in the acts they were missing. He would give a quick synopsis of the ofttimes convoluted plot and reassure his wife that she was not missing a thing. Later, when Alma happened to witness one or another of these operas through to its conclusion, she almost always went away agreeing with Gustav. The first act or two had been quite enough.

Equally important as the routine of the Mahler household were the finances, and these too fell to Alma. In spite of her complete inexperience in this area, she displayed a natural talent for keeping records and controlling the budget. She was appalled to find out how bad their financial situation actually was. Gustav had sent money to his brothers and sisters with such regularity and generosity that he, the one who was earning a princely sum, had virtually nothing left for himself. Beyond that, he still owed his three living sisters their formal shares of the family inheritance and had yet to begin to pay for the building of his summer house in Maiernigg. Gustav seemed to have no conception of money, and it took Alma five years to put the family ledgers into a reasonably respectable shape. This was a challenge she quite enjoyed, except on the days when it was necessary to tell her husband he would have to do without something because they simply could not afford it. Her father, too, had lived beyond his means, but for Gustav the new regimen came as a rude awakening, one he did not always accept graciously.

With all these details of daily life to master, Alma was busy during the first months of her married life in Vienna. Soon she found that she had time on her hands — too much time. The changes taking place in her pregnant body were mysterious, and often unpleasant. As soon as he had fit himself back into his regular routine at the Opera, Gustav had seemed to approach her differently. Alma thought she might have sensed some change even when they became formally engaged, but it became more and more evident to her that spring in Vienna. Gustav no longer seemed to be the same man who had courted her, charmed her, flattered her, and told her so often he did not want to live without her. He acted more and more like a teacher, determined to make her into his own version of what a wife should be. Alma could not say she had not been warned, but as she sat alone in their apartment she thought how pleasant it would be to work on her music, even to begin her regular lessons again. However, she did no such thing, having promised that there would be only one composer in the household. Gustav was evidently not going to express any further interest in seeing her songs.

Additionally, he was not eager to meet her friends, except for those whom they happened to encounter on their frequent visits to the Molls' home, where Gustav always seemed comfortable and relaxed. When the Mahlers entertained in their own quarters, the guest lists were limited almost exclusively to people whom *he* wanted to see; and even these were not the ones to whom he had felt close during his bachelor years, since he had broken ties with most of them when he and Alma had married. While Alma became more and more dissatisfied, Gustav seemed to react in exactly the opposite manner. He thanked his wife for the peace and quiet she had brought him. Though his blessing could give her a new faith and hope, she realized that the very things she had to do to provide this peace were what made her feel so deprived. Finally she mentioned some of her darker thoughts to her husband, and, wanting the best, he promised to help her find new ways to make her life seem more satisfying and productive.

As her pregnancy advanced, it became less possible for Alma even to consider a new project. She sometimes tried to tell her mother how lonely and useless she was feeling, but Anna responded by reminding her how lucky she was to have found and married a man like Gustav. Both of the Molls felt great love and compassion for their new son-in-law. When they were all together it was often Alma who felt she was the odd person in the family.

Alma enjoyed listening to plans being made for a festival that the Secession was sponsoring in honor of Max Klinger, the painter, engraver, and sculptor. All of the contributions were to have something to do with Beethoven. Gustav would lead the opening concert and present his own arrangement of excerpts from the finale of Beethoven's Ninth Symphony, scored for winds and brass. Klinger was deeply moved by Gustav's contributions to the festival, and he spent pleasant hours with the Mahlers. Alma saw then how hard it was going to be to maintain Gustav's schedule and at the same time cultivate new friends. It would have been difficult enough during one of the earlier, more relaxed periods of Gustav's life; now he had begun to fret over his scores until the last possible moment. Detailed and tiring under any circumstances, this work was especially anxiety-ridden as Gustav gained public recognition as a composer and found himself near, not quite at, the plateau that would promise lasting success for his own music.

During those weeks, Alma went with Gustav to Crefeld, where he would conduct the first public performance of his Third Symphony on the twelfth of June, 1902. In this small city near Cologne she would learn that whereas the citizens were delighted to have the famous Herr Director from the Opera in their midst, they were much less happy to welcome the man who had written a symphony too long for provincial comfort. It hurt Alma to see Gustav hailed and honored for what he did on account of other people's music, but doubted and scorned on account of what he himself had created. Furthermore, the Mahlers had left Vienna in the midst of a particularly oppressive heat wave. Alma, heavy with child, found the journey almost unbearable. On the train Gustav tried to tease her into believing they were almost at their destination; so when they arrived in Cologne and approached the Dom Hotel, Alma could not believe they had actually arrived. She attended all the rehearsals with score, and Gustav came to her for comments and suggestions after every movement. She had wise advice to give; he was pleased with both his work and hers. One day, a little boy sat behind Alma and surreptitiously looked over her shoulder to glimpse the music the orchestra was playing. Alma moved the pages so the child could see them. Many decades later, the great pianist and teacher Edwin Fischer thanked her for her kindness at that rehearsal when she let a boy watch the mystery of musical creation.

To whatever extent it was possible on tour, Gustav kept to the schedule established in Vienna. Because the rehearsals for the performance in Crefeld consistently tended to run later than scheduled, because Alma was not vigorous, and (not incidentally) because they drank more wine than usual with their midday meal, the couple's afternoon escapes turned from walks to drives. They took great pleasure in getting out into the German countryside, then returning to the privacy of their hotel rooms. Just before the performance, however, they moved from the Dom Hotel into the house of a rich industrialist in the town of Crefeld, and there they felt uncomfortable and burdensome. Worse, everywhere they went they found curious crowds of students and townspeople. Never again did they agree to spend their days away from home as the guests of strangers. Hotels, however ill-equipped or noisy, were preferable.

Gustav was always the object of attention, but on this trip Alma's dresses also inspired public curiosity. She was wearing maternity clothes of the "reform" style designed by her friend Kolo Moser. The ample garments had not necessarily been intended for pregnant women, but they fitted Alma's needs perfectly — they were cool and loose and comfortable. The children of Crefeld found the costume exceedingly odd, and they gathered to see Alma walking along with Gustav, who always looked wrinkled and disheveled and was in the habit of carrying, never wearing, his hat. One afternoon, he happened to leave this much-watched hat in a tearoom, and was told of his oversight by rowdy youngsters who had been waiting for the Mahlers to emerge. Gustav thanked them gallantly, retrieved the hat, and led Alma to the hotel rooms that had been taken by Arnold and Justi Rosé. Humor was not a major part of the lives of these four persons, but that day they giggled at the prospect of revenge. They lined up at the hotel windows and poured buckets of water onto the heads of the taunters.

With this trip, Alma gained understanding of the obstacles and inconveniences Gustav faced when he was away from home. The man who so needed his routine and privacy was deprived of his peace, and was in constant demand. One day when a knock on the door announced another unanticipated visitor, Gustav asked Alma to hide in a curtained area of their room while he dispensed with the intruder, the composer Hans Pfitzner, who had come to plead with the honored Director for a Viennese production of his opera *Die Rose vom Liebesgarten.* Gustav responded to Pfitzner's pleas coolly and negatively. The visitor persisted. Alma felt great sympathy for the guest, however; she sensed that Gustav could rescue him from despair with merely a few kind words. She emerged from behind the curtains and took Pfitzner's hand in hers to reassure him. Gustav made no promises or guarantees, but Pfitzner left encouraged. To Alma's surprise, her husband was not angered by her indiscretion. Eventually, Gustav did produce *Die Rose vom Liebesgarten* in Vienna, and Pfitzner became one of Mahler's greatest supporters.

When Gustav put down his baton after the premiere of his Third Symphony, Richard Strauss led the applause and stepped toward the podium to offer his stamp of approval. The two musicians were long-time acquaintances, never really friends. That night, Strauss began the ovation and left the auditorium before the cheering stopped. Later, as the Mahlers dined at one of the few inns in Crefeld, Strauss walked past them with a lordly bow but no comment.

Instead of going back to Vienna, Alma and Gustav went on to their summer house in Maiernigg, where another schedule had to be established — this one even more strict than Vienna's, since Gustav counted on getting most of his creative work done during the months in the country. The lakeside house not only was unpaid for, it was uncomfortable. A kind and well-intentioned neighbor on the Woerthersee had built the house for Gustav, and though it might have suited a bachelor, it did not accommodate a family. Alma despised the ornamental fretwork surrounding the kitchen cupboards, for example, so she arranged for the removal of it and other similar atrocities. The house seemed even worse to Alma when Anna von Mildenburg, the soprano of Gustav's less constrained Hamburg days, established herself as their neighbor and announced her intentions to visit.

A long as the days ran smoothly and on his schedule, Gustav was blind to domestic issues. He was delighted to be free from obligations at the Opera and to be able to devote himself fully to his creative projects. In the country, he arose at half-past six each morning, went quickly to his work hut, and waited for the cook to deliver his breakfast silently and inobtrusively. He worked until noon, when he swam or went boating, always wanting Alma to be with him, though he knew that she took care to avoid the sun. After lunch, they would embark together on a hike, then Gustav would work a bit more, have supper, take an hour or so for music or conversation, and go to sleep. In the country as in the city, everything revolved around his schedule. Alma's assignment was to keep things running so smoothly that her husband barely noticed anything other than his own work. While Gustav composed music in the hut, Alma copied the parts of his latest symphony, the Fifth, filling in occasional notes which had been only sketched or suggested. As the summer weeks passed, Alma became so proficient that she found herself working apace with the pages Gustav brought back from his hut each evening. When he reached the end of a movement, or solved an especially difficult problem, he fetched her and they walked with ceremony to the piano in his tiny workroom, where he sought her approval of what he had written.

Guests arrived, but rarely. The intrusive Anna von Mildenburg visited, so did Anna Moll. Any social engagements had to be kept within the very strict perimeter of Gustav's working hours and Alma's health. She hated to be restricted, especially when she had little to do, and wanted to take advantage of every opportunity to be with her family and friends. Alma went walking with Gustav for three or four hours at a brisk, eager pace, cutting under bushes, over fences, and off the marked paths. Although Anna tried to dissuade her daughter from these excursions, Alma insisted on going. Free and private times with her husband were rare, and he was relaxed and happy when they were out in the meadows together.

When Alma was uneasy, she returned to her diary. On July 10, 1902, she wrote that she longed for a person who would think only of her, help her discover what was important for her. She felt as if she had gone astray, and wanted to be at home. Feelings of waywardness increased. She told Gustav what she had been thinking, but he did little to lessen her restlessness. When he came down from the hut on July 13, he found his wife crying and decided she did not love him enough. "How often I myself have doubted that," Alma wrote in her diary. "Still, I know that a person has never been as dear to me as he is. If only I could find my own inner balance! I disturb both myself and him. He told me yesterday that he has never worked as easily and as surely as he is working now . . . From now on, I won't tell him anything about my inner battles. I shall pave his way with peace, pleasure and equanimity . . . But there are always these tears. I've never cried as much as I cry now, even though I have everything that a wife could want."[3]

Early in August, Gustav composed a song especially for Alma on a poem by Friedrich Rueckert, "Liebst du um Schoenheit." She was touched by the gift, especially at the point where, with the words "love me always," her husband had repeated "always . . . always . . ."

In Vienna in October after four months in the country, Gustav prepared Mozart's *Zaide* for the Opera while Alma prepared for the birth of their first child. Maria was born on November 3, 1902, after a long and difficult delivery. Outside the room where Alma was in labor, Gustav raged and cried in terror that he would lose both his wife and his child. Eventually, he heard the infant's cry and rushed in to see mother and daughter. Hearing that Maria had been a breech baby, Gustav laughed uproariously: she had shown the world the part it most deserved to see, very first thing.

From the moment of her birth, Maria was her papa's favorite. Gustav personally nursed her through the illnesses of infancy and early childhood, from runny noses to ailments of greater consequence. He was convinced it was only his singing and talking to her which led her back to health.

Alma had a harder time adjusting to motherhood than Gustav did to fatherhood. Her convalescence was prolonged. On November 25, she wrote in her diary, "I still haven't found the right love to give [my baby]. Everything in me belongs to Gustav. I love him so much that all seems dead next to him. And I can't tell him that."[4]

Shortly after Maria was born, Gustav began work for the Opera's production of Tchaikovsky's *Queen of Spades*. The project provided both the novelty and the intellectual stimulation he and Alma needed. She went to the rehearsals whenever she was able, and they played the score on the piano in their parlor each night after supper. Alma was recovering from an attack of what she reported to be gallstones. She felt that she had to have a life of her own, to be more than just the wife of the Director. She asked Gustav why he had never gone on to insist that she show him her songs, especially after he had seemed so very interested in them on the night when they had met. His response was not satisfying. Writing in her diary on December 15, 1902, she accused her husband of wanting to live only his own life, of not wanting to share a life with her. As she sat at the desk in her room with the governess tending little Maria across the apartment, Alma convinced herself she was not needed, even by her own child.

The Mahlers saw the Molls, Rosés, Zuckerkandls, Burck-hard, Klimt, and Richard and Pauline Strauss whenever they happened to be in Vienna. In the first weeks of 1903, Gustav went to Wiesbaden to conduct his Fourth Symphony, and Alma stayed at home with the baby, since such a short trip would have cost too much money and effort for her to accompany him. One night when Alma was to be at home alone, Justi Rosé came to keep her company. After Alma had played part of Wagner's opera *Siegfried* on the piano, Justi asked whether Gustav had written it. Her sister-in-law's musical ignorance appalled Alma.

The easiest and happiest place for the Mahlers to visit was the home of the Molls. It was there that Gustav met the artist Alfred Roller. He arranged almost at once for his new friend to be commissioned to design the Opera's production of Wagner's *Tristan und Isolde,* which would have its premiere in February — a *Tristan* still remembered in the annals of operatic productions. It led to Roller's being appointed the Opera's stage designer. At the first performance, on February 21, Gustav was exhausted and during intermission he lay on the sofa in his private room and wished to give up and go away from all the problems of his position. Standing over him with Alma, Justi commented, "One thing delights me — I had his youth, you have him now that he's old."[5]

Gustav and Alma found a new friend in Gustave Charpentier, the French composer who traveled to Vienna for the final rehearsals and the premiere at the Opera of his *Louise,* which was to remain one of Alma's favorite works. The first performance was scheduled for March 24. From Alma's accounts, Charpentier was bungling, sometimes crude, and as unlucky as those people who step on the toes of others when they are about to whisper something most kind and appropriate. Yet she saw his genius, and found him captivating.

Both she and Gustav thoroughly enjoyed their new friend's company, and they all looked forward to a reunion.

Again in April Gustav had to go away to conduct, and Alma did not join him. He headed toward Lvov with suitcases packed by Poldi, the housemaid, and Elise, the cook. All things considered, even with the baby, the Mahler household seemed to be running ever more smoothly, the system perfected to the point where Gustav — who tended to suffer from migraines when he was traveling — could grab aspirin from a certain corner of a certain bag without really looking. While Gustav was gone, Alma used the time to prepare for their summer stay in Maiernigg. Before they could all settle together in the country that year, he had to make another trip, this time to Amsterdam, where he met the conductor Willem Mengelberg, and then to Basel, where Alma joined him. In Basel, Gustav conducted his Second Symphony in a magnificent cathedral. There, too, Hans Pfitzner again found the Mahlers and they all met for supper, this time without awkwardness.

Maiernigg afforded what Gustav called "splendid isolation,"[6] where he could settle in and begin serious work on his Sixth Symphony. Alma saw to it that the routine was established, but soon thereafter she was drawn again into her memories, specifically of Alex and the hours they had spent together. She wanted to resume her own musical life. "I love *my* art," she wrote on June 15, 1903.[7] Gustav was so preoccupied with his work that she envied him, and, no matter what he had asked and what she had promised, there was no way in which she could come to think of his music as hers.

Pfitzner had sent a score of his First String Quartet. It impressed Gustav, and reminded Alma of something she had meant to do but forgot. Late in the summer, when Gustav returned to Vienna to resume his work at the Opera, leaving Alma in the country with little Maria for a few extra weeks of relaxation, she took out the score of Pfitzner's opera *Die Rose vom Liebesgarten,* which had been left near the piano under an ever-growing pile of books, periodicals, and music. Alma suspected that there was something to the opera, and as she played it through and studied it, she realized how right she had been. When the family reassembled in Vienna, she saw to it that the score of Pfitzner's *Rose* was always sitting on the music stand of the piano for Gustav to peruse; she knew he would pay attention to whatever happened to be in front of him when he sat down at the piano. After many evenings of playing through Pfitzner's opera, Gustav decided it was worthy of a production at the Opera. Alma and the work's composer rejoiced.

In September of 1903, Alma became pregnant with her second child. This time there was no social embarrassment and she knew what to expect. She enjoyed the time, reveled in the changes in her body, and stayed active. Through Burckhard, she and Gustav met the author and dramatist Gerhart Hauptmann and his future wife, Margarethe Marschalk. During that winter, too, Alma saw Zemlinsky. They spent happy hours talking and playing music. He addressed her with even more respect now that she was a wife and mother. Gradually a friendship grew between Gustav and Alex, to Alma's pleasure and relief.

In the early spring Alma could still travel in comfort, so she and Gustav made a long-contemplated trip to Abbazia with Maria and a maid, then returned to Vienna to await the birth of their second child. Alma could not help being worried about her imminent confinement, remembering the pain she had experienced with the birth of Maria. One night after returning home late with Gustav from the theater, she recognized that she was in labor. Anna Maria Mahler was born at midday on Wednesday, June 15, 1904, when the flowers were in bloom and the birds were singing. This time the birth was easy. The baby was given the nickname Guckerl, or Gucki, an affectionate diminutive of the word for peepshow, because she had such large blue eyes, so like her mother's. She seemed to take immediate pleasure in what she saw in the world around her.

Alma remained in Vienna until she, the children, and the nurse were ready to join Gustav at Maiernigg. Alone in the country, he had spent most of his time supervising the building of a playground for his two little girls, with protective enclosures and a soft, sandy floor. He was very proud of this project and involved himself in it with more enthusiasm than he had shown when the house itself was being built. Gustav and Alma had considered the possibility of spending more time in the country, perhaps even of making Maiernigg their principal residence, but Gustav wrote to his wife of his concluding this would not be a good idea: the environment there was so relaxing that they might never get anything accomplished.

He was correct. Alma, Maria, Anna, and the nurse had barely made themselves comfortable in the country and become established in their summer routine when Alma started feeling restless. She read over her diaries from years gone by, thinking wistfully of the people whom she had so enjoyed and hardly saw anymore. She wished that Pfitzner lived in Vienna, and that she could be in contact with Alex and Schoenberg more frequently. Then she heard a rumor to the effect that Klimt had married, and even more of her past came back to mind. Though the reports turned out to be false, Alma read them with the feeling that a chapter was closing in her life. She decided — not for the first time, and not for the last — that her youth had reached its end. She was jealous of the lady who was said to be Klimt's bride. "I thank him," she wrote in her diary. "I am grateful to him for my awakening." But, she went on, "nothing has reached fruition for me. Neither my beauty, nor my spirit, nor my talent!"[8]

She wrote these words as Gustav was playing the piano version of his Fifth Symphony for Bruno Walter in the parlor at Maiernigg. Alma resented the men's friendship. Gustav, she thought, "is letting him look into his very soul. I went out of the room. Walter, all of these people, everything is foreign to me! Even the music! Today I realized something very strange. — I am not happy — and not unhappy. It came to me suddenly that I am living what only appears to be a life. I hold so much inside of me, I am not free — I suffer — but I don't know why or what for. My ship is in the harbor, but it has sprung a leak."[9]

In October 1904, Gustav went to Cologne for the rehearsals and first performances of his Fifth Symphony. Alma was to join him for the last few days of preparation and the premiere, but she was ill, and with little Anna only four months old she thought she would not be able to travel. "Leave nothing undone — sweat it out — swallow brandy — gobble aspirin — you can get over a chill in two days and still travel on Monday night and be here for the concert on Tuesday!" Gustav advised her.[10] His advice and remedies did not have the desired effect, and Alma never made the trip.

Gustav had so wanted his wife to be with him. He was afraid no one would understand his symphony. This was to him *their* music, the work that had absorbed him during their first summer together. The problems at the first rehearsals caused him to predict, correctly, that generations of conductors and orchestras would be defeated by the symphony's Scherzo. More or less seriously, Gustav began to wish he were in some other place, doing something different to earn his living. "Oh, that I might give my symphony its first performance fifty years after my death!" he wrote to Alma.[11] With this remark, he began his frequent references to a line from Gustav Albert Lortzing's opera *Zar und Zimmermann*, "How blessed, how blessed, a cobbler to be!"[12] Gustav wanted at that moment to be almost anything other than a composer and conductor, especially as he presented a long work that was likely to be neither well performed nor well received. He was not made happier or more content by his wife's absence, or by the prospect of returning to the Opera to face chiding by the officials who found his involvement with his own music superfluous and even deleterious to his primary appointment.

Bruno Walter and Arnold Berliner, a physicist who had become one of Gustav's greatest supporters, arrived in Cologne to offer their companionship and assistance. Heinrich Hinrichsen, director of the publishing firm of C. E. Peters, expressed enthusiasm not only over the Fifth Symphony but also over the forthcoming Sixth. The actual performances far exceeded Gustav's expectations, and as he prepared to travel on to Amsterdam he charged Walter with giving Alma all the details of what he considered to be a triumph.

After a time with the Mengelbergs and double performances of his Fourth Symphony, Gustav had to go to Leipzig for his Third Symphony. He found himself increasingly homesick. It had been difficult to accustom himself to the presence of two demanding children, and he had been strict with them, himself, and Alma as he fitted the girls into his schedule. He worried that Maria and Anna would not even remember their papa by the time he returned home. He wanted constant news of his family; Alma's letters didn't satisfy him. He was proud that his status as a composer was rising, but he did not like having to be away from home alone. Alma missed her husband, though more than that she resented his frequent absences, feeling that he was out in the world while she was chained to children, home, and the practicalities of his life.

Alma had turned twenty-five in 1904. Her world revolved entirely around her husband and family. Early in 1905, both children fell ill, and while Alma felt needed as she cared for them, she lost both strength and patience. On the fourth of January, Alma and Gustav had a long talk. She told him that from the start of their time together his odor had been repulsive to her, probably from his cigars. He smiled, and said that what she was saying to him was the key to many things. In staying with him she had gone against her own nature. "Only I know how right he was," Alma wrote in her diary. "He was a stranger to me, and much about him is still strange to me — and will, I believe, remain so forever . . . I wonder that we can continue to live together, knowing this. Is it duty? Children? Habit? No, I know that I do really love him, and only him . . . To start my previous life again seems an impossibility." [13]

When she saw Alex, she was reminded only of her former suitor's weaknesses. She went to hear the dress rehearsal of a concert that would pair Zemlinsky's *Seejungfrau* with Schoenberg's *Pelleas und Melisande,* and as her appreciation of Schoenberg's work continued to increase, she was ever less enthusiastic about Alex's. She remembered Gustav's remark about Alex's lacking a chin in his music as well as on his face. At the same time, a program of Gustav's songs was in rehearsal, and Alma thought that they might be his finest works.

When Pfitzner arrived in town and visited Alma in the company of the Hauptmanns, she looked forward to an evening of light conversation and gossip, and was disappointed to realize that the composer had apparently fallen in love with her. She let him embrace her, and was attracted by him, but the affair went no further. On one of their midday hikes, she told her husband about Pfitzner's advances. Gustav was jealous, and he stalked away, headed back to the Opera, and left her alone in the street. Alma kept walking, and as twilight began to settle she noticed a handsome young man behind her, apparently following. Later when she told Gustav about this innocent adventure, he accused her of always taking the side of the other man. He was right; she knew it. She went to her bed, sorry for what she had said. After a short time, Gustav came to her — something he rarely did before he thought she was fast asleep. He told her that she should read *The Kreutzer Sonata* by Tolstoy, and made love to her. When he left to go to his own bed, Alma lay awake, fearing the future, feeling that she was on the verge of losing her courage and her will to survive.

In March of 1905, the Mahlers took another trip to the beach at Abbazia. Alma and her daughter Maria (called "Putzi") went ahead with Anna Moll; Gustav joined them after a performance in Mainz. On holiday there was little to do but play with the child, ride bicycles, and rest. They thrived on the freedom. In June they parted again. Alma and both children went to Maiernigg with Grandmother Anna while Gustav filled an engagement in Graz. It was Anna who wrote to her son-in-law with the news he so coveted about his family's adjustment to the country. Alma spent a good deal of her time complaining to her diary, feeling that she had been unfaithful to her husband in her heart and mind. As if to make up to him before he arrived for the summer, Alma spent her free hours copying the parts to his Sixth Symphony from manuscript. One night, very late, she tipped over the paraffin lamp and set the carpet and couch afire. A servant heard her screams and helped to stifle the flames.

At the end of a productive and peaceful summer, Gustav returned to Vienna to begin to prepare for the season at the

Opera, leaving the rest of the family in Maiernigg. He spent his days in the office and his nights at an inn outside of the city, where he felt as if he were still on holiday. These retreats were precious times when he could be completely alone, and he didn't push himself. He relaxed in the knowledge that his wife and children were safe and healthy, especially in the weeks after he had been writing the *Kindertotenlieder* ("Songs on the Deaths of Children"). As Maria and Anna played and laughed in their sandbox, the subject of these songs had put bleak thoughts and fears into Gustav's mind, and even more into Alma's.

Gustav was relieved that Alma was gaining strength from the discipline and routine of their daily life, and they were finding more peace together and apart. A coterie of admirers made every effort to travel to each of the important performances of Gustav's works. These included the young pianist and would-be conductor Ossip Gabrilowitsch, whose company was particularly welcome.

While tending the children, the houses, and the daily routine, Alma had found some new friends. First among them was still Pfitzner, who dedicated his First String Quartet to her and visited her whenever he was in Vienna. One day Alma played some of her songs for him. He was impressed, saying that he wished the two of them could have worked together, since he might have been able to help her refine her talents. In return, not long afterward, while Gustav was working at the Opera, Hans played his own songs on Alma's piano. He played each song over and over again; he and Alma became so engrossed that they widely missed the hour at which they should have met Gustav and Hauptmann for supper.

This bit of thoughtlessness did not help what was already an unsteady relation between Gustav and Hans. The latter seemed to do things that he knew would irritate Alma's husband; Gustav, in turn, did nothing to ease the awkward situations. One afternoon, Hans left a rehearsal of his opera on the pretext of urgent personal business, which turned out to be an irrepressible need to buy a red rose and take it at once to Alma. On his way to the Mahlers' apartment, he encountered a parade of workers celebrating the first of May, and was so disconcerted by the sight of the marching proletariat that he shut himself into Alma's bedroom and refused to emerge. In a scene reminiscent of some operatic farces that had made Gustav and Alma giggle, the husband returned home exhilarated by the May Day crowds, only to find himself confronted by the closeted Hans.

Gustav knew that Hans did not like his music; her friend's opinion only heightened Alma's own skepticism about her husband's creative prowess. Nevertheless, Gustav did everything in his power to promote Hans's *Rose.* After the opera's premiere, the Mahlers feted the composer, inviting the celebrated Max Reinhardt, Roller, the Zuckerkandls, Molls, and Rosés to supper. During the meal Gustav left the table and went off to read a book. None who knew him well were surprised, but the guests who were not used to their host's eccentricities were offended and confused.

When Alma and Gustav went to Strasbourg for performances of his Fifth Symphony, they again crossed paths with Richard and Pauline Strauss. Both Strausses were very concerned with what they thought was a yoke that composers were forced to bear: they created masterpieces and received few rewards. Richard and Gustav continued to have a strained friendship. Strauss was more celebrated as a composer than Mahler, but the Director of the Vienna Opera was the most influential man in the area of music where Strauss had the most success. Since Gustav had not written for the theater with any persistence, the scales were at a tenuous balance. Richard never forgot that the productions of his works in Vienna depended on the approval of this rival. Pauline resented everything about the situation, and found it unfortunate that the man she had married had chosen music as his life's work, so underpaid and unappreciated was he.

In the summer of 1905, while the two-year-old Maria played with little Anna in their sandbox at Maiernigg, their father wrote his Seventh Symphony, to sketches he had begun the year before. The country house now seemed almost ideal, and the Mahlers felt entirely freed from the tension surrounding their lives in the city. The next summer, after he made the preliminary sketches for his Eighth Symphony, Gustav had to cut short his retreat to conduct Mozart's *Figaro* in Salzburg; after that, his autumn and winter schedule was fuller than ever, and there was never a day when he was not catching up with work at the Opera, preparing to leave on tour or be away from home in other music interests. Alma felt she deserved her husband's company, but Gustav was short with both her and the children. He could not find the time to talk with any of them. Though he insisted that his daughters join him for meals, he demanded that they be silent. The baby Anna became so accustomed to her father's requirements of silence that she could not eat with pleasure until she was an adult and free on her own.

Stable though their domestic situation seemed, it could not go on. Except for the excursions into the countryside on summer afternoons and a few rare evenings spent with friends, the Mahlers' lives were almost totally lacking in flexibility. Gustav had to admit that he could not continue to hold his position at the Opera and still be husband, father, and composer. His health was not reliable; the doctor had diagnosed a heart impediment, which, though not serious at the moment, could become life threatening. The overseers of the Opera were more reluctant to let him leave his office during the season to present works they regarded as his, not theirs. Alma argued that he should leave his job; Gustav finally agreed. He was facing a critical point in his creative work: the completion of his Eighth Symphony. That would bring him to work on one with the number nine, a task that had signaled death for Beethoven, Schubert, and Bruckner before him. Though he refused to succumb to superstition, Gustav faced the challenge with dread.

4

New York – The Metropolitan Opera

WHETHER BY LUCK or by very astute timing, Hans Conried, the manager of the Metropolitan Opera in New York, strengthened his campaign to lure Gustav to America. The Mahlers' resolve to leave Vienna had intensified since Gustav had come to realize that he would be able to secure a position offering more financial security and more time for his family and his creative work. Alma encouraged him to be receptive to the possibility of such an offer, but both knew it would take time to find the right position.

In January 1907, Gustav went on a tour taking him to Frankfurt and Berlin for concerts that included his own works, while Alma and the children remained at home in Vienna. Just before Gustav was to leave, Alma dreamed that her husband had fallen in love with a younger woman. So when Gustav and his companion Berliner returned to their hotel from a visit to Louise Wolff, widow of a well-known concert manager in Berlin, Gustav sat down immediately to write to Alma that this lady could not have been the one of whom she had dreamed, and that he was not about to fall in love with anyone else. He had dreamed of Alma the night before, and had seen her wearing her hair as she had worn it during her girlhood. Alma had taken to pinning her long hair on top of her head in a style she thought more fitting to the status of a married woman than the long, half-tied-back tresses of her youth. Gustav found her new hairdo Semitic, and he wanted to avoid this impression as best as he could.[1] Many people in Vienna and across European musical society did not take seriously his purported conversion to Christianity; he was intent on reassuring them that he did not ascribe to what might have been seen as elements of Jewishness.

Alma continued to wear her hair up most of the time. She met the recent news of Alex Zemlinsky's marriage with equanimity, perhaps because she sensed she and Gustav would soon be leaving Vienna. She was at the station to meet her husband when he arrived home, and they went to their apartment for the midday meal with the children before he set off to the Opera. The prospect of departure was strengthened when he found letters and telegrams from Conried piled on his desk.

The American manager's invitation to meet during the first week of June in Berlin was accepted. Gustav and Alma discussed at length the possibilities of starting a new life on another continent. When Gustav went to Germany he wrote to Alma immediately after the first meeting that Conried was full of fire and ideas. "First and foremost, [he] wanted me on exactly the same footing as Caruso. — Then 8 months (180,000 crowns) — then 6. Finally we got to this: 3 months (15th January to 15th April) for which [they pay] 75,000 crowns net, journey and all expenses paid (first-class hotel)!"[2] The major questions revolved around the length of the proposed contract; Conried wanted four years, whereas Gustav wanted only one. Gustav's letter to Alma closed with a diagram making it very clear what part of the offer from New York her husband found the most important: [3]

<pre>
kiss   kiss
         4 years & 6 months @ 125,000 Crowns
                making ½ a million Crowns
            or an annual guest visit of 6–8 weeks
                  50,000 Crowns fee
           making 200,000 Crowns in four years
kiss   kiss
</pre>

For a man who had just escaped from the chains of long years of debt, the prospect of such large sums for so little time was attractive. And to Gustav, chafing and impatient with the regime of the Opera in Vienna, the prospect of being wanted and indulged was irresistible. He confirmed the agreement. "I am going because I can no longer endure the rabble," [4] he wrote to his friend Berliner. Alma was pleased with the decision to leave, and from the country on July 4, Gustav wrote to Berliner, "The most I risk is being rather miserable for *three months* in the year, to make up for which I shall have earned 200,000 Crowns *clear* in four years." [5] He submitted his resignation to the Opera with no regrets. It was accepted on the condition that a successor be engaged before the Mahlers departed for America. Felix Weingartner received the appointment toward the end of the summer, effective in January 1908. With their future apparently secure, Alma and Gustav planned the life they would share when they no longer had such pressing obligations in Vienna for eight months of every year.

They had been together in the country for barely a week when little Maria became seriously ill with what was diagnosed as scarlet fever and diphtheria. There was little that could be done for the child, but she hung on and seemed to gain some strength. Hope for her recovery mounted, then she suffered a serious relapse. Anna Moll arrived at once to offer her help and support. The dying girl, on the verge of suffocation, was moved into Alma's room. Gustav could not stand to witness the suffering of the five-year-old who was his favorite, and he retired into his own room and almost never came out.

The doctor ordered a tracheotomy. Alma and the nurse prepared the child, while a servant stood watch outside Gustav's door, lest the father fall witness to the grisly event. During the operation Alma fled from the house and walked to the lake in tears. At five in the morning the nurse fetched her. She went back to her room to hear her firstborn gasping and choking, staring at the ceiling in distant agony. Maria lived for one more day, during which her father dared occasionally to approach the door of the room in which she lay. He was unable to bring himself to go in, so much did he fear the dreadful sounds of death. Alma, Gustav, and Anna Moll lay together on the bed in Gustav's room, unable to stand being alone.

Maria died on July 12, 1907. On the fourteenth, Gustav ordered Alma and Anna to take a walk by the lake, using a tone of voice that permitted no discussion. Beside the water Anna collapsed, exhausted. Alma tried to revive her mother and heard footsteps on the path. As she turned to see Gustav approaching her, Alma also saw why he had so peremptorily ordered them to leave: Maria's coffin was being lifted into a hearse. At that moment, to Alma, who had been numbed by the events of the past week, it seemed as if her own life was being drained from her body, and the doctor was summoned to treat both women. The older woman was pronounced fit and strong: she needed only a good night or two of sleep to regain her usual hardiness. Alma needed complete and protracted rest and peace, however. As if to indicate that he would not be left out of the group of mourning convalescents, Gustav invited the doctor to examine him, too. He lay on the sofa and the doctor's expression rapidly turned grim. Gustav's heart was critically weak.

On the seventeenth of July, Gustav was back in Vienna for consultation with a specialist. He took a room at the Hotel Imperial, feeling isolated and abstracted. He could not even see Carl Moll, who was at home tending his own little daughter because there was no way to be sure that the highly contagious infections fatal to Maria had not spread into the Moll household. Anna Mahler, three years old, had visited her grandmother and the family on the Hohe Warte, and she might have been carrying the germs. Young Anna could hardly understand what had happened, but she had heard her elders' conversations and knew they were concerned about something she had done, or might still be doing. She was being kept away from other people and it seemed to her that she was being punished. Maybe she had done something to kill her big sister. For years Anna felt responsible for Maria's death.

Alma and Gustav wanted nothing more to do with Maiernigg, so horrible were the memories of the events that had taken place in the house, but any decision about where they would go or what they would do hinged on the verdict of Gustav's doctor. Alma, in the country pending further instructions, found the tension and indecision difficult. Gustav warned her not to try doing all the packing by herself, but wanted her to make sure the suitcases they would have with them would hold what he would need for the rest of the summer — music, books, and his bicycling suit. That suit would never be worn again. The Viennese doctor confirmed the prognosis of his country colleague and told Gustav his life was in danger if he did not take great care.

❧

To the man who had just stood by the grave of his first and favorite daughter in the cemetery at Grinzing, the doctor's words seemed to be a malediction. He was about to embark on a trip that would take him to a new job on a different continent, prepared to leave his home, perhaps indefinitely. His wife was ill, his remaining daughter might be carrying some dreadful disease, and he was an invalid, forced to give up his beloved hikes, swims, and bicycle rides. He felt he had lost himself. He was no longer Gustav Mahler, Director of the Opera. He was not even Gustav Mahler, in a sense, for that man had never acted old and sick.

Alma and Gustav found a house in Schluderbach in the Tyrol where they could spend the rest of the summer pondering the changes in their life. Slowly, and without much enthusiasm, Gustav went back to work and started to sketch settings for German translations of Chinese poems, a symphony for voices and orchestra that would become *Das Lied von der Erde*. By not calling this his "Ninth Symphony," Gustav convinced himself that he would not be tempting fate and summoning death.

Friends visited the Mahlers to try to bring them some cheer. After Roller brought news from the Opera, the young Gabrilowitsch arrived. One evening, while Gustav was still working, Alma and her guest stood together at a window to watch the moon cast its shadows over the mountains. Turning to each other, they kissed. They both realized a mutual attraction, but each felt a loyalty to Gustav that precluded the possibility of betraying him with any sort of illicit relation. Ossip idolized Gustav; and Alma felt that her husband had been even more deeply affected by Maria's death than she had. The two drew apart, and Ossip left the next morning.

Gustav still had a few obligations at the Opera, but when they were back in Vienna in the autumn Alma viewed each performance and each appearance as a kind of farewell. The controversy accompanying Gustav's years at the Opera reached a peak. Those who had ardently supported him resented his decision to leave; those who had objected to his innovations and presentations could hardly wait for him to depart. There were many empty seats in the house on the nights when Gustav conducted. The respect that had gone along with the position at the Opera was denied to him, even contradicted, with snide remarks. Although these hurt Alma and Gustav, they could not allow themselves to be disturbed or distracted, so busy were they preparing to leave for New York. They would not concentrate on the past, but had to look to their new life.

In October 1907, Gustav went to Wiesbaden to conduct works of Beethoven and Wagner, after which he went back to St. Petersburg to lead his own Fifth Symphony. There a young musician named Igor Stravinsky was in the audience. On his next stop, in Helsinki, Gustav met Jan Sibelius, for whose music he could never summon much sympathy. While her husband was away Alma went to take some rest at a spa near Semmering, in the hills. Gustav wanted her to have the relaxation and luxury of the resort, but she left a few days earlier than planned. She knew how much had to be done in Vienna to prepare for their journey and feared that her stay at the spa was costing them more money than they could spare.

In fact, Alma's financial worries were unfounded — not only because the contracts with the Metropolitan Opera would be lucrative but also because the commander-in-chief of the Opera in Vienna, Prince Montenuovo, had arranged for Gustav to receive a pension greater than that to which he was actually entitled, as well as a sum of 20,000 crowns when he relinquished his office on January 1, 1908. In addition, Alma would be granted the pension that would normally have gone to the widow of a Privy Councilor upon her husband's death. If something should happen to Gustav, she would be more than adequately provided for.

Gustav's farewell offering at the Opera was Beethoven's *Fidelio*. On November 24 he conducted his own Second Symphony in the large hall of the Musikverein as his final presentation in Vienna. There was more packing to be done; the apartment had to be closed, and little Anna had to be moved to the Molls' house, where she would live during her parents' absence. Gustav wrote a farewell letter to the members of the Vienna Opera and personal notes of tribute to Anna von Mildenburg and Bruno Walter. There were a number of messages of good wishes from friends and gatherings with Berliner, Schoenberg, Zemlinsky, and their wives and pupils. On December 9, 1907, a group of young musicians, friends, and admirers met at the railway station to wish Alma and Gustav well as they boarded the train to Paris on the first leg of their trip to New York.

That day, Bertha Zuckerkandl wrote in her diary, "When we said goodbye to Mahler for the last time, he said: 'After all, I take my home with me, my Alma . . . And it is only now, when I am released from the crushing burden of work, that I know what will henceforth be my dearest task. Alma has sacrificed . . . her youth to me. No one can ever know with what absolute selflessness she has subordinated her life to me and my work. It is with a light heart I go on my way with her.' "[6]

In Paris, the Mahlers were again met by the devoted Gabrilowitsch. When he and Alma were alone in the hotel, he told her that he loved her in a manner overpowered only by his devotion to her husband. Alma knew that the young man was embarrassed and confused, but she was flattered and appreciated being reminded she was still young and attractive, especially since she was about to leave Europe in the company of a man who seemed to be prematurely aged. She let Ossip hold her hand in the dark room. Suddenly Gustav burst through the door. Alma feared a dreadful scene, but, instead, the evening was spent most pleasantly, as the three shared memories and prospects for the future. The next morning Alma and Gustav took the train to Cherbourg and boarded the SS *Augusta Victoria.*

Gustav hated to travel quite as passionately as Alma loved it. A rough crossing posed the threat of seasickness, and to avoid the worst of that malady, Gustav took to his bed and lay stiff as a corpse throughout most of the voyage. Alma, in the meantime, enjoyed the food, the companionship of her fellow passengers, and the sensation of motion. The first glimpse of the New York skyline was to Gustav the blessed sight of land that would bring an end to the horrid rocking and his misery. To Alma, the sight was pure excitement, a new beginning and a challenge. She loved everything about the city even before she saw it.

Their temporary home, booked for them by the Metropolitan Opera, was on the eleventh floor of the Hotel Majestic. The suite had been equipped with two good pianos and the staff had been alerted to the importance of the Majestic's new guests. Alma and Gustav went off to have lunch with Conried and the Opera's business manager, during which Gustav learned that his first performance in New York would take place on January 1, 1908, with Wagner's *Tristan.* The arrangements were most satisfactory, and the newcomers were alternately charmed and amused by what they took to be American customs and habits. How could the Mahlers have known that the suit of armor illuminated from within by red lights which Conried kept in his parlor was a sign of his own eccentricity of taste, not a standard of American decoration?

Alma walked with her husband to the opera house, left him there, and was delighted to discover that New York's numbered streets made it simple for her to explore by her-

self and still find her way home. Such an expedition would
have been difficult for a visitor to Vienna, where concentric
circles form the city's grid and the streets change names from
one block to the next. Alma had not learned, and never did
learn, more English than was absolutely necessary. She could
ask directions and usually understood the answers. She could
make basic purchases in stores. But she could not converse
comfortably in the language of the country she would call
home, and she never really wanted to, or felt that she should.

Gustav set himself up at once in his office at the Metropolitan and began to define and settle into the routine that
was so important to his life. He was pleased with the musicians with whom he was working (the great majority were
not native Americans) and delighted not to have responsibility for the administration and the general running of the
company. He attended performances and noted the audiences' "crudeness and ignorance,"[7] but he remained optimistic about his new surroundings and felt he could help the
New Yorkers to greater sophistication.

It took hardly any time for Gustav to learn that the Metropolitan was quite as filled with political problems as the
Opera in Vienna, and, willy-nilly, he found himself in the
middle of them. Conried, who had wooed and hired him,
had been publicly discredited. The Board of the Metropolitan wanted to dispense with him and lure Gustav into assuming more responsibility, tasks of precisely the magnitude
that had convinced him to leave Vienna. After refusing their
request to take charge, Gustav emphasized the need for a
strong, imaginative stage designer, specifically Roller. He
participated in preliminary negotiations with his old friend
and colleague, advising him how to respond to the New
Yorkers' overtures, but no agreement was reached. This was
the first of several occasions when Gustav would work in
order to bring a European friend and colleague to America.
Most of these efforts turned out to be in vain, but each time

he touted the virtues of the United States, and not incidentally allowed himself to look forward to the prospect of having another friend and supporter near him in New York.

Alma had not been feeling entirely well, and though she did not close her mind to the attractions and vitality of Manhattan, she spent long hours and days in the hotel suite with little to do and no one to talk to. She was dreadfully concerned about her daughter Anna, even though she knew that she could trust no one more than her own mother to care for the four-year-old child. She had built up irrational fears since Maria's death and convinced herself that something horrible would happen to her only remaining child during her absence. Alma watched the mounting Christmas activity and the glittering lights with feelings of loneliness and sadness, dreading the prospect of having to face one of the most important holidays without any company other than her husband's. Gustav had hardly cared about Christmas, and had acknowledged the traditions of the day only for the sake of the children. Alma always had seen to it that their house was decorated and presents were under the tree. On this Christmas of 1907, there were no children, they were alone in a strange city, and Alma had no reason to celebrate. She found herself feeling desolate, drained of strength and optimism. Although Gustav had barely noticed his wife's previous lethargy, after the holiday he concentrated on trying to help her live a fuller life. The attempts to boost Alma's spirits were well intentioned, but by no means as successful as they might have been, had his own mood been better. He immersed himself in the challenges of the Metropolitan, all the while still deeply affected by his daughter's death. Memories of Maria and her suffering seemed always to be in his mind.

Yet there was great excitement surrounding Gustav's first performance at the Metropolitan, and Alma found herself eagerly anticipating the *Tristan* of New Year's Day. She put on her best gown, and the Mahlers left their rooms prepared to be presented to New York. As they walked down the hotel corridor toward the elevator, Gustav stepped on the train of her dress, and they had to hurry back to the suite to patch the rips. She wanted him to go on without her, since there was no time to spare, but he waited and they hailed a taxi that got them to the theater only a few minutes late. The performance was magnificent; Alma was happy and proud, and both felt more confident and encouraged about their future.

Under doctor's care, ordered to take to bed for four weeks, Alma could not hold on to her good feelings. Again, while Gustav was working at the Opera, she was left in her room to wonder what her future might hold, longing for the life she seemed to have lost. She wanted friends, family, and people to talk to. She missed Alex and Schoenberg and Ossip — particularly Ossip. She wanted to see her daughter, her mother, and stepfather. She knew the Molls could have reassured her about the future and convinced her that she had done the right thing by marrying Gustav. Separated by an ocean from the persons she trusted, Alma began 1908 feeling utterly alone.

The Metropolitan's season, then as now, included a spring tour, so the last weeks of the Mahlers' stay in America found them traveling with the company. They stopped in Boston, which Alma found stodgy compared to New York, and made several trips to Philadelphia. On one of these, at another performance of *Tristan*, Alma sat near enough to Gustav to sense that he was conducting in great pain. Panic over his plight caused her to faint. Dr. Leon Corning, the discoverer of spinal anaesthesia, led her from the auditorium into one of the dressing rooms, where she rested. As the lengthy act progressed, Gustav noticed the empty seat. He became quite as worried about Alma's fate as she had been about his. At intermission, he rushed out of the pit to find his wife. Reunited, both felt better, but any scare of this type had a more lasting psychological effect on Alma than it did on Gustav. In contrast to her strong constitution, his was frail. He lived in constant danger of death, worked too hard, and, Alma feared, did not follow his doctors' advice.

It was still Gustav who wrote the letters to "Dearest Mama," Anna Moll, reporting on himself and Alma. At last she had found some Viennese in New York, so she was more independent and busy. Gustav was heartened by the new path he had chosen. Even during the first spring in New York, he wrote to Anna of the possibility of being given a symphony orchestra of his own in America, a prospect with great appeal: "Everything now depends on the New Yorkers' attitudes to my work. Since they are completely unprejudiced, I hope I shall here find fertile ground for my works and thus a spiritual home, something that, for all the sensationalism, I should never have been able to achieve in Europe."[8]

Shortly before they were to sail from New York to Cuxhaven, a journey that would take them from the last days of April into May 1908, Alma and Gustav met Dr. Joseph Fraenkel, a Viennese who had moved to New York a decade earlier to specialize in the emerging, controversial field of neurological and psychiatric diseases. The three became friends at once, and planned the time they would spend together in New York the next winter. Fraenkel was a devoted patron of the arts and a knowledgeable guide. He also had a theory about humans' ears: all the organs of the body except the ears were under the control of their possessors, he pointed out, so only the ears could reveal the complete truth about a person. This proposition gave Gustav and Alma an amusing challenge to which they responded with glee. They went around carefully inspecting the ears of everyone they encountered, trying to find the truth about friends as well as strangers.

The journey back to Europe turned out to be smooth and sunny. Everything seemed brighter. Some of the obstacles from their past no longer appeared to be confronting them, thanks to their New York adventure.

❧

Upon landing, Gustav went immediately to Hamburg to conduct his First Symphony; Alma joined him after a few days and was happy to be reunited with Berliner, and especially with Ossip. However, the main thing on her mind was the health of her little daughter and plans for the summer. After the trip to Vienna and a brief but emotion-filled stay there, Alma and Anna Moll traveled on to Toblach to look for a house where the Mahlers and Molls could spend the next few months out of the city. Only after an exhaustive search did the two women find an eleven-room farmhouse on the outskirts of town, with a separate garden studio for Gustav's work. They secured the house, had two good pianos moved into the main dwelling, and put a third, smaller one in Gustav's hut. Since so much of what they would need was already packed and ready to be transported, the process of settling in was easy.

Gustav returned to work on *Das Lied von der Erde*. Berliner had a large load of books delivered to the Mahlers in June, and Gustav wrote, "So it is true and for the remission of your sins you are now doing good works, spreading culture among your friends. — Actually, Alma pulled a face when she saw all those books (a prize-giving ceremony at which she was afraid of being left empty-handed) — but then, when the miniature edition of Goethe's works came to light, her face smoothed out and brightened and she forgave you."[9] Since her father had first tried, against her mother's wishes, to give her a copy of *Faust* long ago in Plankenburg, Alma had felt a particular affinity for Goethe's writing. To Bruno Walter, Gustav reported with qualms:

> I have been trying to settle in here. This time it is not only a change of place but also a change of my whole way of life. You can imagine how hard the latter comes to me. For many years I have been used to constant and vigorous exercise . . . like a kind of jaunty bandit, bearing home my drafts. I used to go to my desk only as a peasant goes into his barn, to work up my sketches. Even spiritual indisposition used to disappear after a good trudge (mostly uphill). — Now I am told to avoid any exertion, keep a constant eye on myself, and not walk much. At the same time the solitude, in which my attention is more turned inward, makes me feel all the more distinctly everything that is not right with me physically. Perhaps indeed I am being too gloomy — but since I have been in the country I have been feeling worse than I did in town . . . and for the first time in my life I am wishing that my holidays were over. — It is wonderful here. If only I could have enjoyed something like this once in my life after completing a work![10]

Carl and Anna Moll were preparing to make the trip to Toblach, and Gustav wrote, "For a time, as you know, things with us were in a very great whirl, and the high jinks seemed to have become a permanent institution, then various bouts of heart trouble and generally jangled nerves, etc., etc., crystallized. — But now the air seems to be fairly clear. — *And even if it were not,* the two of you really ought to know that your presence is *never* a disturbing element . . . Quite the contrary, it even helps us to bear all the unpleasant things . . . Almschi is fairly active again, thank goodness, and so I am hoping for (at long last) a restful and pleasant summer."[11]

At summer's end, Gustav prepared for performances of his Seventh Symphony in Prague and Munich, while Alma undertook the task of selling their old house in Maiernigg. She went there, confronting its grim memories, to supervise the removal of everything they had left, and she was glad to close the door behind her, knowing she would never have to see the house again.

In the midst of all the planning and relocation that would accompany the new fall season, Alma and Gustav took one of their rare holiday trips together, traveling to Salzburg on the new railway and staying in the beautiful town where Mozart was born, taking a garden room in the Hotel Nelboeck without work, family, or visitors. There was only one obligation to be fulfilled: having heard that Burckhard was ill, Alma resolved to visit him in St. Gilgen, the scene of her childhood summers. She made the brief journey there without Gustav. Greeting her alone came as no shock to Burckhard, since he and Gustav had often found themselves at odds in the past, and since the older man suspected Alma's husband was still jealous of the influence he had exerted on her during her formative years. Rather than send a car and driver to retrieve Alma on the next day, however, Gustav went himself to pay respects to the former director of the Burgtheater and man of letters. The conversation among the three was so animated and friendly that the Mahlers convinced their host to accompany them back to Salzburg. Halfway through the drive, Burckhard asked to be let out of the car. Alma wasn't sure whether his action was merely an eccentricity, whether he had been offended, or whether he was feeling especially ill. This was the last time they met. Burckhard died in 1912.

Gustav went to Prague a full ten days before the first performance of his Seventh Symphony, which would take place on September 19, 1908. His time was riddled with duties and distractions. Since he usually persisted in revising and reorchestrating his music until the final hour, his rooms were strewn with papers and parts. He found the city in general, and his room at the Hotel Blauer Stern in particular, intolerably noisy. With interrupted sleep he became tired and irritable. Good-willed friends and colleagues arrived to keep him company, including the conductor Otto Klemperer, the composer Alban Berg, and Berliner. When Alma arrived for the last rehearsals and premiere, she knew that what she had to do was simply to support her husband through the first performance. This was only a *succès d'estime* (the Seventh remains Mahler's least popular symphony), though it was at least tolerable enough to raise Gustav's hopes for the subsequent performances in Munich.

Anna Moll accompanied him to that city while Alma went back to Vienna to prepare for their departure to America. Munich proved much more congenial to Gustav than Prague had, and from the elegant Hotel Vier Jahreszeitsen, Gustav wrote to his wife to raise the question of whether they shouldn't leave Vienna and settle elsewhere in Europe. "Munich, which is situated at a height of 600 metres, has, as I've always noticed, a superb climate; and I always feel at the top of my form here . . . The more I think of it the more the idea of perhaps settling eventually in Munich grows on me . . . You can buy a castle in a park here for 3000 marks, and life is actually twice as cheap as in Vienna. With our income, we could live here like princes. In the middle of Europe — with first-rate communications in all directions." [12]

The Mahlers' journey to New York would begin in Hamburg. Gustav and Anna went there so he could conduct one last predeparture concert. Alma joined them with the stern English nurse and little Anna, who would be spending the winter in America with her parents. Anna had been enrolled in a school in Vienna during the previous winter, after her sister's death, but she had missed so many days of classes and her mother had been so worried about her being contaminated by germs, that she had been taken out of the academy and was again in the tutorial charge of her family. As the tender took them to the large ship, Anna cooed with delight. Hearing the nurse order his daughter to be quiet and sit still, Gustav grabbed the little girl, lifted her up to let her feet dangle over the railing, and told her, in a voice quite as firm as the nurse's, to be very, very excited, and he would be excited with her. Anna had a wonderful voyage.

❧

This second year in America the Mahlers moved to the Savoy Hotel, where many of the most famous Metropolitan singers, including Enrico Caruso, were also in residence. There was many a congenial evening spent with the legendary tenor, drawing vivid caricatures but refusing to show them to his subjects for fear of offending them with his sharp perceptions. The free-spirited Anna tried to evade the clutches of her nurse and take over the Savoy much as the fictional Eloise would later occupy the Plaza. Her parents saw old friends and met a number of new ones. They were especially eager to renew their friendship with Dr. Fraenkel, and spent as much time with him as Gustav's schedule would allow. They marked Christmas Eve with the physician, then went on to celebrate Christmas Day with a group of singers at the home of the soprano Marcella Sembrich, whose Christmas tree caught fire. An Atlantic blizzard raged outside on New Year's Eve, terrifying Alma, who had never seen anything comparable. In January 1909, Gustav wrote to tell Anna Moll he was depleting his strength in his work but that he was being careful and felt quite well. Grandmother Anna was preparing to join the Mahlers for the last few weeks of their New York stay and then for the trip back to Europe, where Carl Moll would join them in Paris.[13]

Neither to the Molls nor to other friends did Gustav indicate the trouble he was having at the Metropolitan. Conried was dying, and Giulio Gatti-Casazza had been hired from Milan's La Scala to succeed him. Gatti-Casazza insisted on bringing with him the conductor Arturo Toscanini, who had extracted a promise he would be allowed to conduct Wagner's *Tristan,* the work that had been Gustav's calling-card and one Gustav thought he had claimed as his own. Gustav wanted no part in this kind of skirmish, so reminiscent of much of Vienna. The authority Toscanini was being given hurt him, along with the vagueness surrounding his own position. He began looking more seriously for another assignment.

Gustav wrote to Bruno Walter, "I find myself less important every day, but am often baffled by the fact that in day-to-day life one keeps on in the same old humdrum way — in all the 'sweet habits of existence.' — How absurd it is to let oneself be submerged in the brutal whirlpool of life! To be untrue to oneself and to those higher things above oneself for even a single hour! But writing that down like this is one thing — on the next occasion, for instance, if I now leave this room of mine, I shall certainly again be as absurd as everyone else. *What* is it then that *thinks* in us? And what acts in us? Strange! When I hear music — even while I am conducting — I hear quite specific answers to all my questions — and am completely clear and certain. Or rather, I feel quite distinctly that they are not questions at all." [14]

Gustav told his friend that it was looking as if he might have his own orchestra; a committee had been formed to this purpose even before he had left New York in the spring. Once again, he was energized by the prospect of change and a new challenge, and when he heard that Roller had left the

Opera in Vienna, he wrote, "Perhaps it is only now that your work will become truly worthy of you, now when you are liberated from all petty considerations and can work purely as an artist. — One can write about 'expectations' and send congratulations, but 'expecting' is something about which one may remain silent. And yet I was perhaps more pleased by that short allusion of yours than by anything else. I always have found it downright incomprehensible that you, who have so much love for children and understanding of what they are like, should yourself be deprived of that blessing. I believe it is only now that your wife too will come into full maturity — high-falutin' though this may sound! It seems to me that you need it only for your happiness — but your wife perhaps for her very life." [15]

Alma too was pregnant again. It was not something Gustav thought he had to tell all of his friends and acquaintances, partly because his wife had evidently thought she might have been pregnant several other times between Anna's birth and that second winter in New York. This time Alma and Gustav were particularly happy and eager about the prospect of another child. Also, with memories of Maria's death, they were both concerned, so they urged and begged Anna Moll to join them in America earlier than had been planned. She arrived with haste. In February, Alma lost the baby. To add to a grim atmosphere, Dr. Fraenkel warned Grandmother Anna that serious kidney problems would be inevitable within a few years if the elderly lady did not follow a strict diet. He gave Anna a list of doctors in Vienna who could give her a second opinion and control her condition. Gustav reported all this to Carl in a letter of March 10, 1909, adding, "Alma is very well. (About her *present state* she has doubtless written to you herself. She has been relieved of her *burden*. But this time she actually regrets it.)" [16]

Anna Schindler with her daughters, Alma and Grete

The statue of Jacob Emil Schindler, Alma's father,
in the Staatspark, Vienna

Alma and Grete Schindler

Alma Schindler in her youth

Arnold Schoenberg, the composer, about 1902

Gustav Mahler

Alma around the time of her marriage to Gustav Mahler

Anna Schindler Moll, Alma's mother

Carl Moll, Alma's stepfather

Gustav Mahler and his first daughter,
Maria, fondly called "Putzi"

Alma Schindler Mahler in the avant-garde "reform"
style of dress

Alban Berg, the composer, with a portrait of Gustav Mahler in the background, about 1930

Ossip Gabrilowitsch, the pianist and conductor

Richard Strauss, his wife Pauline, and their son Franz

Alma was not ill, but she was depressed and smitten with doubts about her womanhood and her desirability. As if on cue, Gabrilowitsch arrived in New York. He visited the Savoy, and after Gustav had gone to bed played Alma her favorite Intermezzo by Brahms, the one in A Major. The two talked on for hours. They both were still too devoted to Gustav to want to disrupt his life and their own, but Ossip confirmed his devotion and Alma was flattered and reassured. Unfortunately, Gustav heard their conversation. After the visitor left, he called upon Alma to defend her unfaithfulness. She did so with enough conviction to placate her husband — she had not, in fact, been unfaithful: she had not wanted to condemn the talented young musician for his attentiveness. The conversation cast a shadow neither Gustav nor Alma could dismiss. Later the same year, Ossip married Mark Twain's daughter, the singer Clara Clemens.

Before returning to Europe, Gustav had in hand a contract making him principal conductor of the reorganized Philharmonic Society of New York, precursor of the New York Philharmonic Orchestra, effective the next autumn. His obligations at the Metropolitan Opera had all but ended, and although he could not realize how much work his new affiliation with the Philharmonic Society would actually require, he was feeling both successful and satisfied. Alma, Gustav, young Anna, and her nurse went to Paris, where Carl Moll had arranged for Gustav to sit for the sculptor Rodin. With the cooperation of Sophie Clemenceau, Gustav was convinced that the artist himself had extended the invitation. Rodin was captivated by his new subject, and compared Gustav's head to Mozart's. The time in Paris gave both Gustav and Alma the break they had needed from routine and obligations. As they began their trip home to Austria in May, Alma fell into a state of panic, and her nerves seemed to snap. The doctors in Vienna advised her to take the cure, so she went with her daughter to Levico while Gustav went on to their summer house in Toblach.

He was very busy, involved in negotiations with Mengelberg for performances of his Third Symphony in Amsterdam in October, as well as with dealings with publishers and preparations for his first symphonic season in New York. All these matters seemed to require inordinate amounts of time, and in addition old friends like Berliner came to visit. Gustav was not good at being alone — he admitted that he took to solitude much as an alcoholic takes to wine — and neither could he accomplish a significant amount of work when he had to fend for both himself and visitors. He resented the time taken up in the country by his having to deal with matters that would otherwise have fallen to Alma; he wanted her companionship and her help in writing letters and dealing with business, in which he was far from expert.

While Alma practiced what she called her "icy constraining" at the spa, where she was enrolled in the strict disciplines of the "cure," she longed for "love or life or anything that could release me." [17] Anna Moll had agreed to deliver to Gustav a case of things that he had left in Vienna, including real honey, ink for his special fountain pen, peppermint oil, and a gadget with which he could put out the candles without blowing wax all over the walls. As he sent his order, Gustav added that "Almschi has been sending me thoroughgoing letters of lamentation, from which I deduce that she is finding the cure very strenuous. Besides, I know being alone isn't the right thing for her at present. It is lucky she has at least Gucki [Anna] with her. If only all of us were together here again!" [18]

Gustav told Alma briefly about the minor domestic crises he had encountered, but he spent most of his letters cheering her on to health. "To gain a spiritual centre — that's the thing. From there, everything has another aspect. And it throws a light on your inner self that you should have turned to Goethe. It shows that you reach up to the light, inwardly as well as outwardly." [19] He missed his wife especially at teatime and late in the evening; he hated spending the hours of darkness alone. On June 27, in response to one of her most melancholy letters, Gustav wrote:

Your moods . . . are very understandable to me, for I myself go through the same thing a thousand times over; this may surprise you, but it may at the same time be a consolation and even make it easier to understand yourself . . . In between the brief moments in the life of the man of genius when these challenges are answered, there are the long barren stretches of existence which wring the soul with unanswerable longings. And it is just this ceaseless struggle and its torments that give the life of these few its character. — Now perhaps you will guess, or know, what I think of the "works" of this person or that. They are, properly speaking, the ephemeral and mortal part of him; but what a man makes of himself — what he becomes through the untiring effort to live and to be, is permanent. This is the meaning, my dear Almschi, of all that has happened to you, of all that has been laid on you, as a necessity of the growth of the soul and the forging of the personality. And you still have a long life before you. Persist in exerting this inner force (as indeed you do); claim as your very own your utmost of beauty and power (more than this none of us can do — and only the elect in any case); "spread yourself abroad"; exercise yourself in beauty, in goodness; grow unceasingly (that is the true productiveness), and be assured of what I always preach: what we leave behind us is only the husk, the shell . . . I don't of course mean that artistic creation is superfluous. It is a necessity of man for growth and *joy,* which again is a question of health and creative energy . . . How often I see you in that joyful mood I know so well, when you have "opened out." [20]

There were signs of love and devotion in this letter, yet there it was again — Gustav's impersonal, preaching tone that Alma found so repellent and frightening. Her husband might have been talking to anyone. He would not understand her need for a life of her own, music of her own. She knew he wanted to help her, but he didn't know how. In her absence he had not even ventured into the hut, finally to get down to his work. Alma suspected him of purposely, stubbornly refusing to compose until she was there to help and support him. She refused to be responsible. Though she could not dispel her guilt, she was also angry.

As Alma had predicted, Gustav settled down to work as soon as she and Anna returned to Toblach. Their routine fell easily into its predictable pattern. Guests included the Strausses, the Molls, and several others. At dinner in town with these visitors, and neighbors whom the Strausses had brought from Garmisch, Richard gestured to Gustav to take a seat next to Pauline. She looked up and said that her host might be allowed to sit beside her if, and only if, he did not fidget during the meal. Gustav was quite as well known for his fidgeting as Pauline was for her ill-considered remarks. This time, unwilling to humor her, Gustav walked ceremoniously to the other end of the table, where he sat next to Richard and engaged in animated conversation. Others were left with Pauline, while the two famous musicians had a fine time.

The Mahlers were leaving for New York sooner than usual in 1909, so they went back to Vienna to prepare for the journey a few weeks before they normally would have left the country. The apartment on the Auerbruggergasse was of very little use to them anymore, since the bulk of their time was spent either in the country or in America. They planned to relinquish their rooms on the first of October, put some of their furniture and possessions into storage, and move the rest of the most necessary and dearest items into the Molls' house, which they would henceforth use as their principal address in Vienna. With the worst tasks involved in this move accomplished, Gustav went to Goeding in Moravia to do the final work on *Das Lied von der Erde,* and Alma and Anna both checked in to the Sanatorium Luithlen to have their tonsils cauterized. "You have behaved splendidly," Gustav wrote to his wife during her recuperation period. "I have heard all about it: 24 incisions without an anaesthetic. I'm delighted for you both; and convinced that it will be of life-long *benefit* . . . Meanwhile, I have settled in here very comfortably . . . this — without the factory and railway [noises] — is just what I'd like for us, a comfortable house, a large garden and orchard, and flowers and vegetables.

"Carl says he will go on hunting until he has found what we want near Vienna."[21]

The longer he stayed in that part of the country, the more convinced Gustav was that this was the way he wanted to live. "But a place like this I must have," he told Alma shortly thereafter. "Carl says he won't rest until he has found it for us. All told, staying here suits me remarkably well . . . human nature must have sun and warmth — I shudder now when I think of my various workshops; although I have spent the happiest hours of my life in them, it has probably been at the price of my health."[22]

The Mahlers were welcome to stay at the house on the Hohe Warte as long as they wanted. Carl was busily searching for another home for Alma and her family, a retreat close enough to Vienna for Gustav to conduct his business in the city but one offering them a sunny and private place in which to work and live when they were not in New York or on tour. Alma and Gustav left for New York in the second week of October 1909, looking forward to beginning his association with the Philharmonic Society, and believing that by the time they returned home Carl would have found a suitable house. Anna was again sailing with her parents, as this time was Theodore Spiering, the violinist whom Mahler was taking to serve as concertmaster of his new orchestra.

In the United States the Mahlers faced another change of schedule. Most of the rehearsals and concerts Gustav conducted took place in Carnegie Hall, which was then less than twenty years old. The Philharmonic Society had arranged to present an additional series of concerts in Brooklyn, a place ever so far away to Gustav and Alma; tours to Philadelphia and Buffalo had already been booked. Gustav set in to work, and was once again relieved to be freed from the problems of work in the opera house. Soon, however, he had learned enough of a new set of problems to be able to write to Bruno Walter, "My orchestra here is the true American orchestra. Untalented and phlegmatic. One fights a losing battle. I find it very disspiriting to have to start all over again as a conductor. The only pleasure I get from it all is rehearsing a work that I haven't done before. Simply making music is still tremendous fun for me. If only my musicians were a bit better." [23]

He had one obligation left at the Metropolitan Opera, which company was still paying for his travel expenses and his rooms at the Savoy. Gustav would conduct Tchaikovsky's *Queen of Spades* in March 1910. The preparations for the production began early, so there was not as much peaceful time in America as Gustav and Alma had hoped for. In addition, the first few months with the Philharmonic Society brought increased social obligations. While many of these turned out to be occasions the couple would happily have missed, some of them turned out to be special. Alma always recalled the trip to the Roosevelt estate on Oyster Bay, Long Island, where they were the guests of Mrs. West-Roosevelt; her brother-in-law, Theodore, was hunting in Africa.

On another evening, Gustav and Alma went with Dr. Fraenkel to one of Eusapia Palladino's séances. In dingy rooms on Broadway, all manner of strange events took place, including Gustav's being knocked in the forehead by a free-flying mandolin — an omen of tragedy. Not wanting to allow themselves to believe in supernatural powers but aware that what they had seen was virtually impossible to explain rationally, Gustav and Alma tried to laugh about the events of the evening and convince themselves they had been victims of an elaborate hoax. Gustav finally came to the conclusion it had all been a dream. This put an end to the Mahlers' conversations about the event, though both of them continued to wonder.

Fortunately, they had little time to muse on potential disaster. They met Louis Comfort Tiffany, another legendary eccentric. One night Ernest Charles Schirmer, the music publisher, introduced them to New York's seediest ghettos and pleasure palaces. Much as both Gustav and Alma tended to shy away from social occasions, they found that they enjoyed the contrast to the isolation that they had previously felt in New York, and they met a host of people with whom they could converse and speak of home. Alma felt less lonely and depressed. Gustav's mind was taken off the problems he faced with his new orchestra. Both felt appreciated and liked. Especially when they were in the company of Fraenkel, they sensed that they belonged in this American city.

Crisis-Walter Gropius

THROUGH THE MAIL word came to Gustav that the Viennese public and press were reveling in gossip about his new life, condemning him for having allowed his talent and energy to be poured into a job with an orchestra unworthy of him. Gustav wrote a hasty letter to an old friend, the musicologist Guido Adler, expressing annoyance with an article printed under Adler's byline. The same Viennese who were now chiding him were the ones who had neither noticed nor promoted his talents during his years in Vienna, Gustav maintained. He accused Adler of misunderstanding and misusing his words, went on to justify his habit of napping after rehearsals, and reaffirmed that he was now doing what he had long wanted to do — leading a concert orchestra of his own.

Why did neither Germany nor Austria offer me this? Can I help it if Vienna chucked me out? — Besides, I need a certain degree of luxury, a degree of comfort in my daily life, that my pension (which is all I have gained from almost thirty years a conductor) would not permit. So I welcomed the chance of the American offer, which provided me not only with an occupation suited to my tastes and abilities, but also with a good salary that will soon enable me to spend what years remain to me in a manner befitting one's human dignity.

And now, closely connected with this, I have to say something about my wife, to whom your views and remarks did a great injustice. You may take my word for it that she has *nothing* but my welfare in mind. And just as during the eight years she spent at my side in Vienna she never let herself be dazzled by the worldly brilliance of my position, not ever, despite her temperament and the allurements of Viennese life and one's "good friends" there (all living beyond their means), let herself be tempted to indulge in luxury of any kind, such as would have been in keeping even with *our* social position, so too her solid and earnest endeavor is at the soonest possible date to bring a conclusion to my efforts (which, I must repeat, do not constitute *over*-exertion, as in Vienna) to achieve the independence that only my creative work can provide. You should know her well enough by now! *When* have you ever found her guilty of extravagance or selfishness? Do you really believe she could have been so utterly transformed since you last saw her? I enjoy driving a motor car just as much as (indeed, far more than) she does. And are we seriously supposed to live on the Vienna Court Opera's charity in an attic in Vienna? Is it not better that I should take the opportunity offered me to earn a decent living by honest work as an artist? I must once more assure you that my wife is not only a courageous, faithful companion who shares all my spiritual interests, but also (a rare combination) a sensible, level-headed manager of our domestic affairs, enabling me to save in spite of all the comforts of our physical existence, the person whom I have to thank for all the prosperity and orderliness, in the true sense of the

word, of my existence. I could prove all this to you by giving
you figures. But to my mind that is unnecessary. With a little
good will (and recalling your knowledge of us) you will be
able to tell yourself all this.[1]

Whatever Adler had said to annoy Gustav so much that
he felt it imperative to write this letter, extravagance was
certainly not one of Alma's vices — not even in her imagination. The Mahlers did spend sizable sums of money in
order to have the best and freshest of simple foods for their
table. Also, they were not miserly when it came to finding
places to live in, where Gustav would have space and peace
for his work and Alma and the children would be able to
go about their daily life and recreation. Although they kept
household help for cooking, cleaning, and tending to Anna,
such a staff seems much more extravagant today than it did
to the Viennese of the early twentieth century. It was certainly not beyond the capability of the Director of the Opera
to employ such help, any more than it was beyond the capability of the conductor of the Philharmonic Society of New
York. Along with this, Alma might have worn couture
clothes and kept regular appointments with the hairdresser
and makeup experts, but she did not. Once Alma had wished
that her party dresses had come from the expensive shops
of Vienna, but since she married Gustav she had known very
well that they could not afford the things considered by some
of her contemporaries to be staples of life.

Alma did not appear in expensive clothes, jewels, and furs,
or with her hair perfectly curled. Because of her beauty,
poise, and what many called a statuesque bearing, she always looked regal, and in this managed to look more expen-
sively presented than she actually was. Only during the worst
of times did she ever suffer — go without soap, a bath or
shower, good hosiery and comfortable shoes. She always

knew what was essential and what was extravagant, and only rarely allowed herself to move out of the realm of what was necessary for her own peace of body and mind.

Gustav began to sense that his energy was again being scattered, and he could not even find time to write to friends. He wrote to Roller, "I hope that in about a year I shall be able to achieve a fairly human way of life. To have a home somewhere and be allowed to live and work there (instead of vegetating and working) and to be, I hope, near enough to my few friends to be able to see them from time to time. Although Alma and I play a new game every week about our future — Paris, Florence, Capri, Switzerland, the Black Forest — extend this list according to your knowledge of geography — I think we shall before long arrive somewhere not far from Vienna, where the sun shines and beautiful grapes grow, and that we shall not go away again." [2]

While he kept peace among the members of the board of his new orchestra and tried to whip the ensemble into shape, he also had to set up his calendar for the months they would spend in Europe. As much as Alma could help him with the basic correspondence and contracts, Gustav had to make the decisions himself. Only rarely could he initiate a bit of fun, as he did one night after he had conducted the Philharmonic Society in a performance of his own First Symphony. Afterward he took the whole orchestra, his "children," to a bistro for a celebration. Conductor and instrumentalists had a fine and rowdy time; Gustav left with a conviction that, in spite of all the problems he had had to face, the orchestra members had consistently done their best for him. He seemed content as he wrote to Anna Moll in the spring of 1910, shortly before they would all reconvene in Paris. "Undoubtedly, Almschi has had a far better winter than for many years. — A few colds, but only very slight ones, which didn't keep her in bed long. The climate does not seem to suit

Guckerl [Anna] too well. She has now, thank God, got over a rather persistent catarrh (even with some fever). Now she is in the best of spirits and again looking splendid."[3]

Alma had been especially pleased that their family schedule in New York had become quite simple compared with the one they had tried to keep in Vienna during Gustav's tenure at the Opera. He now had rehearsals only every second day, and he had the luxury of being responsible only for the programs he himself would conduct with the orchestra, not for other people's lapses or errors. So she felt better than she had in several years as they all sailed back to Europe early in April 1910 and headed for Paris, where the Molls awaited them. Gustav conducted his Second Symphony at the Trocadero. In the middle of the performance, Claude Debussy, Gabriel Fauré, and Paul Dukas stood up and walked out, making it known that they found the music much too Viennese for their tastes. Gustav was disturbed by his colleagues' actions. He and Alma traveled on to Rome, where a meeting with Mengelberg eased the pain.

Alma was exhausted by all the travel, so, while Gustav enthusiastically installed himself in the white farmhouse in Toblach and prepared for his work in Munich, she consulted a physician, who ordered a long rest. She was suffering from what she called "the wear and tear of being driven on without respite by a spirit so intense as [Gustav's],"[4] and feared she was on the brink of complete collapse. At the end of May she checked into the spa at Tobelbad. Even the final minutes spent with her husband taxed her nerves. Gustav wrote:

> When I told you the last morning at Tobelbad how nice you looked, it was the expression of a spontaneous delight as I saw you coming to meet me and looking so sweet and charming. But you know me by this time. In art as in life I

am at the mercy of spontaneity . . . Four years ago, on the
first day of the holidays, I went up to the hut at Maiernigg
with the first resolution of idling the holiday away. . . and
recruiting my strength. On the threshold of my old work-
shop the *Spiritus Creator* took hold of me and shook me and
drove me on for the next eight weeks until my greatest work
[the Eighth Symphony] was done. — One summer before that
I made up my mind to finish the Seventh, both Andantes of
which were there on my table. I plagued myself for two weeks
until I sank into gloom, as you well remember; then I tore
off to the Dolomites. There I was led the same dance, and at
last gave it up and returned home, convinced that the whole
summer was lost. You were not at Krumpendorf to meet
me, because I had not let you know the time of my arrival.
I got into the boat to be rowed across. At the first stroke of
the oars the theme . . . of the introduction to the first
movement came into my head — and in four weeks the first,
third and fifth movements were done. Do you remember?
You see, my love, you know enough of me and my ways not
to be wounded by me. And particularly when you can see
for yourself that I live only for you and Gucki, and that
nothing can ever come between you and my love. Everything
else is so insipid . . . Living and loving are as the flowers
of a tree which grows higher of itself, or often spreads
abroad; flowers, or fruit that falls in winter — you have only
to wait for the spring in the full assurance that they will bud
again. [5]

With obligations in Leipzig and Munich, Gustav worried
about when he might be able to visit Alma in Tobelbad. He
was concerned that she stay there to complete the cure and
wanted her to come back to Toblach only when she was
fully strong. He missed her and needed her, and feared that
her treatment might go on longer than he could sustain himself. A drive happened to take him past her childhood home
in Plankenburg, where he barely managed to keep himself

from bursting into tears. "But I have made up my mind," he told her. "In September, when things are better, I'm going to do the whole trip again with you . . ."[6]

Gustav fretted all the more because Alma didn't write to him about the details he wanted to hear. From Munich in June, he wrote to Carl Moll asking him to have a certain design made up into a tiara he could give to Alma in time for her birthday on the thirty-first of August. It was unusual for Gustav to remember any date with a gift, and it was even more unusual for him to splurge on a lavish project with such foresight. To Anna Moll he wrote, "I am so perturbed by Almschi's letters, which have such a peculiar tone. What on earth is going on? . . . Please drop me a few lines at once saying whether you think I had better go to Almschi in Tobelbad. I should prefer it, and it would be better for me, to have peace and quiet for a while in Toblach . . . However, if Almschi's condition so requires, I shall certainly go straight to Tobelbad."[7]

Without giving away the full extent of his concern about her condition, Gustav sent Alma a long and circular discourse on Plato. It was evidently inspired by something she had written to him, though he was always complaining to her that she wrote too little and told him nothing. Again, the letter was impersonal and pedagogical, and it is difficult to tell whether Alma had any idea how concerned her husband was about her well-being, or whether she knew he would make the trip to Tobelbad at a moment's notice. He did not go then, and a letter written to his mother-in-law some weeks later suggests that Anna herself visited Alma, or had been able to send Gustav enough news of his wife to comfort and reassure him. He wrote back to Anna:

What a shock I had today when I got Almschi's letter! — Afterwards, when a second somewhat calmer one, and especially your sweet letter, came, I felt a little easier, and am not assuming I can stay on here for these last few days without worrying. But I am terribly sad about the recurrence of this tormenting ailment. — I live here, as you know from my letters to Alma, much occupied with you all in my thoughts . . . But now everything possible must be done to get Alma well and strong again! I had completely forgotten about my birthday and only your letters reminded me of it so suddenly that I couldn't help smiling at the thought of how unimportant that day seems to me and yet how lovingly you all remember it. Thank you a thousand times for your sweet words, and always remain what you are to me, friend and mother (as dictated by a peculiar whim of fate).[8]

Gustav did go to visit Alma in Tobelbad later in July, and reported to Anna, "I found Almschi much fresher and fitter and am firmly convinced that her cure here is doing her a great deal of good. Please make her stay here for as long as you can . . . Please don't forget to have a similar bed-table made for me and sent to Toblach when it is finished."[9]

Precisely what had made Alma go to Tobelbad and what it was that Gustav referred to as her "tormenting ailment" is not clear. Through most of her life, she attributed ill health to her nerves, gallbladder, and later her heart. She often excused herself from social occasions by pleading illness. Since her youth she had been nervous among strangers and very sensitive about her impaired hearing, convinced that she didn't act her best in large groups. She was reluctant to seek professional advice or assistance, and she seems to have been quite robust and healthy throughout most of her long life. In reading about these illnesses and the subsequent retreats to spas and places where cures were given, one should keep in mind that "female problems" were not discussed in those days, not even within close families, and that retreats to such places are still much more common curative measures in Europe than they are in America. Then, too, it is not surprising that Alma grasped the opportunities to withdraw to places where she would be by herself, away from her family and everyday life, where she could stroll in the woods at a pace much slower than the one Gustav had liked to set for them, and partake in the healthy environment without concern for her husband, knowing that she was doing good for herself.

Nevertheless, Alma's concerns at Tobelbad extended beyond her own physical recovery. Among the people there who were eager to accompany her on long walks was a young architect named Walter Gropius, who was twenty-seven, very handsome, filled with imagination and talent, the son of a respected German family. In Alma's view, he would accomplish great things. When she began to sense that he wanted to spend time with her, she was flattered and fascinated. However, he was about to fall in love with her. There is no way to be certain of the depth of their early friendship. Nevertheless, Walter's presence and affection made Alma feel girlish, most unlike a responsible wife and mother. She experienced pangs of guilt on behalf of both Gustav and Walter, for she knew that she was leading the young man on, and would soon leave him.

At the end of July, Alma went to Toblach and her family. Gustav met her at the station with an embrace. She was healthy again, and her presence meant that he could resume his summer's work. The routine fell into order at once.

In less than a week, a letter arrived addressed to Gustav. Alma left it on the piano in the main house, as always, for her husband to open when he returned from his hut. When he broke the seal, Gustav was shocked to find that the note came from the young Gropius, who was asking, in effect, for permission to marry Alma — as if she were his daughter, not his wife. Surprised and confused, Alma tried to make light of the episode. Such an action was totally out of character with the man she had met at the spa. Gustav, who had wondered about details of his wife's long cure, saw no humor and could not dismiss the incident.

Guilt and suspicion filled the household. For the first time since the critical days shortly after they had met, Gustav found himself preparing to lose Alma and knew that he would suffer terribly should he have to live without her. Alma recognized that this was the first time in her marriage when she had been strongly drawn to a man other than Gustav. Ossip, Hans, and Alex all thought of her as Gustav's wife; not one could overlook the gigantic presence of Mahler or seriously expect to take her away from her husband. To Walter, however, she was simply Alma, the woman who had convalesced at the spa. Although he was not unaware of Gustav's name or position, he was not a musician, and Gustav did not affect him. Walter wanted only her, and he didn't care a whit about meeting her great husband. Alma had wanted him, too, and her return home was, to her, a symbol of devotion to her husband and family.

Alma and Gustav walked and talked at great length. As she told her husband how she perceived their life together, he came to realize the necessity of making significant changes. Virtually everything in the household was arranged around Gustav's work, needs, and desires. Alma had, in many ways, been treated no better than a servant or a child. She had made all of the concessions. He would not pay attention to birthdays, Christmas, or anniversaries, even though he knew that they were special to her. Alma was not convinced that he cared for her any more than he might have cared for a secretary, a business manager, or a good housekeeper. He did not even lie in bed with her and make gentle love to her; he preferred to come to her when she was already deeply asleep. Time would reveal that Alma had adapted so well to

Gustav's concept of the ideal marriage that she would hold
to many of his principles throughout her life.

They tried to work out these matters by themselves, but
finally called for Anna Moll to come and help. She was there
at once, as they had known she would be, and offered both
of her children a full measure of support. The day came
when Alma could say that the interlude with Gropius had
not affected her love for her husband and she could promise
not to leave him.

Just at the time when peace seemed to have been restored,
Gustav collapsed in the middle of the night outside his bedroom door, holding a burning candle. Alma happened to
hear his movement and found him in time to prevent a disastrous blaze. She got him back to his bed, wrapped him in
blankets, gave him the medicine she thought appropriate,
and telephoned first to the doctor, then to her mother. Dawn
was breaking when the doctor reached the house. He prescribed only rest. Anna arrived on the first train, but she
could be of little help; the situation seemed to be in hand,
so she didn't stay long. She wanted Alma and Gustav to be
on their own. The episode had lasting effects on all of them,
tolling through their memories like an omen of doom.

After a few days, Gustav was able to restore his routine,
including the drives that had replaced the hikes of previous
years. One afternoon, from the car window Alma spotted
Walter Gropius lurking near a bridge. She knew at once why
he was there: he had come to get a response to his unfortunate letter of a few weeks ago. She waited until they got
home to tell Gustav what she had seen. He went directly
back to town, found the young man, and brought him back
to the house, guiding the way through the dusk with a lan-
tern. Alma watched from her window as they entered the
house. When she went downstairs, Gustav retreated to his
room, where Alma later found him reading the Bible by can-

dlelight. In his most controlled and reasonable voice, Gustav told his wife the time had come for her to make a choice. Whatever she decided would be right, and final.

With Walter waiting in the other room, Alma looked at Gustav and knew that she would not leave him. She showed the younger man to one of the farmhouse's guest rooms, then drove him to town the next morning to see him off on the train. Walter sent Alma worshipful telegrams from every stop on his journey home. She did not foresee the likelihood of their meeting again and apparently did not respond to his ardent messages.

Gustav was overwrought by the events of recent months. He chastised himself for the ways in which he had treated Alma and others who were close to him. He became almost obsessed with the possibility of losing his wife and, with her, the security he treasured. He wrote appeals to her in the pages of his drafts of the Tenth Symphony. Anxious, nervous, frightened, and convinced that he had to do something, he arranged a consultation with the esteemed Dr. Sigmund Freud. Freud had outlived his reputation as a fashionable eccentric and proved the worth of his principles of psychoanalysis to the intellectual and forward-looking Viennese. Mahler and Freud met in the Dutch town of Leiden and walked together for four hours along the tree-lined canals. Quite apart from anything else, each enjoyed the wit and intelligence of the other. Freud posed the challenge: "How dared a man in your state ask a young woman to be tied to him? . . . I know your wife. She loved her father and she can only choose and love a man of his sort. Your age, of which you are so much afraid, is precisely what attracts her. You need not be anxious. You loved your mother, and you look for her in every woman. She was careworn and ailing, and unconsciously you wish your wife to be the same." [10]

Mahler had to admit to sometimes wishing Alma had shown in her face the same lines of toil and childbearing his mother had worn, though he knew signs of age evoked dread in his young wife. Memories of his mother's illnesses probably made Gustav more frightened by, and less responsive to, Alma's ailments than he might otherwise have been. In Gustav's mind, a woman's maladies brought back the death of his mother, and he could not separate such memories from fears of being deserted.

Gustav stopped sending his wife notes having to do with Plato or a "higher ideal," and left by her bedside such loving tokens as "My darling, my lyre, come and exorcize the spirits of darkness, they claw hold of me, they throw me to the ground. Don't leave me, my staff, come soon today so that I can rise up. I lie there and wait and ask in the silence of my heart whether I can still be saved or whether I am damned." [11] He wanted Alma to visit him in the hut, which had previously been out of bounds for her. He insisted that the door between their bedrooms be open at night so he could hear her breathing. He wandered to Alma's bedside early in the morning and gazed at her while she slept. He begged her to rescue him from his anxiety and fears.

There were other notes. "My Almschilitzili, do stay in bed today. That will be the best rest for you. I'll stay with you and not go out all day. I'll look out something to read too." And, "Beloved, I have had a wonderful sleep and yet my feelings were not for a moment interrupted. And I believe there can never now be a moment when I do not feel the happiness of knowing: she loves me! That is the whole meaning of my life. When I cannot say that, I am dead!" [12]

Letters filled with adoration and concern came to Alma from Munich when Gustav went there early in September to prepare for the premiere of his Eighth Symphony. He said he was afraid of sounding like a "schoolboy in love," but he did not hide his delight. "Freud is quite right — you were always for me the light and the central point! That inner light, I mean, which rose over all; and the blissful consciousness of this — now unshadowed and unconfirmed — raises all my feelings to the infinite." [13] He suspected that he loved his wife more than she loved him, and therefore it was up to him to summon her back into their marriage and to work to improve their life together.

One afternoon as Alma walked toward the farmhouse in Toblach, she heard her own songs being played on the piano. It took her a moment to realize what had happened. Gustav had gone to the case of manuscripts she always carried with her but rarely opened, and delved into the part of her past that he had so summarily ended before their marriage and ignored ever since. Long though she had wanted to share her music with him, she now thought he was invading her privacy, and she was afraid of his verdict.

Almost a decade earlier Gustav had written a song to a poem by Rueckert with a message that might occasionally have been directed at Alma, but which she could now turn on him:

> *Do not peek into my songs!*
> *See, I cast my own eyes down*
> *as though caught in doing wrong.*
> *Even I cannot presume*
> *To watch them grow.*
> *So your curiosity is treason!*
>
> *Bees, when they construct their cells*
> *Do not do their work in public,*
> *They don't even watch themselves.*
> *Finally, when the honeycombs*

can be brought out to the daylight,
You will be the first to glimpse them — only then, only
then. [14]

His "treason" notwithstanding, Gustav was delighted with
Alma's songs. He insisted that she sit with him while he
heard certain ones again and again. Then he turned to her
and ordered her to begin composing again. He was as strict
now about his wife's going back to her music as he had been
nine years earlier when he insisted that she give it up. In
both instances, it was essential that she oblige him at once.

What Gustav noticed in Alma's songs was a lovely combination of youthful talent and enthusiasm, more promise
than achievement. Most of her music was destroyed in later
years, but nine songs remain in published versions and are
performed on rare occasions. Four carry dates indicating they
were written in the years 1901 and 1911. There are no important differences in the styles of those allegedly written
before her marriage and those purported to have come a
decade later. All show more affinity to Zemlinsky's music
than to Mahler's. The songs show why Zemlinsky had called
Alma's music "dramatic," and why she had a hard time ac-
cepting the naive tendencies in her husband's work. Her music moves and changes its tonal base in a manner that frequently seems nervous and unsure of itself. The best of the
songs are the simplest ones, those that would remind the
listener of Zemlinsky's connections with Brahms. The least
successful songs sound a bit like the early works of Schoenberg; it was this other student of Zemlinsky who was able
to develop such early uncertainties into a strong musical language.

Alma knew the worth of her songs. She knew they were
the work of a student — albeit a student who was an excellent pianist — and she knew they revealed only the beginnings of a talent that might have become serious had it been

developed. She thought Gustav was overestimating her accomplishments; it was probably just as well that the space her composition had taken up in her life had since been filled by other ventures. She never found the courage or the time seriously to return to writing music.

Gustav's enthusiasm was not to be quelled, and he saw to it that the Universal Edition, his new publisher, brought out five of Alma's songs that same autumn. In addition, he dedicated the Eighth Symphony to her; although he had previously written songs just for her and had mentioned that other compositions had been written with her in mind, he had never given her a gift of official dedication. Gustav's Symphony No. 8 and Five Songs by Alma Maria Schindler-Mahler were printed simultaneously, with the same title-page design. Alma had mixed feelings when she saw the two editions sitting side by side, the songs of her youth looking so like the symphony that both she and Gustav knew was his greatest achievement.

The first performance of the Eighth would take place in Munich's new Exhibition Hall, where there was plenty of space for the huge orchestra, eight vocal soloists, three choruses (including a children's chorus), and organ. Before Gustav left to take up residence at the Grand Hotel Continental and immerse himself in preparations, he gave Alma the diadem he had had made in honor of her thirty-first birthday. He took from her the wedding ring he had given her, meaning to wear it himself until they were reunited. When he first saw the published version of his Eighth Symphony, he looked at the dedication and wrote to Alma, " . . . I want it taken seriously, as a token meaning far more to me than a lover's extravagance. Does it not make the impression rather of a betrothal? Doesn't it seem more like the announcement of an engagement?" [15]

The pressure he was under in Munich began to take a toll on Gustav's health. He felt worse when Alma misread a telegram he sent her, and wrote, "But Almschilitzilitzilitzili! How did you read the 'ominous' telegram then? Didn't you see at once it was a joke? I couldn't mean such absurd bombast to be taken seriously! You ought to have cut that inflated balloon adrift at once!" [16] As always, she was not writing frequently enough to please him, and when she finally did send two letters that arrived on the same day, she warned that it might be another week before she would join him. "I'm a dead man if you stay away for another whole week . . ." he responded.

> Almschili, if you had left me that time, I should simply have gone out like a torch deprived of air . . . schoolboy in love though I am, there is still something left in me of the father of a family, or husband, or whatever you call the thing, and it wants to know how my dearest and my dears are getting on day by day.
>
> . . . Oh, how lovely it is to love! And only now do I know what it is! Pain has lost its power and death its thorn. Tristan speaks truth: I am immortal, for how could Tristan's love die? . . .
>
> I think of the moment all the time: "Is it true? Are you mine once more? Can I grasp it? At last! At last!" . . .
>
> Our rooms are very nice and unbelievably quiet. It's the first time in Munich I've known peace at night. The windows actually give on to a courtyard. But, to please you, Almschi, my love, I've taken a small reception room opposite, facing the street, where we can spend the days and have meals and receive people . . .
>
> Your letter of today was so dear, and for the first time for eight weeks — in my whole life, for that matter — I feel the blissful happiness love gives to one who, loving with all his soul, knows he is loved in return. [17]

Alma went to Munich as scheduled. When she arrived she found that Gustav had filled the rooms with her favorite tuber roses and placed a score of the symphony with its dedication to her on the table next to her pillow. By the bed that would be Anna Moll's, Gustav had left a piano reduction of the Eighth with the inscription, "To our dear mother, who has ever been all in all to us and who gave me Alma — from Gustav in undying gratitude." [18] The Molls had to delay their arrival for a few days, which turned out to be a small blessing, since they could be called upon at the last minute to bring with them the coats Gustav and Alma needed for protection against Munich's autumn chill.

The premiere of the Eighth would take place on September 12, with a second performance on the thirteenth. Tickets for both were completely sold out. Anticipation mounted in the three or four days before the performance to such a point that Alma and Gustav chose to hibernate in their rooms, avoiding everyone but family. Gustav was concerned about the reception his new work would receive. Considering both its size and the amount of public interest, he knew the reaction would not be mild. He would have either a great triumph or an utter disaster. Alma took her box seat for the first performance just in time to see the entire audience rise to its feet as her husband mounted the railed podium from which he would conduct. Through the long symphony there was hardly a sound from the audience. Then, at the work's conclusion, there was an ovation approaching the proportions of a demonstration as thousands of people surged toward the composer and the stage.

The Mahlers had to struggle to leave the auditorium. Back in their hotel, scores of well-wishers were waiting for them. A celebration had been planned to include only close friends and family, including Berliner, Roller, Max Reinhardt, and the Clemenceaus. The following evening, friends arranged a party in the Hotel Vier Jahreszeiten specifically in honor of Alma, to whom the work was dedicated. There, the proud and happy wife was offered her choice of gifts. She selected three baroque pearls on a gold chain. Gustav, newly aware of how important such trinkets and presents could be, insisted on trying to buy the necklace for Alma, but the party had been Berliner's idea, and he remained the donor.

Another gift followed the premiere of the Eighth. Thomas Mann, who with his wife had met the Mahlers for the first time just after the symphony's premiere, sent a copy of his latest novel, *Koenigliche Hoheit,* with a note calling the book "certainly a very poor return for what I received — a mere feather's weight in the hand of the man who, as I believe, expresses the art of our time in its profoundest and most sacred form . . . Perhaps it may afford you tolerable entertainment for an idle hour or two." [19]

6

Gustav's Death

IN VIENNA after the triumph of the Eighth Symphony, Alma, Gustav, and Anna took up their temporary residence with the Molls on the Hohe Warte and prepared to leave once again for their season in America. Schoenberg and Zemlinsky visited them, deeply impressed and moved by the newly presented opus. Schoenberg took the opportunity to thank Mahler for having intervened financially on his behalf, thus expressing both his concern and his support for the younger man's efforts.

A great deal of time was spent discussing the ideal home Carl was trying to find for his "children." It had become increasingly evident that it would be impossible to find a house meeting all the specifications — one close enough to Vienna to allow for easy access, but still far enough out of the city to promise privacy and a garden, with a place where Gustav could work and enough space to give all of them the feeling of freedom they needed to counteract the months they had to spend in hotels and temporary residences. Gustav and

Carl involved themselves in endless conversations about the prospective Mahler homestead. They decided to consider another plan: buying a plot of land and building the perfect house. The men became ever more enthusiastic about the idea. Alma was dissociated from the preliminary planning stages, partly because the others were having so much fun discussing it between themselves, and also because she had so much to prepare for their departure.

One of the new difficulties she had to face was the sartorial fastidiousness that had recently befallen her husband, one of several manifestations of his new outlook on life. No longer would Gustav be satisfied to use his clothes as stuffing in the trunks and suitcases holding more important items such as manuscripts, sketches, and scores. Now he was concerned with fabric, style, cut, and press, and it fell to Alma to see that every bit of clothing was perfectly prepared for the trip and would arrive on the other side of the Atlantic Ocean ready to be worn.

Gustav went ahead to conduct concerts in Bremen before meeting Alma and their daughter for the trip to the harbor in Cherbourg. The ocean voyage no longer caused the family much concern; they had discovered how to take advantage of the time to rest and prepare themselves for the subsequent strenuous days. Sunny afternoons at sea were spent walking on deck, taking photographs, and gazing off into the horizon. Gustav had been approached by the directors of the Vienna Opera to return to his old position on a limited basis that might have met his requirements, but he was so much enjoying his newly found ability to play and relax that he decided to put off giving the proposal any serious consideration.[1]

In New York they went back to the familiar Savoy, where Gustav could waste no time beginning preparations for the opening on Tuesday, November 1, 1910, of the Philharmonic Society's sixty-ninth season. Mahler was to introduce new programs on Tuesdays at 8:15 P.M. and to repeat them on the following Friday afternoons. Sometimes other programs were presented on Sunday afternoons, and there were tours with stops in Pittsburgh and Buffalo. For the opening program of the 1910–1911 season, Gustav decided to present music of Bach, Schubert, Mozart, and Richard Strauss. At once he began preparing this program and others.

Good news from Vienna gave all Mahlers something to look forward to. On November 3, an agreement had been signed between Emil Freund, who was acting as Gustav's representative, and the owners of "farm no. 17" for the Mahlers to take possession, for the price of 40,000 crowns, of a modest house and the accompanying gardens, meadows, and pastures at Breitenstein on Semmering, south of Vienna but conveniently located to the city. Gustav wrote to Carl Moll:

We received your precious news today . . . and there is a fair and true aim for all our desires. Almschi will be writing at length about everything. This year I have literally not an hour really to myself, but I am very well and full of energy despite — or, indeed, perhaps because of — all this work.

I should like now, before you finish the plans for the house, to urge you to be sure to include a bathroom (with a W.C.) each (no matter how small) for Almschi and for me, for I can hardly find any "residence" comfortable — or, indeed, really hygienic — without such a convenience . . . I beg you to spare no pains on this point . . . I do not feel under the least obligation to . . . the Vienna Opera, since I have always emphasized that I can only make a decision when I have a clear view of the situation from an artistic standpoint . . . Alma is now for the first time really doing something about her health, and I am *very* satisfied with her progress. She is also in very good spirits and full of hope.[2]

Gustav wrote to his agent Freund to remind him that the
land should be registered in both his name and Alma's, and
to say that, no matter what the newspapers had reported,
he would not be returning to the Opera in Vienna under the
old conditions. With some questions about their future answered, Gustav and Alma went off with the Philharmonic
Society on a tour that took them to Niagara Falls. They
enjoyed some hours of peace watching the violent waters,
though they still felt as if they were under a microscope, the
objects of attention not only for the American reporters but
also for European correspondents. A Viennese, Maurice
Baumfeld, wrote an article for the German-language newspaper telling of the Mahlers' life at the Savoy, which read,
in part:

> His best hours were when he had just conducted a successful
> concert and was able to gather round him, in the corner sa-
> lon in the Hotel Savoy, a few people who he knew under-
> stood him and respected his true nature. People with whom
> he could be as he really was. He used to like to lie on the
> divan until he began to feel tired. Then he got up: "Right,
> ladies and gentlemen, now you can enjoy yourselves and be
> merry, I am no good for that. If you get too merry I shall
> throw my boots against the wall. Then you will know you
> are making too much noise." A few hearty hand-shakes and
> Herr Mahler went to bed. Of course that remark about mer-
> riment, which he said he was no good for, was not true. He
> had a strong sense of humor which could run the whole
> gamut from savage mockery to childish glee. When he was
> in a good mood and took off on well-known contemporar-
> ies, especially of course other composers and conductors, we
> just could not stop laughing. He never shrank from the hard-
> est words and the most grotesque mimicry.
>
> But, on the other hand, anyone who saw him playing with
> his little daughter fully understood the gentleness, indeed

lovableness of this basically taciturn nature. To entertain children so that the child is really the one entertained is rightly considered a special gift. Now whether Mahler was the magician or the fairy, the wild beast or the faithful dog, whether he improvised his utterly funny tales from the present or tried to turn them into a parable with a didactic purpose, he always showed that fine understanding of the child's awakening soul which he was able to express in so many of his compositions.

His relations with his wife Alma were equally deep and tender; though this was not until after many a struggle and crisis. The beautiful Frau Alma, herself a brilliant musician and a more than usually talented composer, did not always have an easy time, for all the love he showed her. It was many years before he recognized her as his equal . . . Their harmony reached an intensity which one would not consider possible. It was for this woman above all that he composed, conducted, worked, lived . . . About Christmas he once took me into his room with an air of great mystery. "You must help me buy presents for my wife. You know her tastes. But, for Heaven's sake, she must not get wind of it." We then arranged a secret rendezvous. I walked around for hours with him in the stores and art shops of New York. Nothing was good and beautiful enough for him . . . Then he filled great sheets of paper with instructions for unheard-of treasures which were to be bought in Europe, above all in Paris, in the presence of Frau Alma herself. He put the whole thing together himself on Christmas Eve, piece by piece, but still doubted whether his treasure was rich and fine enough.[3]

Regarding the proposed new house in Semmering, Baumfeld wrote:

This house must have been built and pulled down perhaps a hundred times with his friends last winter. Plans had been produced by people in the artistic circles in Vienna from which Frau Alma came, and also by American architects. For it was to be something special, and above all something quite personal . . . We argued, often to the point of acrimony, about every single chair, about wallpaper and carpet designs . . . "As long as you leave my study alone," he used to say, "you can go on building to your heart's content. But the room where I am going to write my next symphonies is something *I* shall decide on . . ."

Mahler often enough had very hard things to say about the philistines and snobs of New York; but he did not close his heart to either the greatness or the special character of the city. He waxed in fact quite passionate about the New York sun. From the corner window of his living room in the Hotel Savoy he had a broad view of Central Park and its greenery. He could sit for hours as if in a trance and stare out on the vibrant life before him.[4]

That Christmas of 1910, for which Gustav had so carefully prepared, was one Alma could never forget. Gustav had never before gone on a shopping escapade, had not even bought his wife a wedding present. When the time came for the celebration in the rooms Alma had so carefully decorated, Gustav and Gucki shooed Alma from the parlor while father and daughter assembled all the presents on a long table topped with a lace cloth and a blanket of roses. They were pleased with their arrangement and called Alma to come back into the room. She was silenced and shocked, so moving was their tribute, and so strongly did it remind her of a flower-draped bier. She found perfume and a few lovely baubles as well as promissory notes:[5]

Bon
to the value of 40 dollars
for a fine spree along Fifth Ave.
From Herr Gustav Mahler on a country ramble with his
Almschili

Bon
for the purchase of a
Solitaire
worth over 1,000 dollars
Gustav Mahler
New York Christmas, 1910.

Alma had long wanted a diamond ring. Gustav had thought the custom of passing such an item from husband to wife was silly, but now his wife would have a nice one, as well as a shopping spree on Fifth Avenue, which lay right outside their window. It was a joyous Christmas, one of Alma's best. They were happy together and felt secure with Gucki there in the hotel with them, even though both Alma and Gustav knew that trouble was brewing in his professional life. He had asked for an extra $5000 to conduct twenty additional concerts in 1910–1911. The Philharmonic Society granted him an extra $3000 and went on to ask who would be their conductor for the next season. The minutes of the meeting reported that Franz Kneisel had said he would be honored to take over the position from the esteemed Maestro Mahler. It remained for Gustav and the leaders of the orchestra to agree on tenure and terms.

In Alma's view, Gustav had allowed the committee of ladies too free a hand in programming the symphony season, and she knew problems both personal and political had arisen among Gustav and a number of the instrumentalists in his charge. A pall was cast over their celebration with Dr. Fraenkel as they marked the arrival of the year 1911. The three raised their glasses to a new beginning in the city they all regarded as their second home. Gustav was about to begin to prepare his own Fourth Symphony for performance with the Philharmonic Society; although the work had been offered previously in Manhattan, the occasion on which it was to be presented under the direction of its composer was considered very important. On January 18, 1911, the critic for the *New York Times* reported, "The performance of the symphony by Mr. Mahler and his men was an exceedingly brilliant one, and after it was finished the applause of the audience burst out in force, and Mr. Mahler was called forward many times."

Frances Alda, wife of Gatti-Casazza, asked Alma for permission to perform one of her songs at a recital on March 2 in New York. Alma was intimidated by the prospect of being revealed as a composer, but Gustav was delighted. When the permission was granted he attempted to persuade the singer to perform all five songs in his wife's published set. That would be impossible because of time, but Gustav offered to coach the soprano in the one song she had selected. When he and Alma went to the Waldorf-Astoria to meet Mme Gatti-Casazza, she paid attention only to her coach and pianist, caring not at all that Alma was the song's creator.

The prospect of a performance nevertheless boosted Alma's spirits. Gustav wrote to his mother-in-law, begging her to confirm the time of her planned visit to New York, fearing that Anna Moll felt unwanted. "I have the feeling that Almscherl is to blame for this, with her temperamental outpourings . . . It would be really too absurd if a misunderstanding and some kind of pique should have arisen between us. We have our posh cabins on the finest ship in the German merchant navy, the *George Washington*, for 20 March, and you will be sure to arrange your journey in such a way that the three of us can return together, won't you? . . .

"This time I can give you the best of news about Almscherl. She is really blossoming — is keeping to a splendid diet, and has *entirely* given up alcohol, looking younger every day . . . Her published songs are causing a furore here . . . Guckerl is also full of life."[6]

This is the earliest mention of Alma's drinking. She and Gustav had now and then shared more wine at lunch than they thought they should have had. She had a penchant to drink more than her husband thought that she should, but she was not given to drunkenness. His concern was most likely part of his program to make both of them healthier.

In January 1911 Gustav was summoned to the home of the chairman of the Philharmonic Society's Executive Committee, where he was soundly berated by several of the ladies of the board and instructed of boundaries firmly limiting his authority from that moment onward. Gustav was infuriated, and although he tried to tell himself that he had to ignore the troublemakers and do only what was right for himself and the orchestra, the confrontation with his employers touched off his latent illness. He came down with a badly inflamed throat accompanied by a fever, and his condition deteriorated. Contrary to Dr. Fraenkel's advice, he insisted on conducting the Philharmonic on February 21. This concert included the premiere of Ferrucio Busoni's *Berceuse élégiac* (*Cradlesong at the Grave of My Mother*). Both this composer and Toscanini were in the audience. Busoni wrote to his wife that Mahler had prodded him to take two extra bows there in Carnegie Hall. Gustav considered the evening a triumph, and, back in bed at the hotel, he took aspirin and went to sleep.

On February 24 the violinist Spiering had to substitute for Gustav on the Philharmonic's podium. Dr. Fraenkel called in Emanuel Libman, Chief of the First Medical Service and Associate Director of Laboratories at Mount Sinai Hospital, for consultation. With a colleague, Dr. Libman took a blood culture that confirmed the presence of *Streptococcus viridians*. In the doctor's words, "the bacterial findings sealed Mahler's doom. He insisted on being told the truth and then expressed a wish to die in Vienna." [7]

Alma was at loose ends. She could do nothing to help her husband, though the irregular nature of his infection gave her inspiration to retain some optimism and believe he could recover. Several other doctors joined in the consultations, and a variety of medications were tried. Dr. Fraenkel, who was with the Mahlers in the Savoy whenever his schedule allowed, discouraged rash experimentation with drugs, and believed, with Alma, that Gustav would best be helped by his inner strength and will. Gifts of food, flowers, and tributes streamed into the Mahlers' suite when word of Gustav's illness passed around the city. The patient was delighted by the attention he was receiving from the public, from his doctor-friend, and from his wife.

Dr. Fraenkel escorted Alma to the concert at which Mme Gatti-Casazza sang. Alma sat in the rear of the gallery and would not go before the audience or discuss the event. When she and Fraenkel arrived back at the Savoy, Gustav could not wait to hear about the concert; he was more anxious about the performance of Alma's song than he had been about presentations of his own complex symphonies. He was elated when she told him that the song had been sung not once, but twice in quick succession, so enthusiastic was the audience's applause.

When the Mahlers realized that Gustav would have to be taken back to Europe for further treatment and consultations, they called for Anna Moll. Hired nurses didn't meet Gustav's requirements, and he would not allow them to take the place of either his wife or his mother-in-law, who arrived in only six days. Anna's presence made a great deal of difference to Alma, especially when she realized how happy Gustav was to have the older woman tending him. "I used to say jokingly when I was first married that if Mahler had gone to my mother and said: 'I've had to put Alma to death,' she would simply have replied: 'I'm sure you were right,

Gustav' . . . It was the utmost happiness when we were all three together."[8]

Dr. Fraenkel came to the Savoy to fetch Gustav and take him to the ship in the limousine of Mrs. Minnie Untermyer, the conductor's greatest supporter within the high echelons of the Philharmonic Society. Alma stayed behind to check their rooms for a final time, tend to the bill, and thank the staff. The management of the hotel had cleared the lobby for Gustav's departure, so sensitive were they to the feelings of their most famous guest, and so fearful, too, of the masses of people who might have been there to pay a final farewell to the dying man. On shipboard, Fraenkel waited with them until the last minute, making sure that Gustav was comfortable, then turning over nursing duties to Alma and Anna with a final sad farewell.

From hour to hour, the worst concern was the zig-zag nature of Gustav's fever, which went from below normal to dangerously high. It was nearly impossible for his nurses to keep him comfortable. Nonetheless, he was strong enough to be moved onto the deck of the ship almost every day, and the captain obligingly created a private space in the sun that was reserved exclusively for the Mahler party. There, Alma took photographs and received messages and gifts, including a bit of amusing counterpoint sent by Busoni, who was also on board. That musician's presence allowed Alma a companion when she had a free hour for a walk around the deck. Busoni pleased her with his insight and goodwill as well as with reminders of times past.

Leaving America was simple compared with arriving at Cherbourg, where Gustav had to be settled into the tender, then a carriage, and onto a train bound for Paris. Alma led their forty pieces of luggage through customs and kept track of Gucki and the nurse. They were all relieved to arrive at the Elysée Hotel in Paris, where Carl was waiting to lend supportive hands. The next morning, Gustav was on the balcony waiting for his wife and family in his morning clothes, ready for breakfast and wanting to find an automobile to take them all for a ride. During the brief excursion, however, he lost strength and had to be taken directly back to the hotel, where he was given emergency treatment. Alma left her mother with Gustav while she consoled Gucki, who was frightened and confused. Gustav talked to Anna, his "dear little Mama," about his grave and tombstone, while bands of reporters waited downstairs in the hotel.

Alma and the Molls tried desperately to reach the specialists whose names Dr. Fraenkel had given them, but it was approaching Easter Sunday, and offices were closed. Finally they located André Chantemesse, a professor at the university and a Fellow of the Pasteur Institute, who agreed to have Gustav admitted immediately to his clinic.

On April 22, 1911, Vienna's *Neue Freie Presse* reported from Paris that on the previous morning "Gustav Mahler left the Elysée Palace Hotel in the Champs Elysées, which is excellently run by a Viennese, Ronacher. He was taken by ambulance-car to the sanatorium which is situated in a magnificant part near the Bois de Boulogne . . . When Mahler arrived in the sanatorium Chantemesse was ready waiting for him to begin the serum treatment as soon as he had examined him . . . I had a chance to see Mahler when he was brought to the sanatorium. He does not look bad . . . Mahler spoke for a long time about these artistic ideals until his wife, who watches over him with touching care, made him rest . . . Mahler knows of his condition. He has succeeded in getting a full picture from the doctors in America, and what he was not actually told his ready perception soon guessed."[9]

Alma and Anna did not trust the nursing staff, so they kept constant watch over Gustav as his condition worsened slowly but steadily. During those hours when he seemed to be stronger, he and Alma would talk about their future — a trip to Egypt, the carefree life they would learn to lead together. But lows followed highs, and she decided to telegraph Professor Franz Chvostek, a celebrated Viennese physician, who arrived the next morning. The doctor tried to feign optimism as he ordered them all to leave for Vienna that night. Anna Moll took Gucki on an afternoon train while Alma, Gustav, and Carl traveled together overnight. The *Neue Freie Presse* again covered the event: "This afternoon Mahler left Paris. He is traveling on a stretcher accompanied by his wife, by Herr Moll and by Professor Chvostek. At his own specific request, he is being brought to Vienna.

"Professor Chvostek agreed with Chantemesse's treatment, but neither of the doctors could refuse the sick man's request to be taken to Vienna . . . The latest examination, which took place in the afternoon before Mahler's departure, revealed that his condition is very serious and that there is nothing to lose by this journey."[10]

Alma, Carl, and the physician took turns keeping watch over Gustav in the compartment of the train. They were constantly assaulted by journalists who wanted a glimpse of the famous musician and a new report of his condition. Gustav had been filled with hope by what Chvostek had said to him, and he took interest in the inquisitive visitors and remained alert. Alma had to admit that hope was unfounded. When they arrived in Vienna, according to the *Neues Wiener Tagblatt,* "Only a few people were waiting for the train . . . The doctor's wishes that he should be kept away from any excitement had been respected. The ambulance from the Loewe Sanatorium, which drove up about 5:30 at the summer platform of Vienna West, also attracted only a small group of onlookers. Shortly afterwards [Arnold and Justi] Rosé appeared, with Court Conductor Walter and Herr Spiegler. A few minutes before 6 the Orient Express arrived. From one of the sleeping cars,

which was located in the middle of the train, Herr
Moll . . . alighted first. Friends went up to him. Herr Moll
said to them: 'The journey was reasonable. The patient is
very weak.' " [11]

Gustav was taken to the Loewe Sanitorium, where his
rooms were filled with flowers and where he was attended
by Alma and Anna, with visits from Berliner, Justi, and other
close friends. Gucki went to see her father, who warned her
to be good, for ever. Dr. Chvostek joined the family on May
18 in what he knew would be Gustav's final hours. As the
moments stretched on, representatives of the press kept their
watch outside the door. Carl Moll stayed with Gustav until
the end. On the doctor's advice, Alma had left the hospital
and been driven to the Molls' home. Just after 11 P.M. she
heard the bells ringing across the city, signifying her husband's death.

Gustav was buried according to his wishes in the Grinzing
Cemetery next to his daughter Maria. His tombstone was
designed by Josef Hoffmann; it bears only his name. Carl
Moll took the death mask. Arnold Schoenberg painted a
picture of the scene of the interment at the cemetery. Alma
did not attend any of the memorial services.

Mahler's estate was valued at almost 170,000 crowns, of
which 139,000 were in securities, 19,000 in property. The
composer and lawyer Julius Bittner estimated the value of
Gustav's manuscripts at just over 10,000 crowns. Alma received the promised pension from the Vienna Opera. In New
York, in her name, Gustav had left more than $100,000. [12]

The Widow with a New Genius

ALMA WAS NOT QUITE THIRTY-TWO, but she would always think of herself as Alma Mahler. There are those who still claim that when Gustav died she bade farewell to the best years of her life. Through much of the rest of her life, she searched for the emotions, privileges, and energies of the decade she had shared with Gustav.

Alma and her daughter stayed on at the home of her mother and stepfather on the Hohe Warte. Since Gustav had ordered that there be no mourning, Alma wore her normal dresses, went to concerts, saw friends, and made every attempt to get on with her life. She was surprised to find among her visitors Dr. Joseph Fraenkel from New York, and even more surprised that he wanted her to wait what might be a respectable period of time, then marry him. She had appreciated his help and enjoyed his company during Gustav's last months, but she had never looked upon this man as a potential lover or husband. Nevertheless, he returned to Vienna a few months later and talked her into traveling with him to Corfu, the scene of the happy holiday of her childhood. They made the trip by ship, and while her companion spent most of his time being sick in the cabin, Alma met an Albanian cabinet minister who told her the proverb that would subsequently play an important role in her life: "Not the murderer, but the murdered is guilty." [1]

Fraenkel was persistent in his attempts to convince Alma to return with him to New York and become his wife, but she was not ready to commit herself and wrote a letter dashing his romantic hopes:

> The fate that parts us is the divergence of our own souls. Every fiber of my heart draws me back into true living, while you are striving for consummate dematerialization.
>
> What is salvation to me is unthinkable to you, with your cerebral makeup; what is salvation to you strikes me as madness. That's how different we are.
>
> My watchward is: *Amo — ergo sum.*
>
> Yours: *Cogito — ergo sum.*
>
> When it comes to living you're a miserable failure. At best, men like you are put between book covers, closed, pressed and devoured in unrecognizable form by future generations. But such men never *live.*
>
> Today I know the eternal source of all strength. It is in nature, in the earth, in people who don't hesitate to cast away their existence for the sake of an idea. They are the ones who can *love.*
>
> I go on living with my face lifted high, but with my feet on the ground — where they belong. [2]

A few months later, Dr. Fraenkel married Alma's friend Ganna Walska.

In the autumn Alma moved with seven-year-old Gucki into an apartment on the Elizabethstrasse, where, for the first time, she set up a household of her own and built a life. Her first important appearance as Mahler's widow occurred in Munich on November 20, when Bruno Walter conducted the premiere of Gustav's *Das Lied von der Erde*. Alma loved the honor accorded both her husband's memory and herself as she assumed the role of his representative in the company of friends, colleagues, and admirers. On the train home to Vienna, she met an old acquaintance, Paul Kammerer. A brilliant and controversial biologist by profession, Kammerer was also a devoted musician, engaging in both composition (his songs were published by Simrock) and criticism. Alma and Paul talked throughout the journey, glad to have one another's company. He was impressed by the fact that he was in the presence of the widow of Mahler, whom he had championed. As the hours passed, however, Paul became enchanted with Alma herself. There began an intense, if short-lived relation. The voluminous correspondence shows that Alma trusted Paul and relied on the man whose intellect and education were different from — even beyond — the level to which she was accustomed.

Paul, in order to be able to spend time with Alma under circumstances he could explain to his wife, and also to help his new friend expand her own horizons and interests, invited her to become an assistant in his biological laboratory. There was no salary involved, and Alma needed money much less than she needed something to do. She found herself working with worms, reptiles, praying mantises, and all sorts of fauna that were not part of the life to which she had become accustomed. Becoming deeply involved in the new and different challenges, she took some of the specimens home to watch more closely and record their habits.

Paul's devotion increased, and he wrote, "You probably think that I have nothing to do with my time except write these endless letters . . . But you should know: 1) I believe that if someone needs me, wants to be my friend, and if I feel the same inclination, I cannot do other than give myself completely . . . 2) I have no time for the things that do not allow me to approach a higher goal, things that are not part of my search for Enlightenment (do you understand what I mean?) . . . I know that every meeting with Alma Mahler is an added boost to my energy for my work. When I am with her, I collect the energy that I need to produce."[3]

Paul advised Alma as she formed the Gustav Mahler Foundation. This organization would help young musicians and serve as a safe repository for the part of Gustav's legacy that was not directly and necessarily Alma's. In this advisory capacity, Paul spent many nonworking hours with Alma, and it was not long before he was sending his love to Gucki and "Frau Mama," Anna Moll. He was allowed to address Alma with the familiar *du*. She was his "most beloved Alma," and he wanted nothing more than to see her more often. Her response to him was enigmatic.

He wrote, "You asked me today during my improvised visit to your table whether you should marry again . . . I did not respond to you as I should have. You think that complete surrender has to depend on your convincing the man, once and for all . . . to belong to you, not to be what you call a flirt or a playboy. But something is missing, something that you have certainly found in your own experience: It is essential that *you love* the man. If I've understood this correctly . . . this component is still missing in the man to whom you are thinking of giving yourself as a wife. And for that reason, after lengthy reflection, I must advise you to say No!"[4]

Paul served as her confidant, but although he was married he wanted to be more.

The possibility that you would love me as a man arose again yesterday and was stated *twice* by your much adored lips

. . . If that were to be the case, and if your words and your deeds were to prove that it might really be so, then I would at once embrace the whole world and throw myself immediately at your complete disposal. But there remains — not on your side, but on mine — the fact that "the rest is painful to carry," and it is too painful to carry because it brings no peace, only unreality, and that derives from my Alma.

Everything that stands here, in this manner, cannot constitute an "agreement of marriage." To begin with, you did give me such a thing once, almost wickedly (not without justification); secondly, I myself am far from that point, and must see what happy hours and companionship lie ahead of us; and thirdly, I want you to be certain, not just to be considering, because I want at least a *suspicion* that the whole thing might actually come to pass.

The fact that I honor you with my whole existence, with every breath that I breathe and everything that I do . . . you already know, or should know.[5]

Alma accused Paul of being in love with love, and merely flirting.

"I love only you," he responded, "and as far as I'm concerned . . . I can't accomplish as much in a whole day as you can accomplish in one glance and one breath . . . You talk about your searching for people; on my part, you call that flirting. But all I am really doing is searching for friends. There is something erotic in it, to be sure, on my part as on yours. But this erotic part is both voluntary and involuntary, and soon the whole thing becomes so sublimated that it all falls on the same level, and is merely a desire for companionship."[6]

Paul was unstable, brilliant, and a good friend to Alma. But she was not in love with him. As a note on the bottom of the final letter she received from him, she wrote, "his world really had little to do with reality. Our relationship was friendly on my side, but passionate on his. There was a time in the year '12 when we all had to tremble for him. He was about to show his love for me irrationally, to become the clown in my circle of friends. Every day, he was outside my home threatening to shoot himself, which he seemed to want to do on Mahler's grave."[7] Eventually Alma telephoned Paul's wife and told her how critical the situation had become. The two women agreed that his pistol had to be taken away from him, and Alma ended the association. Two decades later, Paul Kammerer committed suicide.

Alma had someone to take his place. She had developed a close friendship with the composer Franz Schreker, a gifted musician and teacher whose work was quickly to be eclipsed for reasons of fashion, which Alma found both incomprehensible and unfair. A year Alma's senior, Franz had been born in Monaco, where his Austrian father was court photographer. The family moved to Vienna, and Franz studied violin with Rosé. In 1908 he had organized the Vienna Philharmonic Chorus, and it was evidently at one of the rehearsals of this ensemble when Schreker heard that Alma was in the auditorium. He went up to the box in which she had taken a chair to pay his respects.

He was on the threshold of what was to be the greatest success of his career, the premiere of the opera *Die ferne Klang* in Frankfurt in August 1912. He was excited and full of promise. Alma enjoyed his company tremendously, even though he was sometimes afflicted by social awkwardnesses in the presence of his colleagues or in large gatherings. He was gifted as a poet in addition to his musical talents and sent Alma poems that were meant as very personal gifts and tributes to her. When he wasn't writing verse, he indulged in romantic dialogues, also meant only for Alma, and only occasionally did his letters to her revert to terse reports on the progress of his work or the details of his life. He was finishing *Das Spielwerk und die Prinzessin,* which would receive its first performance in Vienna on March 15, 1913. He told Alma about the progress and turmoil of this preparation. Much as she respected this man for his talent, she had patience for him, not love.

In the early months of 1912, Carl Moll told Alma about a hungry young genius who was gaining a great deal of attention in the Viennese art world. Perhaps he might like to paint her portrait. She recognized the name Oskar Kokoschka from the bits of his work she had seen, and from stories she had heard about the commotions he had caused during his years of schooling and at various exhibitions. He was seven years younger than she, born in 1886, the son of a skilled goldsmith from Prague and an Imperial forester's daughter. Oskar grew up in a matriarchy and felt he had inherited the gift of "second sight" from his mother and grandmother.

He loved music and showed some talent in this direction, but it was through his skill for drawing that Oskar came to the attention of his schoolmasters. He was offered a scholarship to the Vienna School of Arts and Crafts, where he could study to become a teacher. The school was itself controversial, since, with its close connection to the cooperative known as the Wiener Werkstaette (where Kolo Moser had designed the dresses Alma had worn during her pregnancies) and with the Secession of Klimt and Carl Moll, it defied the superiority of the Imperial tradition. There, Oskar assured his reputation for unorthodoxy by ignoring the prescribed curriculum. Nevertheless, the Werkstaette published his graphic series *The Dreaming Youths* in 1908. That same summer he was represented in the first International Exhibition with a tapestry cartoon and a painted clay bust, *The Warrior,* an anguished self-portrait with an open mouth into which spectators threw chocolate drops and candy wrappers. The sculpture was bought by Adolf Loos, the architect who would become Oskar's supporter, patron, and friend.[8]

Loos came into the habit of taking Oskar's paintings from him, as the artist recounted, "not with the intention of collecting them, or in order to sell them for me, but rather to prevent my painting over them for a lack of a new canvas."[9] Oskar was poor but attractive, so he took some assurance in knowing that he would always be able to count on a large circle of friends — poets and artists as well as bank clerks — and they would take care of the bills that grew during their long evenings in Vienna's cafés. In his early years of manhood, Oskar was fascinated by both the ideal and the reality of women:

> Beyond, more dangerous and intriguing depths remained to be explored. The erotic advance of the female principle almost at once put my hard-won equilibrium in jeopardy. Strangely enough, for me men always had only one face, which showed their character, experiences, passions, even when the face was a mask. No man could lead me, as a woman could, into a guessing game . . . To me, one thing was certain: the instinct for self-preservation which begins with the first movement in the womb and ends with death. I could confront reality and come to terms, as many others do, with the fact that life is a mortally dangerous thing. Thus, I was spared the panic which strikes those who refuse to open their eyes, and I suffered none of the erosion of self-confidence which periods of uncertainty tend to inflict on the mind. Fear makes for inactivity, but behind that shadow of Thanatos, which had dogged me from my childhood onwards, there lurked the ever more enticing abyss of Eros.[10]

In this state of mind, Oskar wrote his first stage play, *Murder, the Hope of Women,* produced in Vienna during the summer of 1909. The semi-improvised presentation might have turned out to be little more than an exercise for its student actors had it not stirred bitter controversy, savage notices in the press, and great notoriety for its creator, who reflected later:

> I was not adult in every sense and different from before, but my curiosity remained unassuaged. An inner voice tormented me, like a hermit in the wilderness, with imaginings about the female sex. In Greek mythology there is a lot about Eros, but nothing analogous to the unhappy story of Bruennhilde and Siegfried, or Tristan and Isolde. And how is one to explain, I wondered, this almost instantaneous transformation when one becomes possessed by another and bestows upon this being such beauty, wit and spiritual qualities as nothing in the world could equal? The power of attraction is strong enough to render passion itself speechless, and you will take any risk, shrug off folly, for the sake of a smile or of words you imagine were never heard before from mortal lips. You can feel icy cold and boiling hot at the same moment. When you timidly try to put an arm around the one with whom you are mortally in love, your heart begins to beat as if you were committing a sacrilege; only God, if he exists, could know how much you suffer.[11]

Roller, Gustav's friend and colleague at the Opera, was director of the School of Arts and Crafts, and it fell to him to tell Oskar he was no longer welcome in those halls — he was too disruptive. Loos encouraged the young man to pour all of his energy into painting. There resulted the portraits of the poet Peter Altenberg, the journalist Karl Kraus, as well as the children of a number of well-to-do Viennese who paid meager amounts but enough to provide the artist with subsistence. Paul Cassirer invited Oskar to exhibit at his influential Berlin gallery in 1910, thus giving a tremendous boost to the one-time renegade's reputation, which Moll had been following closely.

In the spring of 1912, Oskar was called to the house on the Hohe Warte to paint Carl Moll, whom he described as

no genius, but a cultivated man. As buyer for the long-established and respected Viennese art firm of Artaria, he was the first to bring Impressionist paintings to Vienna . . . He had a true eye for quality and the content of a work of art.

I painted Carl Moll in his patrician residence, with its neo-classical mid-Victorian decor . . . I was often asked to stay for dinner. I liked the atmosphere of the house, although its slightly Oriental magnificence was less reminiscent of Schindler's time than of the age of Ingres and Delacroix (or Makart, whose pupil Moll had also been): Japanese vases, great sprays of peacock feathers, Persian carpets on the walls. The table was elegantly laid; there were always flower arrangements, gleaming silver, sparkling glass — and good wine. The concertmaster of the Vienna Philharmonic, Arnold Rosé, and his family, were close friends of the Molls, and there were often chamber recitals. The table talk was usually about art, especially after Moll's step-daughter, Alma Mahler, returned from abroad . . . It must have been very difficult for her to take leave of the little man [Mahler] on his bier and to find herself suddenly removed from the atmosphere of fame and consequence that she had shared with her husband. What had bound her to Mahler was perhaps not so much a great love as a great passion for music. In the last years of his life there had also been the excitements, intrigues and feuds of a small section of Viennese society, the sort of thing she revelled in all her life . . .

Following Mahler's funeral she had cut herself off for a time from everybody; but she was young, and now she wanted company again. She was curious to meet me.

After the meal she took me to the piano in the next room, where she played and sang — for me alone, she said — Isolde's *Liebestod*. I was fascinated; she was young and strikingly beautiful in her mourning, and lonely in spite of all the people she saw. When she then proposed that I paint her portrait at her home, I was at once overjoyed and perturbed. For one thing, I had never before painted a woman who seemed to have fallen in love with me at first sight; and for another I felt a certain shyness and apprehension: how could one man find happiness where another had so recently died? [12]

On April 15, still addressing Alma with the formal *Sie,* Oskar wrote, "My good friend, please believe in this decision, just as I believe in you.

I know that I am lost if I go any further with the present confusion in my life. And I know that I will lose even those capabilities that I should direct to another sacred purpose, you and me.

If you can esteem me and want to be as pure as you were yesterday, when I knew that you were above and better than all of the women who only wanted to drive me wild, then bring to me a true sacrifice and become my wife, in secret while I am still poor. I will thank you as my comforter when I no longer have to hide myself. You must keep your joy and your purity as refreshment for me, so that I do not have to resort to the decay that threatens me. You must save me until I can really be the one who does not take you down, but, rather, lifts you up. Since you asked me yesterday to do that for you, I have believed in you as I have never before believed in anyone except myself.

If you, a strong woman, can help me from this spiritual confusion, the beauty that we both honor that transcends our knowledge will come to bless you [here, the familiar *du*] and me with happiness. Write to me, that I may come to visit you and I will take that as an agreement.

I remain in reverence,

Your,
Oskar Kokoschka[13]

What would follow was different from anything Alma had known, or would experience. Some friends maintain that Oskar was the great love of her life. Their feelings for one another remained deep until her death. Oskar was Alma's match in many ways the others were not. She was beautiful, wealthy, adventuresome, well traveled, a bright conversationalist. She looked for men who were geniuses; Oskar knew he was one. He was good-looking, worldly, very sensuous, articulate, fascinated by women — he also needed money, social status, and physical love. Alma and Oskar could offer each other reciprocal promises, awakening strong sexual drives in one another. She promised financial stability and a circle of cultured admirers, while he promised talent, productivity, and a future that she had thought she might not find. They feared each other as much as they loved. Alma had rarely been stricken and shaken by anyone as much as she was by Oskar, but she kept thinking of the two people who had earlier frightened her: Gustav and their daughter Maria, both of whom had made her tremble. She protected herself. She rarely spent complete nights with Oskar. If he visited her in her apartment in Vienna, they went to bed to have sex, then she expected him to go back to his own quarters. When they were together in her country house or in hotels, she expected they would have separate bedrooms. This was not at all uncommon in an era when space was more plentiful than it is today. It signified Alma's need for independence, as well as her need to control. More often than not, the money for the rent of the rooms was hers.

In order to have more peace and time to build her life on her own, Alma had enrolled Anna in a school for talented children. She would not remain there for long, so unaccustomed was she to formal education, and so worried was her mother about her contracting disease from the other children. Now alone, Alma took out her old songs and worked on them a little; she also tried to get out to meet people. She could summon little enthusiasm for either project, especially in light of Oskar's sudden presence in her life and the demands he was making on her. In another of his early letters, he wrote,

> Alma, I happened to go by your house at 10 o'clock and could have cried from anger because you continue to surround yourself with satellites and to leave me in the dirty edge . . . I can have no strange deities near me. Love, you must force yourself to give up every thought of every production from your past and of every advisor prior to me, before it is all too late. I can't look on another mind when I see you . . . I want you very much when you find your own being, your peace and your freedom in *my* existence. If you have to look back and become impatient before it's time, then I warn you, you will become a martyr, and that is something that I do not want for you, so I warn you to decide whether you want to be free from me, or in me. I would have loved you incredibly strongly
>
>   Alma Oskar Kokoschka[14]

This was the beginning of Oskar's habit of signing letters with both of their names, as if to fuse the two identities. He was jealous of the men who might have been Alma's lovers, and of everyone who took her time and energy away from him. He was grateful whenever she agreed to see him alone. When she went off to Paris in the company of her friend Lili Leiser, he wrote, "Alma, it is not good for me that you have gone away. I didn't want to ask you to stay here because you should have every pleasure you can have." He noticed every French-derived word in any conversation and bought the Parisian newspapers to see if the weather happened to be fine where Alma was, and to learn what music she might be able to hear. "Please be happy, but do not distance yourself from me in your heart because we are separated. I am what you are; if you are away from me, I am nobody, I am without a world." On the next day, April 27, he asked, "Alma, do you still love me? You have been gone so long. I would be very happy if this awful impatience that I am always trying to fight were done away with by you, my dearest. I call out your noble name, Alma, loudly and often, and that, for a moment, makes me well again." [15]

As the hours passed, he became more upset. "Oh, my dear Alma, you have not written to me today, and I wanted a letter from you so very much. If you write to me again, tell me everything you do during the whole day long, and who you talk to, and tell me even the things that you think unimportant. For me, every little thing is a breath of life from you . . . Don't make me even weaker, Alma . . . Love me even more, if you can . . . Love, give me your warm hand; I am so tired. When you go to sleep, I hold your dear, tired face in my hands and look at you. Read this letter in the evening. Good night, Alma, Oskar I am with you." [16]

Alma confessed that being in Paris had tired her, and she was not enjoying herself. He answered, on April 30, "Dear woman do you know that I believe in you and trust in you and am rich as no other man? . . . Be one with me forever and irrevocably bound to me forever in eternal joy." [17]

Lili, the traveling campanion, was among Alma's few female friends. Most women seemed only to be interested in talking about the things that did not concern Alma — hairdressers, gowns, and trivialities. Women also seemed to be envious of her and her position. But Lili herself gave Alma cause to be wary of females. A wealthy woman who lived more ostentatiously than Alma at the time, Lili had lesbian inclinations, which she revealed to Alma on that trip to Paris. Alma was not interested in a homosexual affair, and she tried to make her aversion clear. She and Lili remained friends under somewhat stressful conditions.

Oskar was in the habit of pacing up and down in front of the building where Alma lived. After he had left her late at night, he would sometimes walk the sidewalk until dawn, ostensibly to make sure no harm came to his mistress while she slept, but also to be certain she had no other visitors. Alma appreciated this kind of lavish attention, which Gustav had not given to her. Nevertheless, Oskar's devotion went beyond reason. He thought of Alma as the prototype of woman, Goethe's "eternal feminine," and most of the females in his paintings of those years bore at least some resemblance to Alma. It was almost as if he were in the clutches of a supernatural force. He wrote of the great passion they shared, and admitted there were times when he could not imagine going on living without her. He put upon her a responsibility that she could not accept.

Though there were people in Vienna who had seen Alma in the company of so many men that they believed she would not be faithful to any one, it was precisely for her faithfulness that Oskar honored her. He envisioned her as a heroine, and painted her in imposing attitudes next to a frail and fragile man — himself. They agreed in the basic principles of religion; both were drawn to Roman Catholicism and its rituals, but neither was a practicing member of the Church. Alma wrote in her diary, "Gustav's inclinations toward Catholicism — his manner of preaching, always against me, during our marriage, and, with that, his own *boundless* lack of hindsight — all of that shows me more and more that he was a great dreamer, but not a man of real accomplishment." [18] These were less her thoughts than Oskar's — and she let her lover dictate to her as she wrote the words in her diaries. They traveled together to Naples, where he painted a now lost landscape with Mount Vesuvius in the background. Alma wrote, "I don't believe that life will ever be more comfortable or more pleasant than it was before — just consider the dusty streets and the automobiles . . . and the dirty air that goes above us and then unfairly comes down on us! So the dirt comes from on high, whereas until now it has always come from below." [19]

In summer 1912, Alma took Gucki and a woman friend, probably Lili, to Scheveningen, in Holland. A letter from Oskar said: "Alma, it is impossible that I cannot see you for so many weeks; I am not used to handling such a hardship." [20] They had quarreled, but he claimed now to see only the beauty in her, nothing hateful. Since the two were actually one, what he had thought hateful in her must actually have been within himself. "Dear Alma, I believe now that you must be bound to me more strongly than any other person on the earth, because today I feel so truly your aura, which also lets me sense myself, and which lets me sense the boundaries of the outer world more clearly . . . [She wrote back that he could not deny her freedom.] Alma, dear, I am heartbroken that you would take me for the kind of fool who would deny you your journey. Would you have said the same kind of thing to your first husband? You should be proud and not ashamed; I am not a sheep who follows. How can what the Jewish, free-thinking world around you might say concern you at all, when you are so certain that I think only *good?*" [21]

Remembering Gustav, and fearing that she was pregnant, Alma had been worried about her relation with the Jews, who figured so prominently in her society of musicians and intellectuals. Oskar wrote, "Alma, my sweet . . . If you should happen to have a dear child by me, it would be a compassionate act of nature and it would chase away everything that is horrid and bring us together once and for all . . . You will have found your health in me, dear, and I will have found my peace in you. We would have the sanctity of a family, you would be the mother, an idea which has long been in my soul." [22]

He convinced her to meet him in Munich in July. She consented because she wanted to see him, and wanted to leave Scheveningen as well, where Lili's presence and her erotic insinuations were becoming oppressive. From Munich, Alma and Oskar went on to Muerren in the Bernese highlands of Switzerland, where they took luxurious rooms giving them a glorious view of the Jungfrau. Alma sat on the balcony while Oskar painted her portrait.

Much as he coveted the prospect of being a father, Oskar could not convince Alma to want to bear his child. She left Muerren precipitously to go back to Vienna, charging Lili with bringing Anna home. There is nothing to prove that Alma was pregnant, but in the early autumn, when she and Oskar were both back in the city, Alma refused to admit her lover to her rooms. She said that she was not quite well. Bad feelings arose when Oskar's mother, who had been used to her son's visiting regularly, railed against his obsession with the woman whom she considered to be nothing but a high-society mistress. Although Oskar would not bow to his mother's wishes, the old woman's attacks made both Alma and himself uncomfortable. When pressed, Alma held to almost bourgeois principles. While she had no intention of ending her affair with Oskar, she had been frightened by the prospect of pregnancy. Contradictory as it was to the way in which she carried out her daily life, she believed that it was wrong to have a child out of wedlock. She had become pregnant before her marriage to Gustav, and Maria had died. To Alma, this meant that those who sinned against the traditional tenets of morality would be punished. Although she might not be able to bring herself to conform to all those tenets, she would do almost anything to avoid the retributions of fate. To many of her friends and to Oskar, Alma's attitudes seemed to be irrational, too highhanded, but she was impelled to be careful. She kept her lover away as long as she could.

On February 7, 1913, Alma confessed to her diary:

> I've eaten very little the whole day, and for supper I had only applesauce. But I had a very strange night. I dreamed that Gustav was alive and that our life together was intense in a way that it never could have been in real life . . . He was conducting Schreker's *Prinzessin und das Spielwerk* [*sic*] at the Opera. I was sitting near him and heard the music clearly in my dream, but it displeased me. I left the opera in the company of others, but suddenly I felt that I absolutely had to go to Gustav. I returned and, after a long search, found where he was living. It was a small house in a garden, and a narrow elevator took me many stories high. I entered that apartment, a place that I had never seen before . . . He came out of another room and cried "my crazily beloved Alm-schi," as he always used to say it, and he grabbed me around the neck. His play of expressions — from very serious to indifferent up to the very happiest — was clearer in my dream than it had ever been in real life.[23]

She later scrawled on that page of her diary an explanation of the dream. During those days, Franz Schreker had wanted to dedicate his opera to Alma, but Oskar would not allow it. He insisted that Alma go to the offices of Franz's publisher and have the dedication page removed. The composer was astonished and hurt by her action, but Alma obeyed Oskar's command. Indeed, there probably was a part of her that agreed with her lover and wanted her name off the title page.

Again in her diary:

> How very far behind me my life with Mahler seems. How very frightfully full of magnified happiness and sufferings.

This man and ever again *this* man in my life! I need the crazy mystique of the artist, and from this I also manage to fill my own head. Take everything only as a symbol, the whole world is ultimately only a dream that turns bad . . .

But what has really happened in my life? A sickly child of a robust mother and a neurasthenic father — I was nervous and clever to a certain point, specifically, I had that Arian cleverness, with all of its limitations. How I managed to succeed when I was in school or taught by others I simply cannot imagine. But with that, a strange realization: Even today I remember a few words of my father, which I never could explain but which fascinated me even then. On the sea in Sylt, on the beach with other people and white-capped waves, he said, "Play to allure the gods." More than that, I cannot remember.[24]

On the plot of land Gustav had bought in Semmering, with the help and advice of Carl Moll, Alma decided to build a house that could eventually serve as her primary residence. It would not be large — only eight rooms — but the environs were beautiful. Alma and Oskar looked on the planned house as their private retreat. Carl and Anna had taken Oskar into the family and were happy to engage him in their planning sessions, especially since Alma was not very interested in the technical details of the house. She faced problems from a woman, most likely the same Lili Leiser. Alma wrote in her diary,

I loved a woman, which is to say that I trusted her; she is rich and I am poor, at least when it comes to money! . . . She . . . did everything in her power to have a house on the property adjacent to mine. I did nothing. She visited me: "You are so quiet — don't you want me to build a house here?" "I am afraid," I said. "Well, I am not!" I was shot down. The idea seemed warm-hearted and kind, but then came the matter of money, and, with that, the usual problems. She bought a piece of land four times the size of mine, out of the patch that might someday have been my own. I had discovered, years earlier, a type of American house that I coveted, and I had searched long and hard for an architect who would build it for me. She said, "Is it all right with you if I also build an American house there?" "All right — good." But her house grew to immense proportions and cost twice what mine was to cost. The architect and I had words on several issues, and whenever he came across something beautiful that caught my eye, he would say, "Oh, that is not for you, that is for Frau X. I cannot give you such expensive things." I told the woman about this, but she seemed to find everything quite fair and in order.[25]

Despite their extensive planning and maneuvering, there is no indication that Alma and Lili actually became neighbors in Semmering.

Oskar had concluded he could not live without being married to Alma. He took her birth certificate and her official papers to the registrar in Doebling while she was in Bohemia taking the cure at a spa and, unknown to his alleged bride, registered their intentions to wed. He visited her at the Franzensbad spa and admitted what he had done. She was furious when he revealed that he had gone through her things and "borrowed" her papers, especially when she had thought he was hard at work. She insisted they return to Vienna at once. She created a new rule: she would see him only once in every three days.

Shortly, she relaxed her demands and the two went off to Tre Croci in the Dolomites in August 1913, where Oskar worked and Alma felt a new peace and satisfaction. She commented in her diary, "Oskar must work! He was put on earth for that purpose! *Life* holds no interest for him, but *I am ready with my own evolution — As of today I cannot*

learn any more! If only I had climbed Mont Blanc! But what a lunatic idea! Where is my own truth?"[26]
And, she realized,

> The stronger a man is, the more he wants to reach out and possess everything. And I too am very strong . . . I have drawn myself together and collected riches and no death will frighten me again. I have found once again that harmony within myself that I possessed as a child, without knowing it — today, it is slightly easier to see. (Thank God not much more.) Every experience has cast small gleams on my own fantasies — and with these rays of light I seem to have been cast into a paradise. The earth gives out the purest happiness, but human beings don't recognize it, they take themselves too seriously. Nobody is *waiting* for me. Every person must find his own level of intensity and make it firm. That is a duty . . .

> I know now that I married Gustav because I wanted him years earlier in my subconscious. Consciousness takes me flying through life, but the subconscious remained true to the ideal and led him to me. I also know now that I will never win the game because I want it only with my conscious mind. I am not able to concentrate on that game even for a second. It is impossible for me. I look at the cards and find only one thing: music.

> I know now that I managed to be invited to facilitate a performance [in New York] because I constantly wished for it without really realizing that I was doing so — but everyone who belonged to music knew that the wish was inside me . . . The most important ideas are found in the deepest subconscious — and in consciousness, growth cannot be discovered or comprehended . . . The subconscious is the fire of the world.[27]

In that year, 1913, Oskar wrote a poem with a Greek title that was a close anagram of the names Alma and Oskar,

"Allos Makar" (roughly, "Happiness Is Different"). The poem defies translation because of its onomatopoetic combinations and its reliance on being read aloud by a skilled orator. It was an attempt by the poet to free himself from what he already realized was an irrational and impossible dependency on Alma. He had learned that he could not get his strength and power from her, but would have to find them in himself. Oskar's mother was increasingly worried about her son's emotional stability, and she wrote Alma a threatening letter saying her son might have had a great future, and, should this not come to pass, there would be nobody to blame but Alma. Maria Kokoschka went on to threaten Alma to release her dependent lover by a certain date, or be shot.

Aware of the threat, Oskar went to Alma's building on the appointed date and found his mother walking up and down the sidewalk with what appeared to be a gun in her purse. It was not really a weapon, only the elderly woman's finger. A reconciliation between mother and son was accomplished, but Oskar had no intention of leaving Alma. His confusion increased.

In *The Burning Bush,* a dramatic dialogue, Oskar had written of the two options open to a woman: she could find herself in motherhood or she could remain a virgin. Alma was neither the mother of his child nor was she a virgin. Oskar urgently wanted to have a baby with her; Alma would not consider making an attempt to conceive. He doted on Gucki. When in May 1913 Alma made another brief journey to Paris, Oskar visited the nine-year-old. Later he took "our Guckerl" with him to meet Alma's train in Salzburg and escort both women home. Being with the little girl only made Oskar want a child of his own all the more.

Alma took her lover to the first public reading of Gustav's Ninth Symphony, with Bruno Walter conducting, but the artist had a dreadful time. "Alma," he wrote, "how can I find peace with you as long as I know that there is another in you, whether dead or alive? Why did you invite me to that dance of death and ask that I gaze at you for hours while you listened as a spiritual slave to the rhythms of the man who was a stranger to you . . . I am not allowed to see you every day because you want to keep alive the memory of this man who is so foreign to me . . . You must begin a brand new life with me, your girlhood, if we are to be forever happy together."[28]

Then, "My Alma, I love you more than I love myself . . . I am prepared, in spite of all the suffering and sadness that Mahler's widow has caused me, to forget everything that you have done out of compassion, weakness and vanity if you will, from this point on, be really mine." And, "My beloved Almi! . . . I must have you for my wife soon, or else my great talent will perish miserably. You must revive me at night, like a magic potion . . . In the daytime I don't need to take you away from your companions. That's when you gather, and I know that this is as it should be. I can work all day, spending what I have absorbed at night . . . Almi, believe me! Don't listen to the reasons and the ways of ignorant people who cannot know what we are good for and capable of. You are the Woman, and I am the Artist . . . I have seen how strong you can make me and what I'll amount to when this force is constantly active. You revive useless people, and I, the one you are destined for, should I go wanting?"[29]

Alma said that she would marry Oskar only after he had created a masterwork. He began to work on *Die Windsbraut* ("The Tempest"). Alma seemed enthusiastic about their plans. He answered:

You are so dear to write and ask whether I still want to marry you, and to say that we'll do it at once. I want it as

much as ever, but you have always put it off and I was so
distracted that in my love I did not realize that it would be
a sacrifice for you, since I would always sacrifice everything
to you and see the possibility for only joy and happiness in
our union — and since I always resented the fact that you
wanted me as a lover whose predecessors . . . would add
him to their list. Since you have been so slow to realize that
I need self-esteem quite as much as you do . . . every event,
every person in your life, every small incident that I wouldn't
even have noticed under more normal circumstances . . .
has become a tragedy, to the degree that my nerves have
been strung out as far as they can go. I hope that you now
know what you want above all, that your intentions have
become sufficiently clear that you will not forget me . . . I
do not seek sorrow, I seek happiness, but I seek my happiness only in you, with you — not against you.[30]

Early in 1914, Alma went to Paris again. Oskar wrote to
her, "If you really want to be my wife, you must become a
bit accustomed to following me, and begin right now by
being your own helper! Almi, please don't send me any
money. You know that I have no taste for luxury, it seems
presumptuous to me. Especially this time, don't buy me anything, because you have no cash with you." She sent him a
gift, and he said he would have been happier if she had spent
the money on herself. "Our heaven is the same, but our
worlds are different."[31]
   The poet Georg Trakl visited Oskar's studio on the Stu-
benring one evening when *Die Windsbraut* was reaching
completion, and wrote a poem about the painting. Oskar
also described the work in words; he sent Alma two poems
while she was in Paris, both love lyrics overhung with ominous clouds:[32]

> *The ripples flutter around the submerged peace.*
> *The heart turns on itself and empties out.*

From the overrun, back,
the earth looks white in the winter sun,
and over that which has not yet flowed, in front,
whirls the same sorrow of a threatening thunderstorm.

A faintness enters the restless picture;
I can say nothing loudly, because she is on my heart.

But now there begins, from somewhere below
loud grumbling.

Two people, a man and a woman
choke on the same serpent.
One wants to have the advantage!
Who should get the head
and who the tail!

One is weaker than the other.
From the billing and cooing mouths of the couple the
serpent emerges.
How did this coddling produce such a viper?

"I can hear no loudness,
Because the beat is coming from the heart."

Smiles on the lips bring peace;
I am still as far in front as yesterday.

The heart welcomes morning.

A flat fish swam by, taking its time.
Someone has held me in the world.

I am asea in the distant flood;
My head floats on the water.
Father! Why did you leave me?
Day and night cannot flow as one
since you separated the child from the father.

In winter, irrational sadness
follows irrational longing.

The two burn together to form a light.
The world suffers only through love.
The attitude feeds on itself.
Wind, blow home!
Water, flow home!

In the dream you were introduced.
So that day and night flowed into one
in the mirror,
And the moon cast off a ray,
That met with something strange.

The noise stopped you, you held still, so
I could speak:
Do not exchange me for another,
You see my complexion yourself.

So we two are bound.
Give the direction to heaven.
I hold you at the precipice.
Hovering ship of the spirit!
The mast and the anchor guide you.
Between hole and hell
The two hang of one soul!

Die Windsbraut, dated 1914, hangs in the museum in Basel. On a swirling, luxuriously colored bed, a woman — Alma — lies with her head on Oskar's shoulder, appearing much larger than he. She sleeps peacefully, covered only by billowing fabric. Fully suited, he is sharply awake, gazing anxiously into the distance, sharing none of her rest.

The nearly completed house at Semmering met Alma's specifications perfectly. The central hearth, built from massive blocks of granite from the surrounding mountains, ran the length of the living room. On the wall above the fireplace, Oskar painted a mural of Alma rising toward Heaven in fiery immolation while he stayed below in Hell, engulfed by serpents. Ten-year-old Anna sat watching Oskar paint, as she so loved to do; sometimes in the afternoon her mother would drop her off at Uncle Oskar's studio, where she would eat chestnuts and sit in rapt silence while he worked. Anna, like Alma, was the child of artists. She knew how to behave in their presence. While Oskar worked on the mural over the fireplace in the new house, Anna Moll was in the kitchen cooking, the servants were sewing draperies, the painters were finishing their chores, and Alma was supervising the various jobs. It was a happy and lively time, a renaissance in a household that had apparently shed the sorrows and trials of the past.

Alma was pregnant. Oskar was so happy and proud that she was carrying his child he could not control his optimism about the future. He thought a child would bring Alma to marry him, and he looked on little Gucki as his stepdaughter, on Anna Moll as his soon-to-be mother-in-law, on the house in the country as his own residence.

Domestic peace was shattered when Gustav's death mask arrived in the mail. Oskar protested vehemently, not wanting anything in the house which would serve as a permanent reminder of Alma's past. She unpacked it and gave it a place of honor at Semmering. They quarreled, and Alma arranged to enter a clinic in Vienna for an abortion.

Her diary on May 17, 1914, reads:

So — that too is over. Something that I had considered to be lasting. Oskar has become a stranger to me. [Her words refer to Gustav's finest song, "Ich bin der Welt abhanden gekommen."] I can no longer find him in myself — he has become a mystery to me. He is so quiet in my presence; I had become comfortable with him and he has isolated me so totally that I have the awful feeling of how little one is really needed in this life . . . I know that he goes on living and

will go farther and probably do better without me. We chafe
one another, but now he can live peacefully and quietly. He
has no one to excite his mind. I believe that he must have
forgotten me! *I* want to forget him! We did not profit from
this, rather we became ever more introverted. Today I was
with very pleasant people. The man played Bach, the room
was dark, with only one candle burning; he did not look at
me and I respected the atmosphere that he had created. That
was the kind of thing that Oskar could never have toler-
ated — pure, noble air.[33]

Three days later, back from the theater, Alma described
the play she had seen as "glorious, but, even more glorious
is my life, which permits me to live my time to its fullest. I
am truly fortunate! I can see through everything, and all is
clear to me. The work of this man is a riddle to my feminin-
ity; with this, I feel at my peak."[34]

After the abortion, Oskar tested and nagged Alma about
her habits. While she was writing the entry about the glory
of the theater in her diary, he was writing to her a discon-
solate letter saying that he had waited for her endlessly both
at her house and at his own flat, and, since she had not
appeared at either place, he had missed the chance to see his
brother. "If you had really wanted to see me, you would
have found me . . . You have to have a new heart for me.
I did not know that a woman could no longer climb down
from a certain position in society, that she would not tire
herself . . . And the real danger is that I will be totally lost
if someone does not have the patience needed for love."[35]

In the midst of Alma's and Oskar's crisis, on June 28,
1914, the Archduke Ferdinand and his wife were assassi-
nated. A month later, Austria declared war on Serbia. Alma
was in Semmering, thinking to the pages of her diary that
she was

completely unharried and peaceful here, which is the thing
that I wanted the most . . . He filled and destroyed my life,
both at the same time. I do not know where I erred. Why,
oh, why did I leave the quiet crowd for a fiery furnace? What
should I do with all of these "we shall's" and the maybes
that I have heard from this man? In a different time, I would
have striven tirelessly . . . I'm afraid that I have already
gone through that foolishness and that darkness!
    But do I still love this man?
    Or do I already hate him?
    Why am I so disturbed about it?[36]

Oskar was working in his studio in Vienna when he heard
the newsboys hawking the extra edition of the newspapers
announcing the declaration of war. He slammed the window shut. Then, unable to quell his own curiosity, he headed
for the neighborhood café, where he knew he would find
the paper and the latest gossip. He reflected, "In 1914 I was
twenty-eight years old, and thus liable for military service.
It seemed to me better to volunteer before I was conscripted.
I had no wife or child to await my happy return. I had nothing to lose or defend."[37] When the radio brought Alma news
of the war, she wrote in her diary, "I sometimes imagine
that *I* have caused this whole upheaval, in order to experience some kind of awakening or reconciliation — and that
might also mean death."[38]

Knowing that Oskar had no money, she sent him some,
though he had always been reluctant to accept her charity.
He wanted her to make sure all of her papers were in order
so that, if worse came to worst, she could retreat to Switzerland with Anna. If she was reluctant to travel alone, he
advised, she might consider going with Lili. Alma didn't want
to leave, not with Anna, not with Lili, not at all. Like most
people, she thought the conflict would be over soon. Alma

had no intention of vacating her new home, and she had relatively little interest in knowing what was happening on the battlefronts.

Contrary to their claims of estrangement, Alma and Oskar settled into a routine druing the first months of the war that would take them from Vienna to Semmering on a regular basis. The trip was not long, but it could not be made easily back and forth in one day. They managed to spend most of the warm months away from the city, and in the autumn and winter to retreat to the country for long weekends whenever they could. In Vienna, they maintained separate residences, although he spent most nights in her large apartment. Oskar talked frequently about joining the military, but he put off acting on his conviction that he should serve. Following a fashion of the time, he painted scenes on fans and gave seven to Alma as a present to adorn her new house. He was also working on his *Bach Portfolio,* which would not be signed and released for several years, at which time it would be dedicated to another woman. The *Portfolio* contains the artist's interpretations of Bach's Cantata No. 60, *O Ewigkeit, du Donnerwort,*[39] with its dialogue between the female Hope and the male Fear. The man, whom Oskar identified as himself, faces Woman and Death with terror.

Alma Schindler Mahler Gropius

ALMA MARKED her thirty-fifth birthday on August 31, 1914. A few days later she wrote in her diary:

The dreadful war is still going on. The earth is being fertilized with blood of the best men. . . . Vienna has become a ghetto. Oskar Kokoschka's words: "Austria cannot win — only lose. . . . The people will think only of themselves. They will ban the effete journalism and art from their lives, and they will rub their eyes and decide that the Germans will ever be Germans and the French ever French. The Romantics will always roam the world, stopping to tell of the internationalism of the globe. But each nation will again find its own individuality, the highest and most beautiful thing that every race has.

I would like to break free from Oskar. He no longer fits into my life. He makes me lose my momentum . . . But just as dear and helpless as he appears when he is the large

child, so unreliable and treacherous is he as a grown man
. . . I know that he has made me sick — for years, sick —
and he was not able to leave me. But the moment has come.
I've caught him in a couple of lies, and that has to be the
end. . . .

But he still pleases me *so* much — *too* much!

God punished me by sending this man into my life . . .

A few weeks ago I finally got back to playing the piano —
Meistersinger. I would give up every man on earth for music. Music means everything to me. Wagner means more to
me than anyone. His time must come once again. This war
must teach us once again to love our masters . . . Sweet,
dearly beloved music. And only the "German music." I
haven't wanted to play since the beginning of the war —
but now I know that I will *sing* only in death! *Then* I'll be
a slave to no man, because I will tend to my own well-
being and to myself.[1]

And on October 6:

I want to find a new man, but one who serves me in that he
goes away, disappears, *before* everything falls apart.

Yesterday evening I ran away from Oskar.

I was not well the whole day, and I asked him not to come
in the evening. At 10:30 at night I went with Lili Leiser to
visit Reininghaus [Karl Reininghaus, an art collector]. I felt
awkward walking into the crowded salon, but at once I saw
Gustav Klimt and Hofrat Sczrigowski [an archaeologist]. I
was comfortable. With these two, almost alone, I talked until 3 in the morning . . . I was actually happy. After the
isolation with Oskar of the last few years this evening was a
cure for me.

With Sczrigowski, I spoke about Gustav and his round-
about move from Judaism. He said, "Mahler's humanity came
out in every word he spoke, never just out of his intelligence.

But do not forget how very much you helped him with that. When he was with you, he was always 'brighter.' I once saw him with Schoenberg and his consorts, when he seemed to be drowned with Jews."

I trembled with joy. I had always felt that it was so, but I was still happy to have it said by another person . . . So my existence with him was nevertheless a completed mission? That is all that I wanted, for the rest of my life.²

What was called the "Jewish problem" was lying more and more heavily in Alma's consciousness and in those of many people around her. Alma felt that her strength, her "good-luck charm," came from the fact that she had been born a Christian, and she felt that she had inherited attitudes and traits that were naturally denied to any Jew. The fact that Gustav had converted to Christianity could not give him the "brightness" with which she had been born. Gustav was a Jew, in Alma's mind and in the minds of others who were concerned with what they considered to be the "problems" of being Jewish. But Alma, by virtue of her marriage to Gustav, had become part of that same "problem," and she could not forget this fact. She was concerned about what price she might eventually have to pay.

Alma received a letter from Dr. Joseph Fraenkel, who responded to a remark she had made, saying, "It is not true that the Jews take more than they give."³ Alma read his words but could not accept them. "What of the Jewish question *now?*" she asked in her diary, as if in answer to Fraenkel. "They *have* received more than they have offered in Europe. The analytical spirit, a thing called Social-Democracy, even liberalism — all of these 'enlightenments' have been discovered by Jews. Today, though, they are different. Without me, they would *never* have become human beings — and so it has gone with all of them! They need help and direction — *brains* and *feeling* from *us!*"[4] At least Oskar was not Jewish.

Alma's ideas about politics were, and would remain, naive, based heavily on comments and remarks she heard at social gatherings. She constructed in her mind a stereotype of a Jew as a diminutive person who swarmed with intensity, dissecting his subject until it was no longer whole. From that she tried to extrapolate a concept of international politics, not realizing the unfairness, the shortsightedness, or, indeed, the reality of the situation. She went awkwardly between general and specific, believing that the people to whom she happened to be speaking or writing would never think that she was talking about them, only about the nonspecific "others." Sometimes, her ploy worked.

At the end of October 1914, she wrote in her diary for the first time a phrase that recurred throughout the decades: Oskar was the "evil spirit," the "evil genius" in her life. "He wants to annihilate me. One cannot make pure what is already soiled, and when he took me in his arms for the first time, everything in me wanted to recoil from his evil glances. But I wanted to make him *good*. And, as a result, I almost lost myself.

"Oh, this fascination with evil. My nerves are ruined, my fantasies destroyed. What monster has he instilled in me?!"[5]

She would not let Oskar Kokoschka separate her from her friends anymore. When Hans Pfitzner came to Vienna to work on his opera *Palestrina,* he wanted to be asked to stay in Alma's apartment, but she saw to it that he was installed in a hotel. There, he complained constantly about the noise from the streets and the waiters' banging of trays. He seemed so upset that Alma relented and offered him her guest quarters. He disapproved of Oskar's portrait of Alma, which she had hung over the sofa. Indeed, Hans disapproved of everything about Oskar, and wanted Alma for himself. She rejected his amorous advances, and he departed earlier than had been planned.

Next, the German choral conductor Siegfried Ochs, whose interpretations of Bach had particularly intrigued Alma, came to visit, bearing gifts including a Goethe autograph, his own score of Bach's Mass in B Minor, and a valuable copy of Duerer's *Christ,* which Alma had coveted. Ochs wanted to see her house in Semmering. When Alma pointed out that the trip to the country and back could not be made comfortably in one day, her guest gleefully consented to an overnight trip. Alma, instead, manipulated him into spending a few hours with her in the Prater.

Her relations with women were, as always, more difficult. Alma turned against Justi Mahler Rosé when the latter engaged her as an accomplice in a meeting with a military officer of whom Frau Rosé was irrationally enamored. Justi seemed to have the idea that she could get her intended lover to become Alma's suitor, then reclaim him for herself. The scheme backfired when the soldier walked off to his own mistress at the same moment when Rosé came to claim his wife. Alma pretended to be appalled that Gustav's sister could stoop so low, evidently not wanting to remember the several fiascoes in which she herself had been a party, and refusing to realize that her own life was lived in public defiance of the era's moral codes.

Alma went back to Reininghaus's salon, where she danced, talked, and listened to music, then went on out to dinner with Lili and Sczrigowski. They had lobster and champagne and, to enhance their pleasure, Reininghaus had arranged to have a string quartet play for his friends from an adjacent room in the restaurant. But, Alma wrote in her diary, "the beauty did not move from the outside in, because there sat the figure of an old, rickety man who wanted me. Ach!"[6]

At the same time, Oskar was pleading with her to come home to him, so that they could "move into our house, the one that you built so that you could live with me. I want to become your husband, and I will be able to thank you, only you, again and again, if I make something of myself. If I have made mistakes and must pay for them to the extent that I do not have you as my beloved and honored wife, that is too much against me, and you have to save me."[7] Alma was uncomfortable with Oskar's begging, and she went back to Bertha Zuckerkandl, the wise confidante who had proved with Gustav that she had a good sense of her young friend's wants and needs. Bertha reminded Alma of the young handsome architect who had courted her, Walter Gropius.

Alma began at once to try to find Walter's whereabouts. She learned that he had joined the military early in the war and was among the wounded. From her diary on December 23: "I wrote to Walter Gropius today. I am seldom alone — I have too much company — I know that I would be able to survive on my own, but I would like to be grateful for someone."[8] She celebrated the arrival of the New Year with Oskar; through the night they talked about his future, and Alma thought that she had been very stern and hard on him. On January 2, 1915, he wrote to her:

> You have a superhuman ability to fantasize. I believe that I have been honest with myself, because I see from you what you have realized or felt was not good enough. But suddenly you conjured, from the clear blue, right around me, in all gentleness, that explanation that I in my directionless spirit had overlooked.
>
> The way in which you took me again into your bed was unforgettably beautiful and incomparable, just as you had advised me so wisely and so well. Your words on the night of the New Year put my whole desire into your sweet beautiful hands, and I mean honestly and seriously all that I promised you, since I love you, want to be a good husband

to you, in order that you forget your own dissatisfaction and want to heighten love in your life, since your beliefs and expectations are true. You will come back into my arms with trust that I have succeeded, am not a shame to you, and will not go wrong . . . My angel, I look into the future with fright, until we are married and all of your belief is turned onto me.[9]

Several days later, Oskar wrote to suggest that they take a trip and try for one last time to find happiness together.

On January 15, Alma commented in her diary that Walter was in an army hospital suffering from an injury and shock. "It affects me deeply. I feel that it is, or will become, something important to me." [10] She decided to go visit him. Meanwhile, Oskar was continuing to send his intense letters, though with increasing hopelessness. He spoke often about his own death, with the implication that Alma would somehow be responsible for it. He believed he had given her the opportunity to save him, and, with him, herself, and she had refused.

Oskar decided to join the army, but even there he was not immediately welcome. "I was not robust enough for the infantry, not good enough at maths for the artillery, so Loos managed to arrange for me to serve in the cavalry, where I would at least have a horse to rely on. Friendships between men are dependable; I had been estranged from Loos during the years I spent with Alma Mahler, but now he did his best to see that I would survive the war. It must have been a real satisfaction to him, after suffering Alma's hostility, to have made it possible for me to post to one of the most prestigious regiments in the Monarchy — the one in which the upper nobility of all the Crown lands, and members of the Imperial family itself, used to serve." [11]

Oskar had to have his own horse, so his mother and Loos went to a dealer and with money from one of Oskar's paintings bought a mare called Minden Lo, the Magyar words for "all horses." The new soldier was then outfitted by a tailor whose shop opposite the Hapsburg residences had been designed by Loos. As he departed for the war, Oskar handed his mother a necklace of blood-red beads that Alma had given him, asking her to keep them for him as a memento of his love. Mrs. Kokoschka carelessly tossed the beads into a clay flowerpot on the windowsill.

Instead of seeing his new venture as an obligation or incarceration, Oskar saw it as an escape, a way of relieving himself from the chains holding him to Alma. Alma barely bothered to say goodbye. She had turned her attentions entirely toward Walter. She wrote in her diary on February 2, "My lonely existence has no point of happines, no child, no man . . . I have the feeling that [Walter Gropius] loves me no more. He sees me as a different woman. I would have had to do much in order to prepare myself always to be 'available' in his eyes . . . This German man will *not* end up untrue to me, as O.K. did. I will get over him quickly." [12]

Alma went to Berlin in the company of Lili, wanting nothing more than to restore a relation with the ailing Walter. It took her longer than she might have hoped to overcome the embarrassment that had surrounded their last meeting and to convince him of her intentions, especially since she insisted on talking about her time with Oskar, which appalled Walter. But within two weeks, she convinced him and felt that he loved her in the way she wanted to be loved. It was not inconsequential to her that Walter's birthday fell on May 18, Gustav's death day.

She told her diary, "I went to Berlin fourteen days ago with the disgraceful intention of getting myself together again with this bourgeois son of the muse. Days and nights I cried. Finally, in the course of an hour, he fell in love with me again. We were at [a restaurant], where wine and good food raised our spirits, and where imminent farewell also helped, because he was to leave in an hour to visit his mother. I went to the train with him — there love overpowered him so much that he dragged me with him onto the moving train, and come what might, I had no choice but to travel to Hannover with him. Without a nightgown, without any of the usual comforts or supplies, I had become, almost violently, the booty of this man. I must say, it did not strike me as truly evil." [13]

Alma went back to Berlin the next day, where she rejoined Lili, who was still trying to seduce her, though in a somewhat more subtle manner. Alma was willing to preserve her friendship with Lili but she was not willing to share her bed. Lili consented to adjoining rooms, separated by a bath.

Walter returned to Berlin before Alma and Lili left, to prepare for his return to the front. She wrote, "I was not happy. He suddenly had the manners of a husband — he did everything to convince me to marry him, and I still quake at the thought that it might happen." [14]

After he left, Alma and Lili went to the suburbs of Berlin to visit Schoenberg. Alma was glad to see him surrounded by a circle of admiring friends and students, but she was saddened to find the composer whose talent Gustav had extolled so strongly living under primitive circumstances. To try to rescue him, Alma proposed a concert in Vienna, which she could sponsor, with Schoenberg conducting Gustav's rescoring of Beethoven's Ninth Symphony. Lili would help to finance the event, and Alma would regret ever having come up with the idea, but plans were begun for it even before the women boarded the train back to Vienna.

At home in a gold hostess dress, Alma entertained Pfitzner, Hauptmann, and other old friends. Oskar wrote from the front to report on his training and the living conditions that gave him none of the amenities to which he had become accustomed. He knew that in his absence Alma was surrounding herself with musicians, writers, and artists more prominent and productive than he, and he was jealous. He could never, he wrote, be one of the "Bachians, Brahmsians or Wagnerites" [15] whom she so revered; Gustav was the only one who meant something special to him — and, perhaps, Schoenberg. Oskar and Alma continued their correspondence, he writing more often than she answered. She avoided him even when she knew he was in Vienna.

Alma decided that she was not living up to her own expectations. She consulted a psychologist, Julius Wagner, but did not feel that she came away with any helpful insights or understandings. She was still wondering whether, in spite of all the difficulties, she should not pledge her life to Oskar, even after she had put such effort into rekindling the love of Walter, who was so talented, so handsome, and so Aryan.

As had become her habit during her times of confusion and change, Alma returned to music — this time to four of her own songs for piano and mezzo-soprano later published by Universal, Gustav's old publisher. This time her songs appeared in print with no title page connecting them to Gustav's work, and there is no indication that they received any attention or were performed. Probably because of the absence of response or praise, Alma did not continue to give serious attention to her composing.

She had other obligations. The prize from the Mahler Foundation had to be awarded. Previously, it had gone to Schoenberg. Now Alma voted to bestow the modest monetary award on Bittner, whose work she admired even though he had never come into close contact with Gustav. She reconfirmed her decision to give the prize to that composer with a concert in her own red music room, to which she invited Siegfried Ochs, Kolo Moser and his wife, and a few other friends. With that out of the way, Alma had had enough of Vienna, and took Gucki off to Semmering. She managed to escape from much of the talk and vituperation that had surrounded the disastrous concert in which Schoenberg conducted Gustav's version of the Ninth Symphony.

She received letters from Walter in which he expressed extreme jealousy of Oskar. Again Alma turned her considerations: "Oskar has a right to be inconsiderate, but this man does not, not this small, ordinary man!" [16] She put down her pen and decided that she could no longer tolerate the emptiness of the country, so she took Gucki back to Vienna. There, in her apartment, a short note was waiting from Walter. Reading it, Alma decided that she loved him. Early in June, she took her daughter to Franzensbad, bought a Bible, tried to read it, but could not keep from questioning her own fate. She wanted to find a place where she could live in peace with a man who made her believe that he appreciated her. She decided to do nothing for a while, to stay with her daughter and build as strong, proud, and satisfying a life as she could find with her old friends.

❧

On August 18, 1915, Alma married Walter Gropius.

She thought she loved him. But they had spent so little time together — even less than Alma had spent with Gustav before their wedding — there was no way for either to be sure of what might happen when the war no longer kept them apart. The question of where they might settle once they lived together remained unasked. By remarrying, Alma forfeited the pension she had received as a result of Gustav's arrangements with the Opera. The loss of that money would not signal poverty, but it did require some compensation; Walter's future would have to be seriously considered, and his career would have to be developed.

Alma had in mind the possibility of moving to America (where they would end up, but separately). She told her new husband as much as she knew about the work of the architect Frank Lloyd Wright and the huge and magnificent buildings that she had seen during her trips to New York with Gustav. Walter had little interest in such phenomena. He was a member of the society of upper-middle-class Germany, a society seemingly so foreign to Alma that she sat at the table in Walter's parents' house nervously braiding the fringe on the silk tablecloth, feeling that these polite and proper people thought of her as a social climber and, worse, the widow of a Jew. The Gropiuses' studied mixture of practicality and gentility impressed the new daughter-in-law, who hoped to learn something from their style. Alma saw that she did not fit in the family, and already she feared she never would.

She had wanted a Gentile husband and a baby. Walter was so magnificently handsome Alma knew that their child would have to be beautiful. Furthermore, she reasoned, marrying Walter would release her from the stigma of Gustav's Jewishness and the chains of Oskar's dependency on her. With Walter, she would find her equilibrium and her own life.

The day after the wedding, she wrote in her diary, "Yesterday I was married. I have landed. Nothing will move me from my chosen course — clear and pure is my will, and I want nothing but to make this noble man happy! I am satisfied, peaceful, excited and happy as never before. God preserve my love!" [17]

Walter was free only during infrequent, short leaves. Alma tried to visit him whenever she could, and at first it made her feel healthy and needed just to be a wife again. Soon she changed her mind. On September 16 her diary revealed:

This is certainly the most remarkable marriage that could have been. *So* unmarried, so free, and yet so bound. Nobody pleases me. Now women are almost dearer to me than men, because they are at least not so aggressive. I would like, once and for all, to find my own harbor . . . Gustav never recognized me as a *living* being next to him. He had his needs: quiet meals, a warm house, and every opportunity to work on his music, day or night. He wanted no more, needed no more, and never thought that I might have wanted something else from life or that I could simply have perished from the lack of love if things had gone on in that way. Then, when I was accustomed to living my life for and by myself, I put all of the guilt for my own sadness on my own inability to make life happier. I wanted music, but our house had to be quiet when Gustav came home from the Opera, tired and drained. I wanted my own music, or music about which *I* felt deeply, because Gustav's music was foreign to me . . . But I worked with him, felt with and for him, was always at his performances and lived so that in me an essentially foreign life of sensations and strange creations grew. I believed that I was old and hateful . . . and suddenly there came a man into my life who was new to me and immediately taken by me. When he first told me that he loved me, I was happy as I had not been in years. This happened right after I had lost my beautiful child. I was destroyed and suffering. I sent Annie back to Mama and went at once to Vienna, where I was overcome that I had no power to do anything, because I had until that time existed only for husband and children. There was no future for me.[18]

Oskar finished his basic training and was sent to the front, elegantly astride his faithful horse. He wrote to Alma on November 7 that he would "have very good reason to spend a few hours in Vienna, since, on February 1st, when I enlisted, I managed to do it in a way that I became not a soldier, but a deserter! At very least, now I can see you once more, and I look forward to that greatly. Be sure that you have no visitors and I shall come for lunch. You sent me money, and I return it to you, since I now, with no opportunity to paint, have no prospect of repaying my debtors." [19]

Shortly thereafter, Oskar was riding his horse across the River Bug near Lutek, leading a group of other horses by their bridles, when he was accosted by a group of enemy Cossacks. He rode away as fast as he could but was shot in the head. To be sure that he was dead, the marauders drove a bayonet into his chest. Oskar lay in the woods half conscious, with his right side paralyzed. He was finally rescued by a group of Austrian comrades, and as soon as he could be moved he was transported to a hospital in Vienna.

There he first heard of Alma's marriage to Walter. He had known that she had had a full life of her own while he had been away, but he had trusted her with the key to his studio and left in the belief that he would return with the possibility of rebuilding their lives on a better ground. His death had been announced in the Viennese press, and, as Oskar later wrote: "Alma did not scruple to have sacksful of her letters carried off at once from my studio . . . It mattered less to me that she also took hundreds of sketches and drawings I had left behind, foolishly believing that the war would not last long . . . She is said to have given these away to young painters, by whom they were unfortunately ruined in attempts to complete them and render them saleable. Perhaps she was trying to appease pangs of conscience . . . Naturally she did not know that someone taken for dead might still come back alive." [20]

Oskar wanted desperately to see Alma and sent Loos to talk her into visiting the hospital, but she would not go. Oskar vacillated between hoping that there would come a time when he and she would be together and marry and wanting to leave behind him everything that had to do with

Alma and all women. She convinced herself that his weakness was not worth her time; she wanted nothing to do with people who seemed to need her help.

She was satisfied with Walter, writing in her diary in the dawn of the year 1916, "I hope that I shall be blessed. Our hours of love seem to go on for months — then this painful-sweet conclusion. There is nothing more beautiful in the world."[21] She wanted a child; little else concerned her. Though Walter had once told her that a man and a woman could never be mere friends, she still took pride in the men whom she counted as her friends. She saw Ochs and the poet Albert von Trentini. If one of the men whom she invited to her house happened to fall in love with her, she considered it not her fault. There had been a number of men who had been her friends and not loved her. But there was one who did love, and she had proof: she was pregnant.

Oskar heard about this, too, and it hurt him. So did the sights of the city of Vienna under its afflictions of the war in the first hours when he was allowed to leave the hospital. He went directly to see his mother and asked her for the beads left with her as a symbol of his relation with Alma. Mrs. Kokoschka picked up the clay flowerpot, dropped it, and withdrew the necklace from the shards. Her son understood the point she was trying to make but could not accept it. He wrote, "For some years I derived pleasure . . . from raking the ashes of a dead grief without asking myself whether Alma's psychic wounds had healed as well as my physical ones. Time and again, I found opportunities to try her. For instance, I would suddenly write her a hypocritical letter offering to forget the past, to wipe the slate clean; or a telegram full of devotion and without a trace of reproach or recrimination; another time it was flowers, and finally an invitation to the premiere of my play *Orpheus und Eurydike* in Frankfurt."[22]

The play *Orpheus* had been inspired by hallucinations Oskar had experienced during the worst weeks of his infirmity. "I saw the woman from whom I had so painfully parted standing there before me. I felt myself succumbing to her powers of attraction, as if I could never part from her. The head wound had impaired my power of locomotion and my vision, but the words of my imaginary conversation with her phantom impressed themselves so vividly on my mind that without having to write anything down I could progressively expand them in my imagination to create whole scenes." [23]

Oskar recovered more swiftly than any of his doctors might have predicted, and he asked to be sent to the Italian front as a liaison officer, from which post he would join a Hungarian regiment whose colonel was a friend. He was endangered several times in Italy. Then, in Hungary, he ventured onto a bridge which blew up while he was on it. After another protracted hospital stay he found himself back in treatment in Vienna from shell shock. Even now, Alma would not agree to visit him. Out of the hospital on convalescent leave, Oskar went to Berlin, then to Dresden, wanting nothing to do with Vienna.

In Semmering and pregnant, Alma was spending more time with women than was her custom — with Nora Draskowitsch, who was, Alma thought, as beautiful as she was spiritual, and with the Countess Gretl Cudenhove, whose warmth struck her. Alma looked at herself — Gustav's widow, Walter's wife — and decided in her diary that "Jews have given us spirit, but have eaten up our hearts." [24] She wondered whether she was still the same woman who had married Gustav. Again, she was in flux.

On October 5, 1916, Manon Gropius was born. She was named after the heroine of Puccini's opera *Manon Lescaut,* and from the moment of her birth, everyone who came in

contact with her fell in love with her. Walter was away, but
he sent a gift, Edvard Munch's painting called *The Midnight
Sun,* which Alma treasured.

Alma had two daughters but no husband, or so she felt.
"He is at the front. We have been married more than a year,
but we do not *have* each other, and sometimes, in fear, I
feel that we are strangers. I am tired of all this living in the
future. Always ifs, ands and buts!" [25] She might have returned to Oskar, but she did not want to. "He has become
a hateful, strange ghost to me! Nothing about his life interests me.

"But I loved him!

"What will happen with all of this?

"I walk and walk and my feet are often so very tired . . .
I cannot rest. I am glad that I have enough peace to remain
faithful to Walter, because I love him and will not leave
him. Every man is the preacher in his own church. The
woman is the receiver — the one who must pray in these
churches." [26]

Alma took account of the men in her life:

> Gustav Mahler — from the struggles of abstraction,
> Oskar Kokoschka, the genius,
> Walter Gropius, the improviser of cultures and wills —
> and Joseph Fraenkel, the genial improviser . . .
> From Walter I want children — from Oskar, works — from
> Fraenkel, the celebration of the spirit that he never offered
> me. I wish that Fraenkel had moved into my house to live
> the rest of his life with me. [27]

Alma went so far as to consider devoting herself to the
Church, but that would not have been possible or wise.
"Only for Fraenkel was I too earthy — for Oskar I was no
longer strong enough otherwise, everything was right . . .

But then, when I look at my two little girls, my heart is touched. They are so dear. That is my happiness now, and there will probably not be another for me. Everything around me is becoming still and soundless. 'Husband' means nothing to me anymore. Walter has come too late!" [28]

Young Anna, entering her teenage years, was beyond needing her mother's care, but nevertheless she was Mahler's daughter, exceedingly special, and she was increasingly like her mother. Anna was quiet and wise, determined and eager to build a life of her own. She had learned independence at an early age, and kept her distance, as if she were a member of a separate circle. Anna enjoyed caring for Manon, and became almost as much of a mother to the baby as Alma was. The teenager was fond of her stepfather, though she saw little of him. When he was at home, Walter was almost always the perfect gentleman, a courtier. He did have a temper, however, and he threw the seventh, last, and most intimate of the fans Oskar had painted of Alma into the fire in a fit of jealousy. Anna could not fathom such outbursts.

As soon as she had regained her strength after Manon's birth, Alma returned to society. She saw Paul Kammerer, Alban and Helene Berg, Schoenberg, and Klimt. She didn't want to spend time only with old friends and musicians, so she went about bringing writers into her circle. Among them was Franz Blei, whom she saw in Vienna and Semmering during 1917 and might have considered taking as a lover. His argumentative brilliance was as annoying as it was compelling, and even Walter, home on furlough, was taken with Alma's new friend. After Blei left, husband and wife called their new affliction *Bleivergiftung,* "lead poisoning." Blei offered up others to join Alma's social gatherings — her "Sundays" or salons — and he promised that he would soon introduce the young poet Franz Werfel. Alma recognized the

name from a poem that she had run across when she had
been in Berlin trying to capture Walter's favors; she remembered the words "Nothing is mine to own;/ I possess alone.
This awareness . . ."[29] Alma mused that she might indeed
enjoy meeting Franz Werfel.

9

Franzl-Poet and Revolutionary

IT WAS AUTUMN before Blei introduced Alma to the twenty-seven-year-old Franz, son of Rudolf Werfel, chief of the glovemaking firm of Werfel & Boehm, with offices in Prague, Tuchków, London, Glasgow, Paris, Brussels, and Berlin. In the service since the first days of war, Franz had spent most of his time with the military in Italy, and he had fallen in love with that country, which appealed to the soft, almost feminine side of his nature. The pampered only son in a Jewish family, with two sisters, Franz had had some difficulty accustoming himself to the routine of the service. Nevertheless, he had distinguished himself sufficiently to have advanced in the command and to have managed to obtain some favorable assignments. Furthermore his superiors, not unlike Oskar's, had taken note of his presence. Franz was already gaining a reputation as one of the best young poets writing in the German language. Commanding officers who were aware of the accomplishments of their young charge tended to treat him kindly, and to enjoy his company.

Franz injured his feet when on a free day he jumped too early from a cable car in the Italian Alps, and was reassigned to the Army Press Division in Vienna, thanks to the intervention of a nobleman who admired his poems. In the press offices, Franz's assignment was far from demanding: he didn't have to wear a uniform, except on special occasions; he lived at the Hotel Bristol with every comfort wartime conditions could allow, and he had plenty of time to socialize. This he usually did in cafés, over endless cups of coffee and cigarettes. Alma had come to hate the café circle, and not only because its members often reeked of smoke and alcohol. To her it symbolized the most unattractive parts of Viennese society: the poverty-ridden, who had no homes and were forced to seek warmth and running water in the city's shabbier coffeehouses; and the cynical, often Jewish members of the intelligentsia who wasted hours sitting around pretending to be clever, engaged in idle criticism of the social order. Furthermore, women were not welcome in the café circles, and to Alma, a society of men only was quite as dreadful as that of women only.

When Blei arrived at her apartment with Werfel, Alma greeted a person who fit her stereotype of the Jew: a small, rounding man whose features and solidity made him look older than he was, certainly not eleven years her junior. He had a growing reputation as a poet, but he was far from achieving the status of Gustav, Klimt, or even Oskar. Franz had gained popularity in certain circles for his readings of both his own works and great lyrics from German literature. For every person who appreciated his very theatrical manner of recitation, however, there were several others who found it exaggerated to the point of being foolish. He was intelligent and, unlike his friend Blei, he didn't seem to find it necessary to dominate the conversation. He had a quiet and subtle sense of humor, which he could graciously turn back upon himself. Alma could not abide his politics. After their first meeting, she wrote, "Werfel espoused at first an awful kind of Social Democratism, but, in the course of the evening, he became better, freer and loftier. And because I love his work, a poem called 'Der Erkennede' which he wrote two years ago, he was completely at home . . .

"Werfel is a rather fat Jew with full lips and watery, almond eyes. But he becomes more and more attractive. His unorthodox love of humanity and speech, such as: 'How can I be happy when there is someone, somewhere, who is suffering,' which I have heard verbatim from another egocentric, from Gustav Mahler!"[1]

Beyond that, Franz loved music with sensitivity and talent that overcame his lack of training. He was especially fond of the works of Giuseppe Verdi, and in a fine tenor voice he could sing large portions of many of the composer's operas by heart. Just before Christmas, when Walter was home on leave, Blei and Werfel made another of their frequent visits to Alma's apartment, and Alma played *Meistersinger* and *Louise* while Franz sang. Then he recited a few of his new poems. She sensed that she had with this new friend a kind of spiritual link she had never felt with Walter. Alma admitted to a strange pang of disappointment when her husband announced he would be able to extend his leave and stay at home through the holiday, which Alma had already arranged to celebrate in the company of her daughters and a few friends. She fought the urge to get rid of Walter to keep him from getting close to little Manon, and she wanted to spend her time with Franz.

When Walter left just before New Year's Day 1918, Alma knew that it would not be long before they would say goodbye for the last time. She did not go to the train with him on that morning; she had more important things to do. Mengelberg and his Concertgebouw Orchestra had come to Vienna from Amsterdam to present a series of concerts beginning that afternoon at the Musikverein with *Das Lied von der Erde,* which Alma and Anna Mahler would attend together. As Alma was dressing, the bell rang at the door. Walter was home. He had missed his train and had to wait for the next one, which would not leave until late at night. He wanted to go to the concert, but Alma would not spare him one of her two tickets. Fearing a scene, she called Anna and Carl Moll and asked them to come for supper after the concert and reception. At Alma's that evening the atmosphere was grim, and Walter left early for the train. From the border he cabled his wife, "Break the ice that is in your countenance."[2] Unfortunately, he had quoted a line from a poem by Franz.

The last days of 1917 were taken up in a busy round of concerts by Mengelberg and his orchestra, including one on New Year's Day which combined Gustav's Fourth Symphony and Richard Strauss's *Ein Heldenleben.* After this event, Alma gave a small supper for the Mengelbergs, then opened her rooms to seventy-odd other guests, among them a generous sprinkling of counts and countesses, Schreker, Bittner, Berg, Wellesz, Blei, and Werfel. The party must have been a success, for Mengelberg, the guest of honor, did not leave until three the next morning. Alma remembered to her diary, "The best moments were those when I could talk, unnoticed, with Werfel. Hail to this enriching man! I have to control my heart, lest I lose it."[3]

That happened, in a sense, only three days later, and Alma confessed it to her diary on the fifth of January. She and Franz had attended one of Mengelberg's concerts separately, but they could not keep from staring at one another, first awkwardly, then passionately. They met at intermission and went to her apartment, where "our eloquent silence brought us to the brink. It was inevitable. He grasped my hand and kissed it and we found each other's lips, and he stammered words that had no meaning or context but which were still so right and so true . . . It had to come that I would love him."[4]

Alma found herself worrying about the difference in their ages, much as Gustav had fretted about a similar discrepancy. "If only I were twenty years younger, I would throw over everything and go with him! As it is, I have to watch with deep sadness as this one who is blessed by the gods goes on his own way. Franz Werfel!" Alma did not retreat, however.

"I love Werfel and want the best for him. *I* do not come into consideration here. If only I have the strength to show him all the beauties of an innocent existence. I feel no peace! I have to burn my path . . . The bourgeoisie defeats me. Now for the first time I live with a full heart. God, permit me *this* life!"[5]

Franz wanted Alma to come to visit him, but she was reluctant to go for fear of being seen — a married woman of significant reputation visiting a young man alone in his room. She found a mission that let her rationalize entering the Hotel Bristol: Franz was far in arrears in reading the galleys of his book *Day of Judgment,* and only when Alma was sitting beside him could she be sure that he was diligently at work. She offered her watchful presence in the January weeks before the military ordered him on a tour of Switzerland, where he would lecture on the strength of Austria's war effort. He left on the eighteenth. Alma was pregnant.

The first time his train stopped, he wrote to her that he had left hearing the music that they both loved, *their* music, Pfitzner's Piano Trio "that you play so beautifully. There is so much of you in this theme. Your *heroism* is there." Their time together had been so short he was afraid that she would forget him entirely, "because you live quickly, Alma, I know that from your music." He pined for her apartment, her red music room, her gold hostess dress. When he left, she had asked him to be true to her, but after he had been away for only one week, she told him that he must be free. "Why should I not feel myself held by you? You may not underestimate my sensibility . . . No! I will not let you get away! I want no mercy, that is weak. *You* must wait for me!!!"[6]

Franz met Busoni in Zurich, and the composer asked after Alma. He was delighted to give reports of her, though it began to seem as if everyone he met asked for her. "Yesterday Ehrenstein, Kokoschka's best friend, told me about O.K., how he had crying fits when you did not permit him to visit you and . . . that K. is still bound to you. This conversation agitated me because I had to pretend to be ignorant."[7]

On February 6, Klimt died from the results of a stroke. "With him," Alma wrote, "a bright piece of my youth left my life. How I loved him — and I never stopped loving him."[8]

Walter had been moved to a position on the front too far away to allow return to Vienna on his short leaves. Though this was no disappointment for Alma, she thought Manon should see her father and wanted to maintain some semblance of a marriage. Whenever Walter's leaves and her own health allowed, Alma took her younger daughter and met her husband in Berlin. He was led to believe that the child she was carrying was his, and he asked few questions about his wife's life. On one of the short visits, Alma felt a strong urge to recover the portrait Oskar had painted of her, which she had given, along with some of his drawings, to a newly established private museum founded by Karl Osthaus, the

Folkwang Museum in Westphalia. She wrote to the founder asking for the picture to be returned to her at once. He obliged. Very shortly after the portrait arrived in Alma's hands, Osthaus died and his museum and collection were dissipated.

As soon as the weather began to turn warm and sunny, Alma took Anna and Manon to Semmering, where she awaited the birth of her child in the early autumn. She guarded her privacy, but often found herself beset by more guests than her country house could accommodate. Semmering was not the best place for Franz to work, so Alma discouraged his requests to visit her, knowing that he wrote only under duress, when he had exhausted all available means of procrastination. Furthermore, when he sat at his desk he worked day and night until his project was done, and his energy depleted. Alma took this to signify a lack of discipline and found it most annoying. She blamed Franz's indulgence in cigarettes and cafés for his laxness. In his letters, he assured her that he was avoiding the company of his comrades and colleagues as much as he could, smoking less, controlling his intake of coffee, and not wandering to cafés.

Franz was ready to visit Semmering one weekend when he happened to run into Walter in Vienna. Knowing that Alma's husband was in the area, probably about to go to the country house, Franz postponed his journey. He decided that his meeting with Walter was fate's way of protecting both Alma and himself. Besides, a husband would naturally visit his pregnant wife as often as he could. Instead of going to Semmering, Franz went to see his family in Prague, where his sister, Hanna Werfel Fuchs-Robettin, had just given birth to a child. The Werfel family tried always to mark such occasions with reunions. Alma didn't like the idea of Franz's going home, since she knew he had spent much time with

Alma Mahler as drawn by Oskar Kokoschka, about 1913

Paul Kammerer, the biologist and musician

Alma Mahler

Oskar Kokoschka in military uniform

The young Anna Mahler

Die Windsbraut, Kokoschka's best-known double portrait, 1914

Walter Gropius, the architect and founder of the Bauhaus

Manon Gropius, Alma's third daughter

Alma with the poet
Franz Werfel

Alban Berg joking with Franz Werfel

Alma walking in the countryside

Franz, Alma, and Manon in Venice, 1920

Johannes Hollnsteiner, "the essence of a priest,"
about 1935

Alma's mansion on the Hohe Warte, Vienna

another woman there, one who had gained the love and approval of his relatives. He wrote to assure Alma he was spending all of his free time alone. At the end of July he made the long-postponed trip to Semmering.[9]

The days and weeks to follow were the worst of Franz's life. Alma met him at her house, proud and happy in her seventh month of pregnancy, intent on making him feel that he was not just another of the many guests. He was given the bedroom next to hers. In the evening, after supper, Alma and her daughter Anna played Gustav's Eighth Symphony in its four-hand version on the harmonium. Franz went to his room earlier than the rest of the company. He waited to hear Alma go to her bed, then went to her and, after months of separation, they made love. Franz went back to his own room feeling proud and sated, optimistic about what life would bring to him.

That night, a few hours later, Alma began hemorrhaging. The maid woke Franz and ordered him to fetch a doctor from town, but he wandered out into rain-soaked fields and couldn't tell where he was or which way he should go. Hours passed before Franz found the sickly-looking physician and convinced him to tend Alma. Meanwhile, Anna had telephoned a Viennese specialist. Franz felt an unearthly combination of guilt and hope as he led the country doctor back to the house where he would try to relieve the woman's suffering. Alma had improved slightly, but she was still not allowed to move. She summoned Franz to tell him that she wanted to keep the child, even if it meant her own death. With that pronouncement, she sent him away.

Franz reached the station where he would board the train for Vienna just as Walter and the specialist arrived. Franz did not get to the city until after eight in the evening, when telephone service to Semmering had been shut down for the night. He had to wait until morning to find out about Al-

ma's condition. He did telephone the Molls to tell them of
the crisis. The next day, the country doctor told Franz the
Viennese specialist had decided that surgery was necessary.
Franz didn't understand the implications of the problem. On
July 31, unknown to Franz, Alma was taken back to Vi-
enna.

Franz had vowed he would stop smoking if Alma lived,
but when he found that she had been moved into a hospital
in the city without his knowledge, he broke his vow. He still
carried on what he called his "thanksgiving" fast, eating only
two meals each day. At least he could now speak to Alma
in the hospital. Over the telephone, her voice sounded faint,
and she was pessimistic about the child's chance for sur-
vival.

Alone at his desk, feeling anxious and useless in the face
of suffering, Franz wrote a poem:

> *Once music was the desire of that flourishing voice.*
> *Now the need creeps in silently, to quell the sound.*
> *Verse that was once overpowering on the lips*
> *Now only crawls to fill the paper.*
> *Gold is the hidden change of the sunbeam —*
> *Its final resting point is on the paper.*
> *Song is only word, the strong sound of the gold.*
> *That matters only when it is put down on paper.*
> *Where is the dear one that has used no paper?*
> *Alma, dear soul, God's song of day,*
> *Death cannot still you.*[10]

That night, Alma went into labor. The next morning she
gave birth to a baby boy. Walter was with her. Franz telephoned again and again for reports. When at last he had the
good word that mother and son were both alive and in stable condition, he wrote another poem, "Alma's Son":

Today a child came into the world —
The trees bow in a strange and holy way.
The light streams out of the tent,
As milk flows with new hope through the dry spaces.
The pain that was everything is lost in one sustained breath.
As hope was born into the world.

Today a son came into the world.
A white petal hangs sacredly on all life,
And every glance is different, somehow.
To have created another: We have been chosen,
Blessed again by God in a new baptism . . .
Because today a hope was born.

A man, a man entered our era.
And the stars and distant races know of the secret.
In the flower-strewn meadow and in the crystalling places of
*   greatness*
Those who sing praise lowered their voices
To the great creation and its inner gleam.
Because hope anew entered our age.

A spirit revealed itself today that breathes with us.
Out of the pains of death he appeared in our lives.
In this hour that which was used was unused,
And a hot wind cooled the crippled legs!
Distortions were made whole, which once lay in iron and
*   fire.*
Because the breath of hope has glanced upon us again.

A son of man creates new heartbeats.
The world lay in sadness, and all was possible for him
But we know: Every day is Christmas.
The hero has struggled from this mother's womb.
He who with a new cry lifts us out of nothingness.
And we pray to his new heartbeat.

A child, a son, a person, a spirit, a son of man
Is, through birth, among us. God himself, in his dream

Of deepest peace, rejoices and arises!
From a woman, from heaven, from streets and shattered trees
An explanation unfolds and reveals itself.
God smiles and with him that which was heading for decay,
Because a saviour has been seen,
Because a saviour has been born to us all.[11]

The baby had been born prematurely to a mother almost thirty-nine years old, and he was very weak. The doctors held out little hope. Alma wrote to Franz, assuring him that this was indeed his son, his child, and inviting him to visit three days after the birth. Franz went, and was stunned by how much the baby resembled himself, so well formed, small, lively, and expressive. It was this visit that Franz had in mind when in his last and greatest book, *The Star of the Unborn,* he posed to himself — the hero F.W. — the question of what had been the greatest moment of his life:

The first thing I saw was the white door that I closed behind me with infinite caution, as though by doing so I could postpone reality a little longer. I had reached this door by way of a long corridor and I had hesitated for a few long heartbeats before I knocked and turned the knob. I was expected. I entered into a deep silence, a much deeper silence than that outside. A bare white room. Many flowers. A small hospital room. The window was open. It was in August, four o'clock in the afternoon, and the humid air of a metropolitan summer day was oppressive. On the white enameled hospital bed lay the woman whom I love. She could barely move. She greeted me with a look that combined a smile of happiness and the horror of the last few days. Her long blonde hair streamed over the pillow. Her face was whiter than white but her beauty was never more glorious. The woman whom I love was not my wife, not yet. I was even obliged to act strange and indifferent in this terrible situation. A nurse was bending over the crib in which the child lay. I had to restrain myself to keep from groaning aloud. How could a person be so convinced of his own depravity as I was and still go on living? At other times I had defended myself against myself by saying: It takes two. But now I know that the woman, even as a sinner, is the heroine and the victim. I was nothing but a frivolous, thoughtless, irresponsible exploiter of the intoxicated feeling I called love. How could it be love? Love only begins at the point where one has something at stake and something to lose. What did I have to lose? I was a Bohemian or something like that. I wrote poems and plays, and upon this cheap and ambitious activity I and the likes of me based the strange claim of exemption from "the civil order." Even at this instant I was sure that other standards applied to me. At the same time, however, I was convinced more icily, more cuttingly from moment to moment, that we two had offended not only against the civil order but against a higher world order. Man — woman — child — the holy meeting of these three should not have been like this. I should not have entered this white room with a smiling nod, with controlled features like any friend or acquaintance. The last time we had seen each other was in the lonely house on that terrible night when she became deathly ill . . . I had finally received permission to see her again, as a good friend like other good friends. I was afraid to look at her, for my self-control was exhausted. One of us would finally have to say something. And then she spoke. But not to me, she was sending the nurse away on an errand. I waited, listening, until the inner door closed, then the outer door, and I sank down on my knees by the bed. This combination of expectant waiting and sudden kneeling struck me as theatrical and made me unhappy, like everything else that I did during those lagging minutes. Her hand stroked my hair. She said: "The child . . . Your child . . ."

I rose. I walked on tiptoe to the little crib at the foot of the bed. Was the nurse listening outside? Why was I thinking of the nurse? I was afraid to look at the child. The physician whom I had asked downstairs had shrugged his shoulders.

"It can hardly be expected to live." But now I was surprised to find this premature child a complete human, an incredibly developed personality, completely limited by its tiny body but more identical with it than a painting with its canvas. I looked at the delicate, pallid face, the high forehead, the extraordinarily round skull with its pulsating fontanels. And I became absurdly convinced that in this spherical little head there resided a unique, characteristic independent permanence that was older than twelve days, that was as old as the world. I was the father and this was my little son. I was the cause and here was the effect, and this chain of cause and effect went back to the beginning of things.

I should now have felt a solemn attachment, the miracle of the nearest relationship on earth, the poignant pain of impending loss. I felt nothing of the sort, although I made a feeble effort to talk myself into it. Ordinarily I was an easy victim to auto-suggestion; now I was quite incapable of producing the reactions that the difficult situation demanded . . . The child was quiet. If it would only cry, everything would be easier. The child was still feverish; its big blue eyes roved. I knew that I had to say something hopeful to its mother. I wanted to give myself some hope, too. "We'll get through all right," I said, or something like it.

Once more, one last time, I bent over the round little head. Suddenly I had a feeling of kinship. I knew this feverish little boy. The nurse had returned to the room. I put on my mendaciously innocent face. The woman on the bed said in a soft voice, "When you stepped into the room before, funeral music was playing outside . . ." These words gave me a chance to walk over to the open window and look outside. The street in front of the hospital was deserted; the trees in the little park were wilted in the drought of the late summer.

"I don't see a thing," I said.

"Please close the window," said the woman.

I closed the window. A silent, dry sob rose in my throat. I pressed my face against the pane . . .[12]

Franz's recounting of the most important moment in his life is a vivid description of the turmoil he and Alma went through with the birth of their son, and the only direct reference to her in his fiction. There are other characters in the writings who might have been taken in part from Alma, but this passage, in a novel unfortunately forgotten today, shows the author in very specific memories of that August afternoon. It is also the clearest indication that Franz recognized his son would not survive.

The parents tried to retain hope. Franz called the hospital several times each day; occasionally he spoke with Alma, but more often he spoke to Anna, Walter, one of the Molls, or to a nurse. Since Walter had rushed home on emergency leave to be with his wife and weak son — who, he still thought, was his own — Franz could not be a regular visitor. He admired Walter's help and concern. Alma was slowly growing stronger and the child's condition was stable. Franz kept a diary in which he could record his feelings to counteract his loneliness and worry. But there arose the possibility he would have to be sent out of Vienna on military assignment. He could not tolerate the prospect, and it put him in a frenzy. Fortunately, these orders never came through.

Alma was weak and disheartened. One moment she was happy and proud of her son, and could feel sure he would survive and, eventually, thrive. Franz often presented this optimistic prospect to her in his letters, either out of his own convictions or out of his desire to help Alma regain her own constitution. Alma was secure with Franz, sensing that no matter what might happen their love would go on. Then she would fear for herself, her baby, and her lover. What would become of them all? Guilt descended upon her as she felt that the sickly infant was her just punishment for all of the evil she had brought upon her husband and her family. Walter had given her Manon and wanted to do the best for her, always in the most kindly, patient manner. When Franz called to find out about Alma's condition, Walter had been happy to report to him, pleased by the concern of a man he considered their mutual friend.

Franz helped Alma decide on a name for their baby, and when she was again strong enough to exchange regular letters, they began to discuss the possibilities. Franz suggested Gerhart (but, he wondered, would that be acceptable to Gerhart Hauptmann?), or Benvenuto (but that was what Hauptmann had named his own son). He also suggested Martin, Gabriel, Daniel, Matthias, Albrecht, Lukas, and Klemens. The couple tentatively settled on Imanuel, but in the end, the infant was named Martin Carl Johannes.[13]

Alma and Franz were discussing possible names for their son one Sunday morning when Walter walked into his wife's room, found her on the telephone, heard her say the name Franz in a most delicate tone, and realized the truth. He asked a mild question or two. Alma would not answer him, but her silence and her expression told her husband everything. Walter said nothing more, then or in the future. He never outwardly succumbed to jealousy or reproachfulness. He did write a note to Franz, asking him to be very careful for the sake of both Alma and the baby. Franz responded to the husband's letter, affirming his love and concern. With pain in his words, Walter answered that the father of "our" child had "a Christian mission," but he asked the Jew Franz to visit Alma frequently, and seemed to be leaving his wife in her lover's charge.[14]

Alma confided to her diary, "The secret is out. My secret that I love Werfel more than anyone — that I belong to him forever." But, she continued, "I want to and will stay with Gropius — my duty calls — while my heart belongs to Werfel . . . The person and the man are equally important to me, and that has occurred for the first time."[15]

Well as he had come to know Walter, Franz was shaken by the husband's dignity. It made the situation all the more difficult for Franz, and increased his feelings of guilt. Alma was distraught, fearful for both herself and the baby, and more than a little annoyed that Franz was entertaining a house guest, and soon thereafter would be host to his sister Mizzi, with whom he would go out on the town and visit friends.

Alma was allowed to take her baby home. Back in her apartment, she was struck all the more by the hardships that had resulted from the war. It was impossible to obtain an incubator for her infant, and she had to deal with shortages of food, paper products, and a number of other items that would have made her more comfortable. Little Martin was too weak and tired to cry for anything that he might have wanted — play, care, even food. Alma found sustainment only in Franz. She wrote in her diary in September, "how incredibly much we are alike. 'Panerotic' he called it yesterday. And he is right." But, she wondered, "How shall I part myself from this marvelous person? I love him. Peacefully, I love him. He does not lead me to my death, as the others did; he is an instigator of peace, like the sea." [16]

She thought she would have to leave him, and wrote:

Oskar Kokoschka was right. He made symbols out of every contact and always saw the deepest erotic meaning in everything — sometimes to my annoyance — but now I see how he alone was right. The fact that I was so deeply influenced by so many Jews taught me this morality, so that I was not in the position to accept this true statement of O.K. Werfel is amoral, without realizing it. Yesterday, Walter brought me to him. He lives in a furnished room, the likes of which I have never seen . . . I was shocked and frightened. The room reeked of immorality — bad, depressing, mystical books by Swedenborg, Kierkegaard and old churchmen who had to spend their enlightened lives there under filthy hands. An awful storm reigned overhead. Everything that is wild and evil over the righteousness of the spirit. One poor, single bed, in which he sleeps, seemed mildewed to me . . . I had the feeling in that room that I would come across an antique mattress.[17]

With this visit, Alma saw vividly how much Franz needed her to provide him with the surroundings in which he could work and flourish. The more he needed her, the more she seemed to need him in return. Walter knew something had to be done, so he wrote Alma a letter proposing that she give him custody of Manon in return for a divorce; she could then take baby Martin and go to live with Franz. Alma was adamant — she wanted Franz, but nothing could make her give up Manon, the one treasure of her union with Walter. On the same evening both Walter and Franz came to Alma's rooms. She gave notice that she wanted nothing further to do with either of them: they should go away and leave her with her children to pursue her own life. Walter went down on his knees to apologize and beg her forgiveness, but Alma was only disgusted that he would humble himself in the presence of a third person. Franz reacted calmly and quietly, and helped put an end to the tension without pushing or asserting himself beyond the acceptable bounds. Alma wrote in her diary, "I love him beyond death. His noble face was peacefully sympathetic but without sorrow, since he *knew* I would not leave him." [18]

Franz could not always remain patient and soothing.

If Walter loved you too, then we would both have to be married [to you], for anything else would be a swindle and has to be recognized as such. What does he want? He only makes you ill. *We,* on the other hand, make each other happy. He does not belong to you and he should see his mistake. Even if I did not exist, he would not belong to you! Tell him that! Don't be weak and agreeable . . . Say to him, "You see that I got sick when you came here. What do you want? . . . You don't understand that I have moved on to another destiny and want more than anything to turn from my obligation to you and into the life that is light-years away from yours. Don't violate me with your own pain!" — And even if you don't say all of that, you have to let him know of your illness. Say to him, "If we had not been married, you would not permit yourself to spend the whole day with me and to make me melancholy and turn my life bitter, or to keep me away from the person with whom I want to spend my time. But only because we happen to be married, do I have to go along with this?" — You shouldn't put up with it and let yourself be made a slave by some foolery of the past. . . If you don't have the courage to change our lives, I do.[19]

Alma did not have the courage. There remained something in the back of her mind that reminded her what had happened to the first child she had conceived without benefit of marriage vows, and then what had happened to the child's father. She stood in awe of the marriage contract, even though she could not live by its vows or its accepted regulations. Furthermore, she hated to hurt anyone, especially Walter, who, despite everything, had behaved better under the most difficult circumstances than she had had any right to expect. She wanted Manon to know and love her father. And if Alma had no doubts about her love for Franz, she was still concerned about the difference in their ages — especially as she faced her own fortieth birthday. Lastly, she knew that the conflicting feelings she and her lover held concerning religion and politics could cause trouble.

The questions of the political situation were to lead to the most heated arguments between Alma and Franz, especially in that November of 1918, when revolution broke out in Vienna. Alma hated the riffraff, the proletarians, and the hoodlums who ran amuck on the city streets. She reached the point where she took with her a pistol whenever she had to go out by herself. On the day after the revolution began, Franz appeared at Alma's door in uniform, ready to fight. She soon learned that he had joined up with the "Red Guard," which had been born in the coffeehouses of Vienna. When he came to her smelling of tobacco and cheap booze, she sent him away. Franz's participation in the revolt caused some commotion among the journalists and society people who knew Alma and wanted either to protect or to embarrass her. Franz became the most articulate spokesman for the cause that finally led to the fall of the ruling Hapsburgs. The police went after him, and it was partly through Walter's intervention that Franz avoided arrest. The situation was distasteful, but, more than that, it accentuated Alma's affiliation with another Jew, who was also a rabble-rouser.

Bertha Zuckerkandl tried to defend Franz in her columns in the *Neues Wiener Journal:*

> For weeks, Franz Werfel the revolutionary has been discussed with a more passionate interest than people ever took in Franz Werfel the poet. The questionings and scribblings have not ceased since he was reported to have joined the "Red Guard." I admire Werfel as a poet, love him as a person, and have the strongest reservations about him as an "activist thinker" — because his thinking wells up from the elemental font of emotion. There is a utopian in him, who will always outstrip the cosmic idea in poetry, but will always founder in action.
>
> That is why "the case" did not interest me much until things took a sad turn. Today — when even diametrically

opposed intellectuals ought to be protected and united — the hue and cry is raised against Franz Werfel as a moral personality . . . The politician Werfel may justly come under attack; whoever plunges into chaos nowadays cannot afford to be squeamish. But Werfel's human value must be upheld, for he is one of the morally untainted.[20]

Alma was annoyed by everything about the episode, especially the publicity. Walter found himself in an awkward and unenviable position. As a highly respected member of the military, Gropius was also responsible for his wife, their child Manon, her daughter Anna, and the new baby Martin. Yet he considered Franz to be his friend, and he recognized the younger man's value in spite of what he considered to be his stupidity.

In the futile hope that they could all be friends and maintain what he viewed as an acceptable way of life, Walter kept in communication with Franz, sending him notes of encouragement, offering him visits, coffee, and the like. Walter was trying to plan a project that might make his career as well as save what was left of his marriage. He intended to move his family to Germany, where he would start a new school of architecture and design, a kind of child of the Secession and the Wiener Werkstaette that would be called the Bauhaus, or the "working house." He would like to have had the chance to discuss his plans with Alma, who had been so intrigued by the emergence of the Secession, but she was completely uninterested. He did not care much about Alma's music; she did not care about his school or his architecture. Whether or not she ever suggested she might consider moving to Germany with Walter, he had come to believe that she would go with him. It was his last hope and his inspiration. She did not dash it.

Walter went off in search of his dream. In her husband's absence, Alma and Franz went to Semmering to revel in privacy and solitude and try to put the revolution and its implications behind them. Alma wanted to install Franz in her house in the country so that he could work without distraction and temptation. She changed her mind about his staying there just after Christmas, when she realized — with memories of Gustav — that Franz would not observe the Christian holiday in the ways she thought appropriate. She felt distanced from this man, even though she had become so close to him. She knew he was planning to go on to Prague to visit his family and could hardly wait for him to leave; she hoped he would not return. She wanted some outside force to come between them and tried to find that force in Franz's family. Alma created an artificial uproar over his planned trip, blaming his unmarried sister Mizzi for causing troubles far out of her realm. Franz argued that his trip would be brief, and was not going to let Alma talk him into changing his plans for her own selfish reasons. To the quiet, rational approach Franz used so often and so well, Alma had no good answer, especially when he impressed upon her that he was going to help his sister in his family position as elder brother and only son.

10

The Complicated Family

As 1919 BEGAN, Alma's thoughts turned to politics and religion. She wrote in her diary on January 9, "I have suddenly and as if from a higher inspiration understood the deeper meaning of bolshevism, the religion of the future. It resembles the beginnings of Christianity, the preparations for which came through the Jews' wait for a new Messiah who would teach them. Now they rise wildly with fire and sword in the world, but then they were carried only by *one* idea: Love thy neighbor as thyself . . . A new Christ will come, but not from among the Jews . . . Everything is ready for him, to crucify him, and it is time that he appeared. If my opinion is not wrong, he will come out of Russia or from slavery. But the Jews are at once an unprecedented danger and the greatest good luck for humanity." [1]

Most likely, Alma had not the slightest idea what bolshevism meant at the time to its proponents. Taking her advice from the passing comments of friends and companions, she was having great difficulty settling her thoughts about the Jews, her own Aryan people, and the rapidly changing political climate.

Household matters also occupied her thoughts. Manon, two and one-half, had reached an age when she wondered where her papa was; "Uncle Werfel" did not take his place. The war had reduced Alma's staff and Anna spent much time tending Manon. In addition, the ailing baby Martin demanded considerable care and attention. Alma called on Anna Moll for assistance whenever she could. The wonderful old woman always arrived promptly, without making an issue of how odd it was her adult daughter could barely cook an egg for herself.

Martin lost strength and was moved to the hospital. On January 28, the doctors performed surgery on the fragile infant, with no success. She would remember in her diary, "The worst thing about this whole time was the uncertainty of whether it was definitely [Franz's] child. I suspected it, hoped it, but was not absolutely sure. But this poor, small, sweet, wonderful child, *his* son, had to live through all of these awful conflicts. That was *my* guilt, the fact that it was even possible that I did not know who the child's father was."[2] She went so far as to think about throwing herself from the window, but had neither the courage nor the will.

Werfel is far from my thoughts, Walter is vague, Fraenkel is lost and gone, and Oskar is near. Why did I never understand that genius? We could have turned the world around together. I believe that I have done him the greatest harm and disservice. Because he believed — believed in me! This evening I read all of his letters through again, and a wonderful boy jumped out at me, but I poisoned his youth.

I have never erred. Everything that I have *really* experienced has been real and true for me, just as on the first day. Everything is simultaneous. I cannot deny any of them — Gustav, Fraenkel, Kokoschka, all were and *are* real! But how I would like to know how I have been put to rest in the heads of these men . . . [As happened so frequently, her mind went back to Oskar.] Was I too old for him? Too used up inside to satisfy such a marvelous youth? . . . And must everything then be worthless? Those many moments of happiness and sadness, in such deep communion with O.K. — where are they? I have only a few vivid pictures left in my mind — his beauty, a landscape here and there, his words — but nothing else . . . Last night I had my scratching fingers clinging in a death threat to the open window. But it is still hard for me to die, although my life, my constantly passing and burning life, is over.[3]

She decided to reactivate her salons, the "Sundays" in which she had lost interest during the months when she wanted to be alone with Franz, and then through her pregnancy. Franz had been uncomfortable at these gatherings, not knowing how he was supposed to react in the presence of Alma's friends. He had fallen into the habit of spending those afternoons when she entertained at cafés, smoking and drinking more than Alma thought he should. This had become a point of contention between the two, but now Alma decided that she needed to have her friends around her again. She invited Schoenberg, his wife, and daughter to lunch; after the meal, other friends and students joined them, and a pair of young musicians played a four-hand version of Gustav's Sixth Symphony. "The whole time I had the feeling that I should open my coffers and ask them all to take whatever they needed," Alma wrote. "I felt horribly guilty because I have more than they [Schoenbergs] do, and because I am more beautiful than all of them . . . Finally I gave that hateful daughter of theirs a platinum bracelet . . . and I will probably give them more, much more."[4]

In her red salon and in her gold dress she was Alma Mahler, not the wife of Walter Gropius in love with Franz Werfel. She wrote on February 2, "Now I know suddenly, and with incredible clarity, that I love Gustav and will love him forever, and that I am always looking for him, even since his death — but I will not find him. Everyone who comes near me is immature and negligible — Kokoschka, Werfel, important artists — they're nothing next to him, and something important is always lacking, so I am always dissatisfied. I have been so stupid even to search."[5]

Martin grew weaker, and the doctor told Alma that there was no hope for him. She saw "the sudden recognition that Werfel must be out of my life — that he is the source of all my unhappiness and that I have let my will to love overrule the more important welfare of my own life. — It's high time to make the turn. I sent him off to work at Semmering, and there he shall stay. I have no wish to see him again. The child is mortally ill. That separates me from him more than anything else. That this child must be buried is the curse of my happiness. I played a card and I lost — but I also lost Werfel!"[6]

During these months one of Oskar's crazy pranks caused further damage to Alma's reputation and laughter behind her back, although she seems to have been either unaware or forgetful of what was going on at the time. The art world knew that Oskar had ordered a life-sized doll, like Alma in every way, to be brought to his rooms in Dresden, where she would live with him, go to the opera and concerts with him, and be everything to him that Alma would no longer be. He was sharing the house of the odd Dr. Posse, who asked his guests to draw pornographic fantasies into his guest book, and had the services of the maid Hulda, whom Oskar

designated as tender to the effigy of Alma. He bought for
the doll the fine Parisian clothes and underwear he had always encouraged Alma to buy for herself, dressed her, and
planned her debut — a large party

with champagne for all my friends . . . there to put an end
to my inanimate companion, about whom so many wild stories were circulating in Dresden. I engaged a chamber orchestra from the Opera. The musicians, in formal dress,
played in the garden, seated in a Baroque fountain whose
waters cooled the warm evening air. We all had a lot to drink.
Torches were lit. A Venetian courtesan, famed for her beauty
and wearing a very low-necked dress, insisted on seeing the
Silent Woman [as the doll was called] face to face, supposing
her to be a rival. She must have felt like a cat trying to catch
a butterfly through a window-pane; she simply could not understand. [The maid] paraded the doll as if at a fashion show;
the courtesan asked whether I slept with the doll, and
whether it looked like anyone I had been in love with. In her
own bedroom, she said, there hung tapestries of pastoral
scenes, and a tiger-skin lay at the foot of her lace-covered
bed, to which I was very welcome if I should ever tire of
keeping the doll warm. In the course of the party the doll
lost its head and was doused in red wine. We were all drunk.

Early the next morning, when the party was almost forgotten, the police appeared at the door, investigating a report that a headless body had been seen in the garden. The
postman, of course! Postmen are always the first to spread
news of that sort. "What sort of body?" I asked. By now Dr.
Posse had been awakened too, and in our dressing gowns we
went down to the garden, where the doll lay, headless and
apparently drenched in blood. Though the policemen had to
laugh, they still reported me for causing a public nuisance.
Thanks to Posse's influence it all passed off smoothly, but
the public nuisance still had to be removed. The dustcart
came in the grey light of dawn, and carried away the dream

of Eurydice's return. The doll was an image of a spent love
that no Pygmalion could bring to life.[7]

This was not the only time that Oskar would draw attention to himself with such escapades. One evening he invited
twelve women whom he had loved to a performance of
Mozart's *Don Giovanni*, then on to his rooms for supper.
A white-gloved servant served the soup with his thumb
deeply immersed in every bowl. Word of this party too
spread wide; the mad genius had found another means of
fighting back at the women who had made him lose his
equanimity. Most of the objects of these antics were infuriated. Alma, the recipient of the sharpest and most discussed
of the blows, was more charmed than maddened, and, fortunately, many of the members of Kokoschka's entourage in
Dresden had no idea of the person upon whose image the
doll had been fashioned.

Alma promised Walter that she and Manon would visit
him regularly in Weimar, near Berlin, where he was estab-
lishing the Bauhaus. Early in March 1919 she decided to
make one of those trips both as an escape for herself and a
chance for Manon to see her papa. A part of Alma did not
want to part from Walter for good; he was her husband,
and it sometimes seemed as if he might be the best available
to her. As she prepared to see him, she wrote, "How often
I have deeply regretted having left Oskar . . . He loved me
more than any of the others, more than Franz, who certainly
loves me . . . But the townspeople cried that it was not
appropriate; Oskar was not appropriate for me, and now
Franz Werfel doesn't seem to be appropriate. But it *is* appropriate to vegetate with Walter Gropius in Weimar for the
rest of my life."[8] Alma resented the standards seemingly im-
posed upon her by society; at the same time she could not
forget the standards and the morality into which she too

had been born and trained. Complete rebellion was not in her nature.

The trip to Germany had to be delayed since Martin became even weaker. Alma felt imprisoned, as if nothing at all was going right for her. One afternoon, Franz and their friend Blei brought the writer Baron Dirzstay to her apartment. After happy hours of music and poetry, the Baron stayed on to deliver to Alma a private message from Oskar: he still loved and wanted her and would not be able to reach his highest capabilities without her, even though he was living with another woman. "I told Dirzstay everything that had separated me from Oskar: his frivolity and his untruthfulness." [9]

But, she went on, "It does seem to me that Franz is not the right man for me physically. He is so young and passionate, and I can't go along with all that anymore." [10] Bertha Zuckerkandl came to visit. Franz had begged her to help him and Alma immigrate to Switzerland. In the back of her mind Alma still felt that if she went anywhere she would go to America; somewhere on the huge continent there had to be a place where there would be peace and contentment. Instead, she made the planned trip to meet Walter in Berlin, where she received a letter from Franz: "Kokoschka's love was elevated and soulful. Gropius's love, Alma, came from lowly desire and, as such, it was wrong and must trail into absurdity." [11] He was encouraging her to make a permanent break from her husband. During the visit, Alma decided a change definitely had to be made. The one she decided on, however, was not what Franz had in mind; she came to the conclusion that she had to find a way to get back to Oskar and go with him to the south.

While Alma and Manon were with Walter, Martin died. Walter, when he broke the news to his wife, said he would rather have died himself. Alma telegraphed word of their son's death to Franz, who was in Semmering at work and planning to visit his family in Prague and meet Alma in Berlin to travel home with her. Before she left, Alma again mentioned the prospect of divorce to Walter, proposing that Manon would live with her in Vienna but spend significant periods of each year with him. The subject was allowed to drop, and Alma surreptitiously spent her last few days away from the Bauhaus in Weimar — having argued that Manon should have time alone with her father — and searched the city of Berlin for Oskar, who was purportedly there. She did not find him, and when she fetched Manon to go home she realized how much she missed Franz.

Settled in Semmering for the summer, Alma looked around her, reflecting "everything breathes the ghost of Oskar Kokoschka . . . The only thing left for me is an open window. I have thrown away O.K. What was my reason?" [12] Oskar wrote to her: "Honored friend, I am returning to you your letters, as you requested. I can't believe that you really wanted anything from me. I hope that you have arranged your life so that you are happy. I want to be fair to you and would doubt that it would be right to meet and see you face to face. The last thing I want is to make you suffer." [13] Alma burned the letters he sent back to her.

❧

Early in July Alma and Franz went back to Vienna, where they spent a few days alone. He had reached an impasse in his work on "The Black Mass," which would remain a fragment, and they sought privacy and recreation. In the amusement park at the Prater, it occurred to Alma to look for a boy whom she had seen there years ago with Oskar. He had noticed a deranged boy sitting behind the counter of the amusement stand kept with his father, and he had predicted that the boy would be a murderer. That evening with Franz,

Alma saw nothing looking like the old game table or the demented youth, but a crowd was streaming toward one of the stands in the distance. The couple joined the throng. The boy Oskar had spotted had just killed his father. Alma remembered the proverb she had been told on her trip to Corfu with Fraenkel: "Not the murderer, but the murdered is guilty."

Immediately, Franz began work on a new project with the proverb as his title. They went back to Semmering, where Alma wrote in her diary how very happy she had been with Franz, "always with the feeling that I cannot bind myself to Gropius at a distance and go on — he is so far from me, and the name Gropius lies on me like a piece of barbed wire. I *am* not Gropius and thus cannot be called by that name. My name is *Mahler,* for eternity." [14]

She wrote to Walter and reaffirmed her desire to be divorced. Franz cheered her on. "Almitschka, live for me! I see my future completely in you. I want to marry you!! And not just out of love! But from the deepest knowledge that, if a person is alive who can fulfill me and turn me into an artist, you alone are that person. — I say this with full knowledge of all the pain and suffering that we have already brought to one another." [15]

She didn't want Franz around all the time, and thought he worked better when he was away from her. He disagreed and said he needed her presence to be able to write efficiently and well. "Franz is like a tiny bird in my hand," she wrote, "with heartbeats and wary eyes, whom I must protect from the weather and the cats." Sometimes he tried to appear to be a hero, but, "I love him more as a little bird — because the other part of him doesn't need me, doesn't need me and probably doesn't need anybody." [16]

Near the end of July, Walter responded that he would consent to a divorce, but still could not think of being parted from his daughter. "His letter is good and honorable, but seems strange to me," Alma said in her diary. "What should I do now? I love Franz and want to have his child. It is like an *idée fixe* in my mind: I must once again bear him a son. Fate has brought me to that. He is the only thing worth living for on the earth. He works with energy and power, and that is more important to me than any good I might find in the world."[17]

Much as she wanted her freedom from Walter, Alma would not be deprived of Manon — the beautiful, special child who had complained one day as Alma was walking across the lawn in a long white summer skirt, "Mummy, you are disturbing the grass."[18] Manon was the only child she had left. Anna was very independent, spending most of her time with the young Rupert Kollner and his family in their country house not far away. When Anna contracted a serious painful ear infection later in the summer, Alma took her into the city for treatment. There she herself came down with an infection manifesting itself as tonsillitis. When they arrived back at Semmering both Alma and Anna convalesced in the care of their beloved servant "Sister" Ida Gebauer. As soon as she could, Anna went back to the Kollners'. Late one night she returned in the cold to announce to her mother that she was engaged to marry the soldier Rupert.

Alma would not deny the two young people their romance; she didn't really take their intentions seriously. She went back to Vienna for the premiere of Strauss's opera *Die Frau ohne Schatten* and for a performance of Gustav's Sixth Symphony. During this trip she happened to meet Fritz von Unruh, a writer whose work she had long admired and with whom she had enjoyed a brief correspondence. She invited him to visit her. It even occurred to her that this might be a man with whom she could happily spend her life. She was taken by his looks, his forcefulness, and his articulateness, until she realized how like her husband Fritz was. With that the friendship cooled. Alma mused in her diary, "O.K. wanted with all his heart to have a child with me, and I let that child be taken from me after three months. Franz never wanted it, but I bore him a son." [19]

Back in the country Alma worked in her yard, more out of boredom than interest. When she saw that Anna and Rupert were not likely to tire of each other and give up their plan to marry, Alma summoned the young man and wished him every happiness and good fortune in his life with her daughter. The prospect of being a mother-in-law and perhaps a grandmother did not appeal to Alma at all, until she received simultaneous letters of devotion from the conductor Ochs and the poet Trentini. These renewed her hope that she herself was not old and ugly, so she could have something in life to look forward to.

In mid-November Alma went back to Vienna for the winter while Franz visited his family in Prague. "Life without Franz is nonsense," Alma wrote. "Not to be able to care for him, not to share his joy, not to know *at once* what he has accomplished. Here, all I have is that eternally damned telephone!" [20] Alma had been among the first to have a private telephone installed in her house. Even though she usually loved the devices that signaled progress, she never learned to use or appreciate this one. The telephone could not replace letters or visits in her life, and at the moment she envied Franz's reunions with old friends, who included the critic and writer Willi Haas, Franz Kafka, and the musician George Szell. He duly reported all of his engagements to Alma, still reassuring her that he was not seeing his former woman friend. He wanted Alma to come to meet his family, but she would not. Her thoughts returned to Oskar, who had sent her a strange and unsettling letter. As she read and reread the pages, her mind was once more flooded with memories of her "evil spirit." She had tried to put him out of her mind. Whenever she managed to accomplish that, he produced a letter that would once again seem to call her to him, and reaffirm the hold he still had on her.

Early in 1920, Franz, Alma, Manon, and the servant Sister Ida went to Italy. Their train arrived hours after schedule. The composer Alfred Casella met them with the bad news that it was almost impossible to find rooms in any hotel. This first leg of the trip was a signal of what was to come. They were plagued throughout the journey by rain and sleet, unanticipated expense, uncomfortable rooms, and head colds accompanied by high fevers. Manon was the sickest of all. When they were finally well enough to undertake the journey home, Alma was glad to leave the country that had always before seemed to be paradisical.

No sooner were they back in Vienna than Alma had to prepare for her next trip to Walter with Manon. It unfortunately had to coincide with the opening of Franz's new play, *The Trojan Women*, at the Burgtheater in Vienna. This journey, too, was beset with bad luck. Very shortly after Alma and Manon arrived at their hotel in Weimar, where the Bauhaus had become a reality, Germany was hit by a general strike, which cast a pall over the already impoverished circumstances of the community of artists and made it necessary for Alma to move with Manon into Walter's small and badly equipped apartment. There were neither lights nor newspapers; riots in the streets left an unbearable stench. Since word of the protests and fighting had not been transmitted far beyond the boundaries of the dispute, she feared Franz would think that she had forgotten him, or had decided to stay with Walter. She made arrangements to leave as soon as it was possible to do so. Franz met them in Berlin, and they traveled home together.

Alma insisted that Franz go to Semmering to work. She sent her servant Ernst to act as his helper and companion. Franz tried to work but had no enthusiasm for it, and he begged Alma to see him either in the country or back in Vienna. She would not give in, and even when he claimed he was not well and getting nothing done, she insisted that he stay where he was, without her. She was preparing to take Anna to Mengelberg's Mahler Festival in Amsterdam; while they were gone Manon and Sister Ida would stay with Walter. There was no place in the plans for Franz.

In Amsterdam, Mengelberg saw to it that Alma and Anna were treated royally, with parties and receptions surrounding each event of the festival and with their every moment tended to by friends and admirers.[21] Alma presented the manuscript score of Gustav's Seventh Symphony to the conductor who had done so much to introduce and promote her late husband's music. She sat through a multitude of speeches and tributes, met the Dutch royal family, and gave her formal blessing to the formation of a Mahler Society. She was happiest, however, in the few hours she had alone with Anna and the Schoenbergs. On May 18, the anniversary of both Gustav's death and Walter's birth, Alma managed to go off by herself to the city's museums. She felt that she should mourn, but was no longer capable of it. She realized that she was tired of being Gustav's widow, holding her court in his honor. He had been dead for nearly a decade. Alma decided that she was much more interested in being the wife of a living, active genius than the widow of a dead one.

She tried to devote herself more completely to Franz and accepted with as much patience as she could muster all of his flaws save one: she would not let him retreat into the caffeine, alcohol, and tobacco milieu of the cafés. In Vienna it was virtually impossible for her to keep him out of those meeting spots, so she preached again the virtues of his working at Semmering, and tried to take him with her when she went out in the city, in order that his hours would not be empty and he would not be led into temptation. She took him to a performance of Schoenberg's *Gurrelieder* in June, and could not but notice how long it took for him to seem even slightly interested in her friend's beautiful, emotional symphonic songs. She kept herself from complaining or rebuking him.

So convinced was she of the necessity to devote herself to Franz, she barely reacted when she learned Joseph Fraenkel had died. She was totally wrapped up in her own life, and she had something to look forward to: her divorce from Walter was expected to be official soon, and that would renew the challenge she faced with Franz.

The divorce was delayed repeatedly, but the mere fact that the process had been begun and was now in the hands of the complex judiciary system relieved Alma's conscience. By the end of 1920 she and Franz were living together. More accurately, they were both living in two houses, since she still insisted that he move between her apartment in Vienna and the house in Semmering. Actually, they were spending no more time in one another's company than they had in the past two years.

Alma thought it was important that Manon see her father, so in October she took her daughter back to Weimar. It was evidently during this absence that Franz wrote what is probably the loveliest of his poems for Alma:

> *Still, all around me,*
> *The devils spin their colors.*
> *Sweetness guides me*
> *From all sides*
> *Wind from the wings of confusion.*

I cannot know in the years of change
The battle of the end
That has meant
So much to me.

You are to me the great rush of the storm
On whose shores I
learn everything of the voice.
You are for me the warm atmosphere of flesh,
Which reminds me of flowers' existence.
You are the sacred golden light
The universal gold light,
Through which I must grow
To become the white light.

From every tomb of carelessness
You collect me anew in your bosom.
Oh, golden light! Bearer
Be as a mother to me
Be the cause of my rebirth! [22]

❧

Alma irritated Franz by writing to him that she missed "you and the Jews." [23] How, Franz asked, could she possibly say "and"? Had she forgotten that he was a Jew? Did she have to put them all in a category suggesting that they were something different, separated from the rest of society? The remark only served as another indication of the dichotomy Alma experienced in her own life. A great part of Walter's appeal had been his Christianity, but on a practical level that meant very little to her. It was with Jews — Gustav, Franz, other friends — that she enjoyed spending her time. However, she could not give up the fear of being denied what she considered her Christian "brightness," that she would be placed with people whom she considered the others.

In recent months, however, Franz had gone from being a young poet of promise to being thought of as one of the most brilliant emerging authors in the German language. He took great pride and confidence in his growing reputation. This helped give him the incentive to undertake a diet that allowed him nothing but milk and an egg for two consecutive days, then regular meals on the third day. He did not lose weight as fast as he had hoped he would, but he felt noble and strong, and he bragged to Alma that he was sticking with it. He had been asked to lecture on Jules Verne's *Twenty-Thousand Leagues under the Sea* and was busy with this work. Even so, he took the opportunity of Alma's absence to see his family, and while in Prague he began to lose patience. "You have been there in Germany for more than fourteen days," he wrote to Alma. "I have written you letter after letter, sent telegram after telegram, asking whether, when, where I should come. (I was ready after only three days here to take my leave and travel.) But only today did I receive from you a letter that was written at the same time as mine . . . which does not respond to any of my questions, but which, rather, asks, 'What shall I do?' "[24] Franz wanted Alma to take responsibility for her own moves, and would only assure her that he would be there to meet her upon request.

Alma feared that having her and Manon so near renewed Walter's futile hopes of their living again as a family. He appreciated too much having a woman in his presence and became very attached to Manon, with whom he had to reacquaint himself anew every time he saw her. Alma thought she should leave, but she was somehow reluctant to pack and go off to Franz. He wrote again: "I am through with this anticipation and wishfulness! Everything here has been made to fit your visit, and even my father is genuinely happy that you are supposed to be coming here . . . Write a word either about my desire to see you there in Germany or about your intentions to meet me here in Prague."[25]

Alma eventually left Germany without her divorce papers. She went on to Franz in Prague, where she began more bureaucratic transactions. Her daughter Anna, by virtue of her father's nationality, could obtain Czech citizenship, and with that she could facilitate getting American permits, visas, and perhaps ultimately citizenship. All this would have to be accomplished before her marriage, since a wife automatically claimed the citizenship of her husband's country. (Alma was considered a German citizen during her marriage to Walter.) Alma tried in vain to obtain Anna's decrees of nationality. She was concerned because her daughter's period of betrothal had not been a happy one, but she was pleased that Anna had begun to devote herself more intently to art and music. Franz promised too that he would try to reform, to be stronger in the face of temptation. In effect, he was promising to be more like Walter.

In the first months of 1921, while Manon had her tonsils cauterized and Anna was wed to Rupert Kollner, Alma shipped Franz off to Semmering. He felt deserted and forlorn and realized how much he missed Manon, whom he had come to think of as his child, his and Alma's. Anna, too, thought of the girl more as her own daughter than as her half sister. Manon beguiled them all with her beauty and with a sense of humor that did not seem to have come from either of her parents. She had a way of bringing the adults around her closer together. Franz had been cautious in his early days in the household, acting almost intimidated by her, but he had quickly relented, and "Uncle Werfel" was now quite as dear to her as she was to him.

The group settled happily in Semmering for the summer. It did not surprise Alma when Anna, the recent bride, wrote to announce she was coming to visit, alone, for a protracted stay. Anna was very unhappy. Apparently she did not get the help wanted from her mother, so she went on to Germany to see Walter and took rooms by herself in Berlin. That outcome was the best Alma could have hoped for. She trusted Walter to help her daughter and thought being away would be the best thing for the young woman.

Alma was more concerned with her own future. The travails of their last trip there notwithstanding, she and Franz both remained partial to Italy, and Alma planned to go to Venice to seek a house suitable for them all. Although she was not lacking the funds needed to buy such a house on her own, she was concerned as to how long her own money would last if she had to go on supporting not just herself, but also Manon, Franz, and the household staff in different locations. Alma was sure Franz would be successful, only it was not foreseeable when that break might come. His drama *Bocksgesang* was to be produced in Leipzig that autumn, and his father was willing to continue providing a small monthly stipend — at least as long as he could afford it and Franz needed the money. Alma didn't buy a house on that trip to Venice, but she went back to Vienna feeling full of hope and energy, thinking of their future in beautiful Italy.

In her red music room she entertained Pfitzner, Maurice Ravel, and Casella, then sponsored two back-to-back performances, with different casts, of Schoenberg's *Pierrot Lunaire* for voice and chamber ensemble. The composers Francis Poulenc and Darius Milhaud were her guests, but the new Viennese styles were not dear to their French hearts. This activity gave Alma much to think about, and took her mind off the pleas Franz was addressing to her from his family home in Prague. He insisted that she marry him at once; he wanted her as his wife, his family wanted her as his wife, and he was unwilling to take no for an answer. Alma did not respond.

Almost all the changes that took place in 1922 were for the better. Alma went with Franz to Leipzig, Prague, and Munich for performances of his play *Spiegelmensch,* and, with encouragement from her mother, she decided to buy a house in Venice on a canal at 2542 San Tomà. The details of purchase of Italian land were made all the more difficult by problems Alma had with the people then living in the house. She persisted, nevertheless, and had no doubt that she had done the right thing. She thought of her apartment on the Elizabethstrasse in Vienna as a place to stay when she happened to be in the city. The house in Semmering was a pleasant summer retreat, though Alma would always associate it so strongly with Oskar that she would not make it her principal residence; it was a good place for Franz to go and work by himself. The house in Venice would be hers with Franz — a retreat that was theirs, together. Even if the house in Italy served them in a relatively casual manner for a few years, they both also knew it would be there to act as a sanctuary when and if the political situation became so intolerable and dangerous they had to escape.

Persecution of the Jews was permeating all levels of society. Though Franz seemed almost unconscious of the threat, Alma was frightened both for him and for herself. The cause for her fears lay not alone in her having been the wife of the Jew Mahler; she was also a Roman Catholic who had been divorced from the good Aryan Gropius in order to live with another Jew, Werfel. To add fodder to what the Viennese gossips viewed as a family tragedy, Anna, Mahler's daughter, had divorced a fine man to live in Berlin with a penniless composer, Ernst Krenek, who would soon become her husband. Alma found herself thinking of leaving her homeland for emotional reasons as well as for political ones.

When Franz's drama *Spiegelmensch* was presented in Vienna, to horrid reviews, Alma was in Venice overseeing the final negotiations for and the first renovations of her house — and seeing Oskar.[26] His works were being shown there at the International Exhibition, and Alma was impressed by the display and by the attention Oskar was receiving. She would have seen more of him had Franz not arrived from Vienna very depressed about his play in particular and his work in general. He and Alma spent a few days together in Venice talking about the novel he was considering about the life of Verdi. Alma was opposed to the idea, not only because she was a partisan of Wagner as opposed to Verdi, but also because she didn't find it an appropriate subject for Franz. He was determined nonetheless, and, seeing that it would give him new purpose, she helped him with the project by playing through the piano scores of Verdi's operas while Franz tried to sing all of the roles at once. They delved into the composer's life, and either visited or tried to construct in their imaginations the places where Verdi had lived and been.

This project continued when they were back in Semmering in 1923, disrupted only when Anna and Krenek came to visit. Conditions were trying, since the house was not big enough to accommodate both writer and composer at work. Franz contrived to make progress on *Verdi*, which was to become one of the first books published by the firm managed by Paul Zsolnay and his family, whom Alma and Franz had met through the Molls. *Verdi* appeared in print in the same month Alma was finally able to live comfortably in her house in Venice.

For Alma and Franz the move into the Italian house on the canal meant a break from the past, a reaffirmation of their ties, and, at the same time, an end to the trials they had led one another through in recent years. Alma prepared the house in Venice while Franz tended their affairs in Vienna; he had added her business matters to his. Alma had prevailed upon Lili to help her finance a significant part of printing the score of Alban Berg's opera *Wozzeck* and in gratitude Alban had dedicated the work to Alma. It was one of Franz's chores to watch the opera's progress during Alma's absence. Anna Moll was happy to see such an able and sensitive man acting on behalf of her daughter. A number of Alma's acquaintances, however, resented Franz's position in her life and made it clear that, when they issued invitations or requests to her, they did not appreciate secondhand responses from a Jew of questionable professional achievement.

Summer 1924 found Alma, Manon, and Franz in Semmering again. He worked on his play *Juarez & Maximilian;* then, in the evenings after supper, he and Alma planned an autumn trip to the Near East. Alma loved to travel, and she thought it was good for Franz. It kept him from staying up all night with his notebooks and cigarettes and gave him fresh inspiration. Their first stop was Cairo, where they heard Verdi's *Aïda* at the site of its premiere. Then they headed up the Nile, past the pyramids, and east to Palestine and Jerusalem. There, Alma appreciated the comfortable rooms in the Allenby Hotel. They both were deeply moved by the city and its people, and vowed to return. Alma, however, found that she took less well to the adventure and unpredictable elements of their travel than Franz did. On the way home, they stopped in Sicily, where Anna Mahler met them and joined in relaxed sightseeing excursions. Alma took pleasure in being able to travel more openly with Franz. There were no more clandestine meetings in Prague or unannounced journeys, and she went with him more often on his lecture tours around the German-speaking countries. At home, Franz was working so well and making so much progress that Alma decided she also might do some work. With this in mind she took three of her songs and considered working them into a symphony. The idea was discussed with Franz, but the project never came to fruition.

Several times each year, the couple parted with the understanding that they would reunite when he had completed or substantially finished his work-in-progress. She was in Venice while he was in Semmering working on "The Whirling Dervishes," a short story. Then, in 1925, after visiting the Italian Riviera and going from Genoa to Nervi, Franz went on to Santa Margherita to write *Class Reunion* while Alma stayed in Nervi to enjoy the company of the ever-growing community of German artists and writers. With this excursion on the Italian coast, the two realized how beautiful and friendly the new area could seem.

They could not miss the first performance of Berg's *Wozzeck* on December 14, 1925, in Berlin. More than having a financial stake in the production of the opera's score, and beyond the fact that she was the work's dedicatee, Alma had come to think of Alban and his wife Helene as her dear and important friends. The tall, ethereal, and talented Alban had about him a very appealing elegance, though he was fastidious to the point of being bothersome. Helene, the illegitimate daughter of the Emperor Franz Josef, was beautiful, sensitive, and in love with Alma. Alma did not return the affection but she did feel close to the fragile Bergs, and somehow responsible for them.

It was probably through Alma's suggestion that Alban was invited to stay at the imposing home of Franz's older sister Hanna and her husband, the industrialist Herbert Fuchs-Robettin, when the composer went to Prague in May 1925 to hear Alexander von Zemlinsky conduct the Three Symphonic Fragments from *Wozzeck* at the festival of the International Society for Contemporary Music. Alban met the whole Werfel family during his visit and had a wonderful time with the Fuchs-Robettin children, a boy and a girl who were awed by having the famous composer in their midst. Alban wrote to Helene about the good wine and the hospitality with which he had been greeted. What he did not report to her was that he and Hanna had fallen in love. Their affair was to last until his death.

On his way to Berlin to begin the preparations for the premiere of *Wozzeck*, Alban had been Hanna's house guest. When Helene traveled to meet her husband in Germany for the first performance, she suspected that Alban had been enchanted with something more than the wine, the lobster dinners, and the wide-eyed children. She too was graciously welcomed as a guest in the Fuchs-Robettin house, and she left eager to meet their new friends again.

The success of *Wozzeck* established Alban's reputation internationally. The occasion, however, had not been entirely comfortable for some of those in attendance, since the circle around the composer in Berlin included not only the cadre of musicians but also his wife, the Fuchs-Robettins, Alma, and Franz. Alma had been filling the role as confidante to Helene, but in the months surrounding *Wozzeck*, she and Franz drew increasingly close to Alban and came to realize the depth and the import of his affair with Franz's sister. Alban prevailed upon Alma and Franz to act as emissaries for the notes and messages he sent to Hanna. The web of conspiracy brought the small band closer together than ever. When Alma and Franz returned to the Italian Riviera in 1926, she paid for the Bergs to travel to join them. Alban was thinking of writing an opera based on Gerhart Hauptmann's play *Und Pippa Tanzt*, and Alma seized the opportunity to put the composer in the company of the dramatist with whom she and Franz spent a good deal of time in Italy. Hauptmann had also been smitten by Alma, and in the presence of his wife he jovially commented that he would be her lover in their next life. To this, Mrs. Hauptmann answered caustically that, even then, he would have to wait his turn.

At the end of 1926, the same circle reassembled for the first performances of *Wozzeck* in Prague. This time, self-assured by his earlier success, Alban took care to make the occasion very special, decking the box occupied by his close friends and family with huge sprays of flowers. Instead of the triumph they all expected, the performance turned out to be the target of an organized riot, and Alban's flowers easily identified the occupants of those box seats as the objects of the dissent. Anti-Semitic shouts were hurled at the guests of honor. Ironically, the protestors had made their plans in the mistaken belief that the Bergs were Jewish. When Alban and Helene made a brisk and early getaway, they left Franz, his sister, and brother-in-law — all Jews — to receive the insults. The Werfels, with Alma, had to be escorted to a car by police officers.

For the first time Franz realized the seriousness of the political climate and the hatred directed toward him as a Jew. Previously, he had not wanted to believe what he had seen and heard, but on this night he was stunned and frightened; there had been a very real possibility that he, his relatives, and even Alma could have met physical harm. He knew this was a problem Alma did not really share: she was not a Jew. As he thought of the beautiful flowers that had been placed around their chairs for what should have been a great occasion in the opera house, he remembered Alma's pronouncement that Jews did not appreciate flowers. In Jerusalem she had not seen as many bouquets and windowboxes as she might have liked, and had decided this must have been because most of the inhabitants were Jewish. Much as Franz could not accept this kind of statement, which was certainly not unique in his experiences with Alma, he also did not want to drag his lover into a danger to which she had not been born. He would not leave her for such irrational reasons, and as he faced this dilemma he decided again that it was best put into the back of his mind.

Alma had electricity introduced into her house in Semmering, only to have riots and a general strike in Vienna knock her house back into darkness.[27] She did not mind; electricity was not yet an essential part of her life, and she felt that her imagination would sustain her as long as she could keep her house in the country and stay at a distance from the violence and the crowds. Alma's imagination gave Franz the fodder for several of the short stories he wrote during this time — a time punctuated by trips from Vienna to Semmering to Venice (in the autumn) and the Italian Riviera. Only two people seemed to be able to disturb Alma: her daughter Anna, who was being divorced from Krenek just months after their marriage; and Oskar, whom she had spotted one day in Venice and who then sent one of his strategic letters asking her to accompany him on a trip to Africa. It was a trip Alma had long wanted to make, and Oskar knew it. She felt that it would be important to his creativity. She didn't go, and wrote in her diary, "Crudeness made me leave O.K., and crudeness will make me leave Franz Werfel."[28]

At Christmas Alma again found herself in the company of men who did not celebrate the Christian holiday, Franz and his publisher Paul von Zsolnay. Alma was depressed and went to her bed, writing in her diary that she could live neither with Jews, nor without them, and wishing once more that she could escape with Oskar. Instead, she went to visit Margherita Sarfatti, Mussolini's mistress, with whom she discussed something they called world fascism, which would transcend the primitive ideals of nationalism and, Alma thought, preserve world order. Although her ideas were naive and undeveloped, she found people who agreed with her and refused to realize the realities of the events around them.

The Essence of a Priest

ALMA WAS BEGINNING, at the age of nearly fifty, to experience the signals of menopause. It bothered her terribly, not so much because of the physical manifestations, but because it made her feel old and ended her hopes of having another child with Franz. She had to realize it would have been difficult for them to tend an infant and maintain their way of life, which was spread among so many houses, hotels, and countries. She also knew that she would give in and marry Franz were she to find herself pregnant; the fates of Maria and Martin had proved how wrong it was to have a baby conceived without the benefit of a marriage contract.

Franz wanted to marry her. To be sure, he was kind, attentive, and understanding of her need for freedom. She occasionally threatened to leave him, but knew she never would. He had aged more rapidly than she, and they now appeared to be close to the same age. Oskar still tempted her, but running off with him crossed her mind less frequently. Alma resisted becoming the wife of another Jew. It had, however, become very embarrassing to have Manon constantly speak to her friends of Mummy and Uncle Werfel.

On July 6, 1929, Alma and Franz were married. Like her previous two wedding days, this one passed without Alma's taking much notice. She had been right in her feeling that marriage would not alter their day-to-day lives. Nevertheless, she had to come to terms with acknowledging that as the wife of a Jew she would more than likely have to face harassment and upheaval of dimensions she might not have felt had she remained on her own.

Shortly after Alma married for the third time, her daughter Anna did the same. As Mrs. Paul von Zsolnay, married into the family of Franz's publisher, she came into both money and social status. This did not concern Alma at all. She was beyond feigning interest in her daughter's personal life, though she expected that this union, like the others, would be stormy. Anna was soon pregnant, and named her daughter Alma. The honoree was not impressed. She disliked being a grandmother, and she wanted another baby of her own.

Alma gave much thought to what she would call herself now that she was married to Franz. She had never used the name Alma Gropius. She had nothing against being Alma Werfel; Franz had lovingly addressed her as Alma Maria Werfel even before they had considered marriage, and she had rather liked that. For almost thirty years, however, she had been Alma Mahler. That was her name, the one with which she had built her life. So she would be either Alma Mahler or Alma Mahler-Werfel. In truth, she was no longer interested in playing the role of Mahler's widow, but in that capacity she had more potential for social and financial advancement than she might have were she to use the name

Werfel or — worse — combine the two Jewish surnames. Ultimately she made no clear decision. If she thought of herself as Alma Mahler, she called herself by that name with no more frequency than she used Alma Werfel or Alma Mahler-Werfel.

Then, too, Franz was about to write the book that would establish him in his time as an equal of Thomas Mann. That novel, *The 40 Days of Musa Dagh,* was considered for the Nobel Prize, but today is remembered only by its title if at all. The idea for the book began on the honeymoon that he and Alma took a few months after their wedding, traveling back to Egypt, Palestine, and Jerusalem, where the now famous King David Hotel was then just being built. Their itinerary also included Damascus, Baalbek, Mount Lebanon, and Beirut. Alma hated the dirt and the poverty and Franz was intrigued and inspired by the plight and the courage of the Armenians; these impressions shaped his new novel. The saga grew in Franz's mind from the discussions he and Alma carried on in subsequent weeks and months about Siegfried, the hero who knew no fear. Alma wove long and eloquent stories about the champion who had inspired Wagner's opera, and Franz took her challenge as the basis for his book.

In Vienna, friends prodded Alma to find a new and better house. The old apartment was no longer sufficient. Though Alma thought twice about leaving the rooms on the Elizabethstrasse rented after Gustav's death, she had to admit that there was no longer space there for Franz's work, her own life, the friends whom Manon wanted to see, and the staff of servants.

Alma found and bought, in her name, an imposing, twenty-eight-room house on the Hohe Warte, very close to the Molls'. Some called the house a mansion. A studio was built for Franz on the top floor, and Alma's music room was below. Early in 1931 they moved into the house with a collection of treasures that could have filled an even larger building. Among them were Gustav's desk and his library of scores (with the manuscript of Anton Bruckner's Third Symphony), books, and works of art. Before everything was appropriately placed, the Werfels had a housewarming party for friends representing the realms of the theater, film, music, and literature. The guest list seemed to announce the position Alma and Franz intended to assume in Viennese society.

Alma didn't think of herself as especially rich, but she couldn't deny that she owned a house in Venice and two houses in Austria, one of them among the largest in Vienna. The house in Venice had increased significantly in value when it was declared a historic monument. Alma's daughter was married to a man of wealth and prestige. Her husband was well off in his own right.

Though Carl Moll had been implicated in a fraudulent art scheme, he and Anna were still Alma's greatest friends. The elder couple loved Franz and Manon, and they were helpful in working out the details of the Werfels' daily life. When Carl had published a book about her father Alma had been infuriated, believing that her stepfather was again infringing on her territory of memories. Nevertheless, with everyone settled in the new house and with her family evidently comfortable and secure, she was satisfied.

On May 18, 1931, Alma sent Rodin's bust of Mahler to the Vienna Opera in honor of the twentieth anniversary of Gustav's death. Clemens Krauss acknowledged the receipt of the valuable gift by conducting the Adagietto from the Fifth Symphony, the movement in Gustav's works that most closely marked his life with Alma. Late in 1931, Manon went to visit her father while Alma traveled with Franz on one of his lecture tours of Germany. While she was away, Alma received word of Anna's determination to separate from

Zsolnay. Much as she hated to see her daughter leave a third marriage, Alma knew there was nothing she could do. Because of the professional association between Franz and the Zsolnays, this rupture would be more difficult for both families than Anna's previous changes of heart had been. The Werfels and the Zsolnays remained friends, nevertheless, and the big radio that Alma and Franz listened to during their evenings in Semmering was a Christmas gift to them from Paul's family.

Franz was much in need of his publisher's support. His play *The Kingdom of God* was produced early in 1932 to another spate of highly critical reviews. Then followed one of his fallow periods, when ideas seemed to seep out of his brain and sparks refused to ignite. He became more anxious about financial problems than probably necessary. He and Alma were property-rich but cash-poor, and though they would not consider giving up any of the houses that gave them comfort and options for the future, they had to face the prospect of curtailing their travel and entertaining, and of cutting back the extravagant sums they both liked to spend on food and wine.

The reasons for the difficulties were several. Franz, like Gustav, refused to concern himself with the details of finance, and he indulged his weakness for the finer things in life. Alma found this trait charming, but she could not be a partner, especially as she saw Franz's income and her royalties from Gustav's compositions waning. In both cases, the diminution was a function of fashion as well as of the growing anti-Semitic movement in German-speaking countries. A good deal of Franz's spending money had come from his lecture fees, but he was no longer being invited to speak in Germany, Austria, or Switzerland, where even his friends and supporters would not risk engaging a Jew.

The Werfels considered renting out their house in Vienna. Before they reached the point at which they would have had to decide on a plan of emergency action, however, checks began to arrive from around the world announcing the great success of translations of *Musa Dagh*. Alma was relieved. This triumph inspired Franz to concentrate on the challenges of the novel instead of on short stories, poetry, and the theater. Alma relaxed further when her elder daughter turned her attention to sculpture, working in large, almost mythological forms that appeared to capture her imagination and give her the purpose she had not found in three marriages. With Franz and Anna engaged in productive work, Alma went back to the trunk containing her old compositions. Looking at what she had written, she saw again the work of a young, immature woman. It was not worthy of further time and effort.

Her thoughts went to Oskar. He still wrote, always reaffirming his devotion, and, occasionally, suggesting they take a trip together and attempt some kind of reconciliation. Alma did nothing to encourage him. There were other women in his life, and he would soon marry Olda Palkovska, the daughter of a doctor in Prague. The Kokoschkas left Czechoslovakia in 1938, settled in London, and spent their last years in Switzerland.

Alma saw the Hauptmanns, the Strausses, and other old friends, trying to reenter the social flow. She and Franz went out to hear Adolf Hitler address a crowd in Vienna. *Der Fuehrer*'s charismatic oration entranced Alma; Franz said nothing. Remembering the conversations she had had with Margherita Sarfatti, Alma decided that she preferred Mussolini to Hitler. Many of her friends, Pfitzner and Schoenberg included, were so frightened by the implications of National Socialism that they were already planning to go into exile. Alma saw no reason to consider the possibility — at least not yet. Franz was working well and undisturbed in the country, and he was capable of keeping his mind on nothing but his writing and his domestic tasks of the day.

For the moment, there seemed no cause for the Werfels to disturb their status quo.

Alma found personal relief from the unrest and anxiety of 1932 by returning to the Roman Catholic Church. She offered her confession to Father Engelberg Mueller of St. Stephen's Cathedral in Vienna, and sensed that she was again protected in the religious community. She took the fifteen-year-old Manon to a spa where they could enjoy a quiet time together, while Franz went to Venice to write. Alma had planned to join her husband and stay on in Italy, but when she got there her presence seemed to disturb Franz's work, so she took Manon back to Vienna. She attended the enthronement of Cardinal Innitzer and marked the grand occasion by giving a luncheon for several of the men who had been involved in the ritual. One of these was Father Johannes Hollnsteiner, a professor of theology in his late thirties, handsome, articulate, and thought by many to be in line to be Vienna's next Cardinal. Alma and Father Hollnsteiner began spending many of their free hours together. Franz was glad to hear that his wife had found such a well-respected and intellectual companion. Alma called Johannes "the essence of a priest,"[1] claiming that she wanted nothing more than to learn from him, to understand the ritual and the blessing of the Church.

Back in Vienna, Franz visited with the writers H. G. Wells and Sinclair Lewis, who was with Dorothy Thompson, the first of many journalists expelled by the Nazis. They partied until dawn. Franz heard, firsthand, about Hitler's atrocities, but he still admitted to Alma that *der Fuehrer* might not be totally evil. He did everything in his power to keep himself from recognizing the destiny, by then virtually inevitable, that would take its toll on him, his family, and of course on Alma. As Hitler's power increased at an alarming rate, the Werfel patriarch collapsed. Franz went at once to Prague to see his father, and he was both terrified and sickened to see anti-Semitic slogans lining his route. It was time he and Alma planned a course of escape, whether to Italy, France, England, or America. Alma could not decide whether this was a mark of Franz's strength or his weakness. She wrote in her diary, "Mahler must have understood what I meant when I told him that I would love him only until someone stronger came along — to which he said, 'So I can rest easy, since I cannot imagine anyone stronger.' Is it the real strength or only an imaginary one? . . . I really believed that I would not fall in love again! What nonsense!

"I was aware of Mahler's weaknesses. *But — they — were — still —* MAHLER'S *— weaknesses!"* [2]

Leaning on Johannes, her new confidant, Alma kept quiet while authorities ordered Franz's books burned and Gustav's music proscripted. She watched while her friend Julius Tandler, who had recently become the commissioner of health of the City of Vienna, ordered that all crucifixes be removed from hospital rooms and decreed that priests would be allowed to make their visits to patients only during the normal hours.

Her real confusion came from her interest in Johannes Hollnsteiner. "He is so free," she wrote. "He has never had to utter the word 'sin.' He does not see things that way — but I, must I be more papal than the pope? We are both bound, he to the church and I to Werfel, whom I love so very much . . . who is so deeply ingrained in my mind. J.H. presented the Mass to me yesterday, and every word that he utters is song to me . . . Hollnsteiner thinks that Hitler is a kind of Luther, even though there is obviously great disparity. Further, he taught me how strange it was that the birth of Christ was moved, in the sixth century, from the sixth of January to the twenty-fourth of December." [3]

While Alma was reentering the Church and its safety, she had fallen in love once again. She wrote, "J.H. is thirty-eight years old and has never yet given himself to a woman. He wants to be and *is* only a priest. He seems quite different to me, and I am glad for that. He said, 'I was never even close to a woman. You are the first, and you will be the last.' I worship this man and would kneel before him. Everything in me wants to submit myself to him, but I always have to deny my own desires. This is the first man who has conquered me."[4]

From this moment, Alma began to censor her own diaries. She wrote that she and Franz had long conversations about Hollnsteiner and that Franz was jealous, but his reasons were not those Alma might have found valid. "He doesn't really believe in infidelity," she wrote, adding, probably for her own protection, "There is none."[5] People in Vienna noticed that Alma was attending Mass with remarkable frequency, and Hollnsteiner's limousine was regularly parked in front of the Werfel mansion on the Hohe Warte. Many also knew that Hollnsteiner kept a small apartment for his private uses, to which he often retired with Alma after Mass.

Alma wrote, "If I consider the tough, incomprehensible workings of a Hollnsteiner, for whom it is all the same whether he sleeps or eats, and if I see that this idea of duty to God is essentially foremost in his mind, then I have to recognize the crass difference between the well-bred and the mongrels. If I consider Hitler, who spent fourteen years in darkness . . . because his time had not yet come, I see in him, too, a genuine German idealist, something that is unthinkable to the Jews." Alma was echoing what Johannes had said to her, just as she had previously written Oskar's thoughts. Years later, she crossed out the last phrase and wrote of Hitler, "Unfortunately, he is stupid!"[6]

In the early 1930s, Alma decided that "every Jew, as a mediocre person, loves Italian music. German music leaves them cold." [7] She knew well that this was not true; she could not have forgotten Gustav's affinity for the music of Wagner — but Franz loved Verdi. Contradictions were raging inside her. Nevertheless, Alma knew that she faced a dilemma. She wrote, "Hollnsteiner is either an angel or a scoundrel. Out of self-respect, I have decided to look upon him as an angel . . . I shall never leave Werfel, and the more harm that is done to him, the less I want to leave him! Fifteen years cannot be erased from a life, especially when a person has been as relentlessly good and pure and noble to me as he has been." [8]

She wanted to convince herself — and certainly to have other people believe — that her relation with Johannes was purely intellectual, tied to her return to the Church. Her older daughter finally mentioned to Franz how remarkably devoted Alma was to Johannes, but Franz just smiled at Anna and shrugged, saying that it would be Alma's last fling.

Early in 1934 Franz was working in Italy at Santa Margherita while Alma was in Vienna. She witnessed the general strikes, occupation, riots even in the vicinity of her own house, and the ultimate takeover by the Nazis. Kurt von Schuschnigg, the minister of justice who would shortly be appointed Chancellor, asked that Alma and Manon come to his house, where, he could promise, they would be completely safe. Alma refused, intending to join Franz as soon as she could travel without danger. She continued to think that the fighting and the gunfire would disappear quickly; when the battle was close to her own front door, Alma opened a bottle of champagne. There always were companions. She felt secure.

During those weeks Alma realized that at least two of the men who had been eager to come to her new house were not especially interested in seeing her; they were intending to court the eighteen-year-old Manon, her baby Mutzi. Alma could hardly fathom grown men being desirous of such a child. When she realized the truth, she had to admit that Manon was beautiful, talented, and clever. The girl wanted to become an actress, and there were many who had noticed the talent she possessed in that field. She read expertly in several languages, and seemed to be able to catch the essence of the written word. Alma's wish was for Manon to become a language teacher, a very appropriate career for a young woman. Alma had forgotten that before she had married Gustav she had briefly envisioned herself as a pianist or a conductor. She could not imagine for her daughter any future more glamorous or exciting than one in the classroom.

In his absorption with Verdi and his music, Franz translated *La Forza del Destino* into German. He and Alma met in Venice, then went to see the new version of the opera performed in April of 1934. When they left, Manon appeared pale and weak, but they didn't worry until they returned to Italy and found her seriously ill. Six days hence Bruno Walter would conduct *Das Lied von der Erde* in Vienna, and Alma wanted very much to be there. As the time approached for her to leave, Mutzi acted stronger and encouraged Alma to go. The young woman did not tell her mother about her severe headaches, or that she had been swallowing aspirin in amounts several times the prescribed dosage. Alma and Franz went to the performance, and she returned to Venice right after the performance, only to find Mutzi pallid and despondent. She summoned the doctors, Franz, and her mother. In only a matter of hours the paralysis of polio had taken hold of the young woman's legs, then moved through her body. Alma could sense the same thing happening once again — loss of someone closest to her.

With the consultation of the physicians, it was decided that Manon should be taken back to Vienna. With difficulty, family and servants maneuvered the patient across the

Venetian waters to the train station, where the Austrian government had put at their disposal a specially equipped railway car that had once been an ambulance for the Hapsburgs. The trip was filled with anxiety, and only Manon eased the tension, as she laughed, bantered with her elders, and remained optimistic. Back in Vienna, under the familiar watch of her grandparents and family doctors, the young woman regained some strength, and her disease seemed to go into remission. So great was the fear of an epidemic that she had been put in complete quarantine. After weeks of lonely isolation and discomfort, she was allowed visitors. She dressed and toured the house in a wheelchair. Visitors included the playwright Carl Zuckmayer, the actor Werner Krauss, and her acting coach Franz Horch. Alma and Franz taught Manon the leading role in his German version of *Forza*, dressing her in costume and staging "performances" in the music room, with Alma playing the piano. Walter Gropius sent his daughter a book, and she wrote to her "dear little Papa" that she was feeling better.

Manon had few friends of her own generation. One of these was Kathy Scherman, the daughter of Harry and Bernadine Scherman from New York. These were close friends of Lincoln Schuster of Simon & Schuster, then Franz's New York publishers. Schuster had visited Austria a few years previously and, seeing Manon, he had mistaken her for Kathy, so alike were the two young women. He had led Kathy and Manon to write letters to one another in French, their only shared language. When Kathy's parents toured Austria and Hungary in the summer of 1934, Kathy was invited to stay with Alma, Franz, and Manon on the Hohe Warte. The American girl's presence was more of a balm to Alma than to the weakened Manon, but Kathy sat by Manon's bed while they talked in French about their schools, friends, boyfriends, and especially their cats. Alma wanted to give

Kathy the same good times she would have liked to give Manon, so she invited English-speaking friends to suppers and evenings of music, took Kathy to the Opera, played bridge with her in any number of languages, and led Franz, Kathy, and a hired escort to dance in one of Vienna's several Gypsy restaurants. Alma considered Kathy much too thin, so she ordered her servants to bring their visitor breakfasts of cream and pâté de foie gras at seven in the morning, after which Kathy was routinely invited to join Alma for morning schnapps — something the girl consistently declined. Schnapps between breakfast and lunch was not considered irregular in Vienna, but it seemed highly improper to a young American girl.

For Alma, a morning libation became necessary. For fifteen years after Gustav had mentioned to Anna Moll that Alma had given up drinking, the subject had not been touched upon in letters or diaries. After Gustav's death, Alma again became accustomed to her after-breakfast Benedictine. She drank only cordials, wine, or beer, but her desire for these beverages extended throughout the day. She was sometimes tipsy, never downright drunk, and much of what was to be called drunkenness in the future was attributable to her deafness and advancing age. She did, however, indulge in Benedictine. One day shortly before she became ill, Manon ran to Anna with the urgent cry: "Quick, the Benedictine, Mummy's thirsty!"

When it was too late, and Manon could move only her hands, Alma and Franz engaged a therapist, who might earlier have helped the young woman regain control of her motor powers. There was no progress. At the end of her resources, Alma had to wonder what would happen should Manon's disability persist, and if she herself would have to spend her life tending her younger daughter.

In the spring of 1935, Manon became more seriously ill, went back to her bed, and lost her spirit. On the day after

Easter, she whispered to her mother, "Let me die in peace. I won't get better again, and you only talk to me about my acting out of pity for me . . . You'll get over it, Mummy, as you get over everything, as everyone gets over everything."[9] She fell asleep and died.

Among the first to arrive to comfort Alma was Father Hollnsteiner. Alban and Helene Berg visited. Berg developed the Violin Concerto he was intending to write for Louis Krasner (with quotations from Bach's Cantata No. 60, the inspiration for Oskar's *Bach Portfolio*) with Manon in mind, dedicating it "To the Memory of an Angel." Johannes delivered the eulogy. Manon was buried next to Gustav and her half sister Maria. As usual, Alma did not attend the rites.

❧

She reflected in her diary on the lives of her children:

The means and the moment of birth are definitive and meaningful to the life of the person. My four children all entered the world differently. My oldest, Maria, was born as the result of great fighting and mortal danger on my part. It was almost as if she was stillborn, all blue and quiet, but then there began her short, dramatic life, which was also to end with storms and drama . . . Anna arrived on a beautiful day in June, at noon. The air was still, the birds sang . . . She was laid on a pillow — it wasn't necessary to comfort her — and the doctor had to come nearer to check on me because the birth had been so sudden. She whimpered quietly and I loved her immediately, all too much.

Then came my ever heroic Mutzi, many years later. I carried her for ten months . . . It was a slow and difficult procedure . . . until finally this beautiful, black-haired child was in the world, and I looked on her with worshipping eyes. Her whole aesthetic way of life, her reticence, her great peace — these were all results of this delivery.

And finally, my son. Fate did not decree that he should have a life, since I had lived in doubt and in conflict with Gropius. His birth was nearly the death of both him and me — and so was his death ten months later.[10]

Franz and Johannes both tried to comfort Alma, but she would not release her misery to them. When either of the men tried to speak philosophically, Alma replied that God was obviously Evil. When either wanted to make love with her, she thought only about how frail human bodies were, how transient the pleasure. Her father, her first child, her only son, her first husband, her beautiful and gifted third daughter, so many friends and lovers — all of them had died. Manon had been right: Mummy would survive, because she always did. Her dying daughter's words rang harshly in Alma's ears. What might she have been able to do for and with all of those people who were now lost to her?

She decided to act, and went to Venice to sell the house there in the hope that with it she would purge herself of the vivid memories of Manon and tragedy. She returned to Semmering feeling that she might be able to free the country house and the other places in her life from old ties, from shadows of Manon, Oskar, Johannes, and the rest. All Alma wanted to do was sleep.

12

Refugees

ALMA HAD TAKEN certain maxims and proverbs to heart:
"Play to allure the gods," from her father; "Not the murderer, but the murdered is guilty," from the trip to Corfu
and later times with both Oskar and Franz; and now, *Jeder
Mensch weiss Alles,* or "Every person knows everything."
She took the last to mean that when she had wanted to be
free from Gustav in those early years, she had known that
he would die, that she had almost willed his death. She took
it to mean that Martin, her illegitimate son, had died for her
guilt. She also felt that everyone with whom she came in
contact knew, on some level, his or her own fate, as well as
other people's responses and reactions. Her lovers had
known precisely what meaning she would have to their lives,
and they to hers.

Alma took this adage one step further and concluded that
the things of beauty in her own life would be taken from
her: Manon; her own youthful beauty and womanhood; the
passionate loves she had known; her magnificent houses; the

ways in which she had once presided regally over men of culture and creativity. Alma read a signal and became more resigned than depressed. Whereas she had once had the red music room and the golden hostess dress to set off her beauty, she now looked for compromises to bring the brilliance and pleasure she thought she could reasonably expect. She had had her hair bleached further to the color of dawn. Her clothes were black. She wore simple shapeless dresses every day, all made to fit her figure from the same pattern by the same dressmaker, with full sleeves to cover her arms, a V-neck, and a flare to hide her wide waist above a skirt still accenting her shapely legs. Over these dresses Alma wore a variety of loose jackets made of silk or brocade in the style of the bedjackets popular in the era. Under her dresses she wore only pink silk slips, on which she embroidered little flowers with matching thread to cover signs of wear, in one of her rare measures of domestic self-sufficiency. She wore black shoes, wedgies, in which she could slide across the floor when alcohol or difficulty in hearing threw her off balance. Her stockings were fine and sheer. She hated corsets, and wore them only when she felt that she had to. She never wore panties; she loved to ask other women whether they happened to be wearing them, and then would brag that she was not then wearing, never had worn, and never would wear panties.

Six months after Manon's death, in the fall of 1935, Alma and Franz sailed for America to tend the production of his *Eternal Road,* a "Biblical cavalcade" that had been ordered a year earlier by Max Reinhardt. The play had turned into a multileveled extravaganza based on the Old Testament, and it was to be produced in the Manhattan Opera House with a musical score by Kurt Weill. At the same time, *The 40 Days of Musa Dagh* was released in America. The success of the novel, which was published in eighteen languages and would sell almost two hundred thousand copies in the United States alone, promised Franz and Alma greater financial stability. Alma looked to the return to America as a trip into her own past, and built up her hopes on what she remembered from thirty years earlier, when she had come to New York as Gustav Mahler's wife. She didn't let herself think of the problems Gustav had faced in America, or even of his last days there. Rather, she remembered walking around the city, looking in the windows of the shops, going to the performances at the Metropolitan Opera and at Carnegie Hall, meeting people who became good friends, being courted and revered.

When the Werfels arrived in New York, everything was very different from what Alma remembered. Whisky on the ship had made Franz ill. Ben Huebsch of the Viking Press met them at the pier as a representative of Franz's new publishing house. When he dropped them off at the Waldorf-Astoria, they found that their hotel rooms were booked at their own expense. The Werfels could not yet afford the tariff, and they worried all the more when they found that, in order to accommodate the production of Franz's play, the theater had had to be torn apart. The producers gave their word that they would be responsible for the liabilities, but before any sets or costumes had been made, more than $500,000 had been spent. The unions, newly strong in New York, were enraged to the point where they saw to it that the entire production fell to the brink of extinction. Alma had no use for either the extravagance or the ultimatums; she thought that the people who would invest their savings in this kind of effort were fools, and wanted nothing to do with them. Franz and Reinhardt worked themselves to exhaustion to preserve their commitments to *The Eternal Road,* but the myriad delays in the schedule made their mission impossible.

The only compensations to Alma and Franz came from the publication of *Musa Dagh,* which was met by many tributes from New York's Armenian community. Included were a solemn Christmas Eve service and supper, a congenial celebration at the home of the son of the late Hugo von Hofmannsthal and his wife — a member of the Astor family — and a dinner on January 5, 1936, at the Hotel Pennsylvania, where three hundred members of the Armenian populace rose to Franz in standing ovations. Those of the German and Austrian communities, having heard of Manon's death and the problems surrounding the production of Franz's play, contributed invitations and friendship. With all these attentions, the couple had no chance to be lonely during the holidays.

Alma slipped into depression when she read in the papers of the death of Alban Berg on Christmas Eve from blood poisoning. She felt again that she had lost a member of her family. The Jewish Forum honored Franz at a dinner attended by two thousand people at the Hotel Astor, with Albert Einstein as the featured speaker, but Alma felt alienated and wanted only to go home. As soon as the production of the play seemed to be reassured, the Werfels made plans to sail back to Europe. They were met in Paris by a group of young Armenians, paying homage to the novel that honored the nation they no longer possessed.

From Paris, Alma and Franz went on to Locarno, where Father Hollnsteiner celebrated the Mass on the anniversary of Manon's death. After all the attention that had been lavished on Franz, the trials of recent months, and the reminders of her own past with which she had been confronted, Alma felt left out. "My marriage is not really a marriage anymore. I live unhappily next to Werfel, whose monologues no longer know any boundaries. It's always *his* intent, *his* words, *his, his, his!* He has forgotten how important *my* words once were to him." [1] At the age of fifty-seven, Alma would not remember how similar were the words she was writing in her diary to those she had written during her marriage to Gustav and her years with Oskar.

She and Franz spent eight days in Locarno so that, in Alma's words, "Franz can find himself after all of the difficulties of the past year. He behaved himself as he has not done for a long time. But he thinks night and day of Mutzi, as I do too." [2] They went back to Vienna where, on the second of June, she continued, "I don't love anyone anymore. My heart is worn out. The thing I love most now is the bit of life that I have left to me. Work and the men who are close to me are not the important things anymore. They don't need me now. I am pleased to be alone in Vienna." [3]

Franz was off in Semmering working on his novel *Hearken unto the Voice* when Alma saw the manuscript of Bruno Walter's book on Gustav. "Mahler comes as a banal conglomeration of styles," she thought, deciding that the characterization was "highly unsympathetic." And, worse,

I am simply not considered . . . Still and always they hate me, the fact that I am a clean, beautiful Christian . . . It doesn't satisfy Mr. Walter and his consort that I was very gifted in my youth. They want also that I produce in my old age. But how similar we are all in the end. The few years before and after our lives end quickly, and they leave only emptiness.
One has parents in order to deceive them.
One has husbands in order to cheat on them.
One has children in order to lose them.
One has a soul in order to destroy it . . .
God, oh God, why do you *so* love all that is evil?! [4]

Alma and Franz spent Christmas in Milan and decided to sell the house on the Hohe Warte. Franz maintained that he had never really been able to work there, preferring rooms in hotels to his huge rooftop study. Both wanted to be in Semmering whenever they could, or, during the winters, in Italy. Alma liked Paris more than Franz did, and she kept returning to the possibility of settling in America. That seemed like a last resort, far away and different from what they were accustomed to.

Early in 1937, Alma saw to the packing of nearly ten thousand books, five thousand pages of music manuscripts, furniture, pianos, works of art, and all the other items that had sprawled to fill her house's twenty-eight rooms and hallways. Just before they left they had another party, duly reported by the press with lengthy lists of the names of the guests — cabinet ministers, ambassadors, princes and princesses, counts and countesses, barons and baronesses, actors and singers from the Burgtheater and the Opera, priests, composers, publishers, writers, and on and on — a strange mixture that recalled past times, when lines of social and political strata were drawn with less attention to religion or affiliations. Few left the party sober; some did not leave until the next day. It was an unusual time to stage such a celebration. Alma was so glad to be able to leave the house she considered jinxed that she went on with the packing and weeding out, feeling that she was leaving tragedy behind and eagerly anticipating what might lie ahead.

She and Franz moved to Semmering, where she had a dream involving her mother and Oskar, to whom she wrote a letter on the twenty-third of July:

> You are fifty years old — without me — and I feel as if we had spent the time together, after all . . .
>
> I know much about you, and you about me. You know of the death blow I have been dealt by the loss of my child Manon — but you hardly knew this wondrous creature. In her suffering she far outgrew us all. She really became the

"angel" to whom Alban Berg's last work was dedicated.
I have known no joy since, and any remaining appearance
of hopefulness or expectancy is deceptive. Now you know
all about me; so please let me know about you . . .
Today I awoke at dawn and saw a globe-girdling rainbow
curve over the mountain, from my valley into another, distant one. It was like a sign of your forgiveness. I beg you
now to drop all unkind feelings, to take my hand — all I
want of you is to know that we are one again, as deep down
as we have ever been.[5]

In July, Franz went to Paris to deliver lectures and to participate in a panel discussion of "The Future of Literature."
His greatest happinesses came from the evenings he spent
singing Verdi with James Joyce. Alma was so impressed with
the text of his lecture that she made a note of excerpts from
it. Franz was speaking of the misgivings he had about the
"barbarization of life" that characterized modern literature,
then went on to discuss something

> even more alarming, I mean the claim to totality which mod-
> ern technological implements of power have enabled certain
> states and their national ideologies to enforce in a previously
> unimaginable fashion. We have witnessed a complete rever-
> sal of values. In the classic era, literature and philosophy
> would influence political events, ceaselessly pressing their
> ideas upon reality; now, in our dark age, it is the new polit-
> ical-party dictatorships that proclaim the inviolable, unalter-
> able dogmas of what they euphemistically call their "idea
> content" and defend by force of arms against the slightest
> opposition. The primacy of politics destroys the spirit. It en-
> slaves what ought to dominate. The intellectual life of more
> than 200,000,000 Europeans suffers this nameless indig-
> nity — suffers without hope, for the awareness of the armed
> ideologies' technical superiority paralyzes even the strength
> to revolt inwardly. There have always been times of opposi-

tion; but the cruelest of them left free thought with sufficient solitude and silence for an occasional home-coming to its own truth. Today it is different. The steady war of propaganda avalanches loosed by press, radio and film makes it impossible for the thought to hear itself. It wavers, weakens and ends up in resignation. And the worst of it is that the evil is not confined to the "totalitarian" parts of Europe, but that it is spreading and infecting the intellectual life of all nations with a strange anarchy mixed of doubt, discontent and confusion.[6]

These words seemed so moderate that Alma copied them as an example of Franz's wisdom and insight, even though there were many points on which she disagreed with her husband. In Paris he was looked upon as a rabble-rouser, and found himself being elevated to a position that would have made him an international spokesman for his cause. Though he was willing and eager to speak his beliefs, Franz had no interest in devoting more of his energy to politics. He had been frightened; he knew that he and his family would probably not be able to remain safely in their homes, but he wanted to get back to his own work in peace. The reaction to his days in Paris told him how high emotion was running throughout Europe. Once again, Alma marveled at how completely her husband could separate himself from events outside his study. Franz was the one whose work, life, and family were seriously threatened; Alma was the one who could not remain temperate. Their battles about politics continued. Franz considered Alma narrow and doctrinaire when she preached fascism as a route to freedom. She could not understand his claims for the power of the common man. It was always Franz who put an end to their verbal matches by rising from his seat, shrugging his shoulders, and leaving the room.

Alma looked for something to arouse her passion as she approached the age of sixty in the absence of many persons who had been important in the earlier and more glamorous years of her life. She went back to music, this time taking pleasure in her ability to do something that had not come easily to Gustav or his daughter Anna: she could improvise on the piano. Divorced from Paul von Zsolnay, separated from her child Alma, Anna was coming to spend Christmas with Alma and Franz in Semmering. Anna had submitted a seven-foot-tall sculpture of a woman to the Paris World's Fair in 1937 and had won first prize. Her daughter's determination and success pleased Alma, even though she knew that Anna, now thirty-three, was not happy. Franz had always said Anna had no talent with men; she asked for something they could not give — comfort, sympathy, tenderness, childlike attention. Alma thought her daughter found men who were not worthy of her instead of those who might have helped her raise her sights and cultivate her considerable talent.

The indefiniteness of her own future worried Alma. Would she have to go with Franz, lock up her houses, and escape from the Nazis? Would Franz be successful enough for them to be able to choose where and how they wanted to live out their lives? What would finally happen to her — would she be Frau Werfel, the Widow Mahler, or an old woman of no consequence in a rapidly changing and unpredictable world? A palm reader predicted she would move to another country, perhaps to another continent, when she was in her early sixties. She would be there with the man with whom she had lived since she was in her early thirties — but she would not be with him for long. After six years in exile, she would return briefly to Vienna, and would want to go back to the place she had come to call her home.

Alma knew at once that the palmist was talking about

Franz, though she wished it had been Oskar, since he had written to reprimand her for not having answered his most recent letter. She had a dream about her "evil genius" and asked her diary, yet again, why she had not seen that he was the one whom she loved. He was the only man who had monopolized both her imagination and her memory. She tried to convince herself that Gustav had been the most important man in her life, but it was Oskar who continued to affect her, and whose spirit seemed to remain with her.

After the holidays at the end of 1937, Alma and Franz went to Milan, where they rented the rooms that had been Verdi's in the Grand Hotel. They went to hear the opera at La Scala and toured through Naples and Capri. While they were in Italy, Chancellor Schuschnigg went to Berchtesgaden to meet with Hitler. Annexation of Austria to the German Reich was imminent. Franz could no longer return home, and he and Alma finally had to face political reality. They prepared to go into exile at once, traveling together as far as Naples. From there, Alma took the next train to Vienna by herself to tend to their affairs at home. Her remnants of idealism were shattered. She stepped onto the platform of the station in her home city to be greeted by no one. Before telephoning her parents, her daughter, and Johannes, she wanted time to look at the city and remember it as it was.

After Alma walked around the Ringstrasse and through the narrow streets she knew so well, she prepared to leave. Her daughter Anna maintained that Alma had no options but to go into exile. The priest Johannes said Alma was overreacting — it would be only a matter of weeks or months until all was normal again. Alma took all of her money out of the bank — never again was she able to trust funds to institutions. She sewed the hundred-schilling notes into the girdle of her long-time servant Sister Ida, and the two women arranged to meet again when they were both safely over the border in Switzerland. Alma packed only what she considered to be the barest necessities, the few dresses and things she would not be able to live without until she was safely in another country.

Alma listened to Johannes espouse political theories even more naive than her own. Wanting the latest news of events directly affecting their fates, Alma and her daughter went to cafés and bars in the evenings to learn the gossip and try to hear the outcome of the plebiscite Schuschnigg had ordered. The vote was summarily canceled. By March 11, 1938, Alma and Anna knew escape was a matter of urgency. Alma spent her last night in Vienna visiting with Johannes in her hotel. His fate under the Nazis would be grim. The priest was not to become the Cardinal of Vienna — he was sent to a concentration camp. Later he left the church, married, fathered children, and died young.

On March 13, Alma and Anna took the train to Prague, where Franz's sister Hanna Fuchs-Robettin met and housed them. They traveled on from Prague by way of Budapest, Zagreb, and Trieste to meet Franz in Milan. All the trains were jammed with people, and whenever either of the women caught a glimpse out of a window she saw their route lined with signs of Hitler's triumphs. As they left their homeland, Alma felt a combination of regret and relief. There was much in Vienna she was happy to leave, but she feared she would never again see the places and persons who had been so important to her.

Carl Moll, his daughter Maria (Alma's half sister), and her husband Eberstaller — even Anna Moll — had actively embraced the Nazi ideology. Alma knew that her family's conversion could have only positive effects on her own immediate future and theirs. To a certain extent she agreed with them, but she did not like having to be the one who was forced to go into exile. Alma had to realize that the politicians' theories were deleterious not only to herself and to Franz, but also to the memory of Gustav, to the lives of many of her close friends, and to millions of others across the continent. During the days when she had wandered around Vienna preparing to leave for ever, Alma wore the swastika given to her by the Eberstallers, ostensibly to ensure her safety. Alma didn't care much about it one way or the other, and was anxious only to attend to her affairs and return to Franz. She gave Moll power of attorney over her property, including some works of art that, they agreed, would go on temporary display in a safe gallery. Despite his alleged lapses of honor, Moll was still a respected member of the art world, highly skilled in assessing and valuing. He had helped and supported Alma so much in the past that she did not worry about his reliability in this time of crisis.

During his wife's absence, Franz tried to go on with his work on a German translation of Verdi's opera *Don Carlos* in addition to many matters that still had to be tended to concerning the American publication of *Hearken unto the Voice* by the Viking Press. He was so anxious about his wife that it had been difficult for him to accomplish much. Accurate reports of the news were impossible to get. Alma had only been able to communicate with him in a code to allow her letters to get past the censors. He knew that she was safe and under great strain, and had no idea of what she had been through. Franz was waiting at the station when the train pulled in well behind schedule. In a matter of minutes after their reunion, they began trying to answer the question that would rule their lives for months to come: Where do we go next?

They didn't intend to stay in Milan. Italy no longer pleased them as it once had. When Franz's younger sister Mizzi, now married and living in Zurich, invited them to come and stay with her and her family, they accepted. But Zurich was not satisfying, so they undertook the tiresome procedures necessary for them to obtain papers to enter France and settle in or near Paris. It took almost a month before they unpacked their belongings in the small Hotel Royal Madeleine near the Louvre, where they slept long hours, enjoyed their privacy, and came to feel quite at home.

From Paris, they conducted a nearly normal life. Anna had gone back to London, where she had settled safely and was working well. Franz gradually returned to his cloistered writing. Alma accepted Mengelberg's invitation to the Mahler Festival in Amsterdam during the first week in May. There she found herself feted and interviewed as the Widow Mahler and also as a recent emigrée who could provide some of the information being withheld about Hitler's conquests and the situation in the east. A Dutch publisher, Albert de Lange, approached her concerning a book of reminiscences about Gustav; this was a project she had discussed with her son-in-law Zsolnay in Vienna, where it now seemed impossible to go ahead with the book. Both the relative peacefulness of Holland and the attention being paid to her late husband in that country convinced Alma to accept de Lange's offer.*

From Amsterdam, Alma went on to London with Franz. The couple attempted to settle in with Anna. The sculptress was quite at home in that city, but the accommodations were not of the nature to satisfy Alma. She was unhappy to the point of experiencing what she called a "nervous breakdown" while Franz went off to see publishers and friends and toured the city's sights and museums. In only a matter

---

*This volume never went into wide circulation, which is especially unfortunate because it is the most accurate to have appeared under Alma's name, and probably the only one in whose creation she played a major role.

of days, his previously rudimentary English improved to a point where he could read the British newspapers and converse with people in restaurants and shops. Alma did none of these things; she pined for her piano, her books, the warm sun that she wanted to feel in the early days of summer, and friends with whom she could converse in her native language. Her husband had a gift for languages; her daughter was almost as comfortable in English as in German. Anna came to prefer speaking English, and tried to convince her mother to do the same. Alma was not interested, especially then, so the Werfels returned to Paris after three weeks.

This time Alma installed Franz in the grand Hotel Henri Quatre in St.-Germain-en-Laye, away from the city, while she went back to the Hotel Royal Madeleine, with easy access to friends and cultural activities. She went to hear Furtwaengler conduct *Tristan* and judged the performance as fine as could have been expected, considering that the instrumentalists were French. She visited museums and found friends with whom she could converse. Whereas London had been too chilly in the late spring, Paris was oppressively hot and humid. Alma decided it was time for another escape, and went to the French Riviera to find a small house. Alma did not want a large or imposing house, and she knew that it would be difficult to find a household staff, or friends to entertain.

In Sanary-sur-Mer around the first of July she found the perfect spot, an old watchtower that had been remodeled in simple but good taste by a painter. It would be ideal for her and Franz. She signed the rental agreement for the watchtower and celebrated that afternoon with Anna Marie ("Buschie") Maier-Graefe, widow of the art historian, who would be her new neighbor in a town where war and its oppression still seemed far removed.

While the two women indulged themselves in looking forward to the days they would have in such sunny surroundings, the telephone rang. Franz was seriously ill. Alma returned to Paris at once. It was his heart; a prolonged period of convalescence would be necessary. An English doctor who had been summoned to the suburban hotel had told him his condition was so grave that he should expect to die. Franz, more frightened than ill, wanted Alma with him constantly. She slept on a little sofa in his room. She was sure that the attack had been caused by his smoking, and plotted how she would keep him away from his beloved cigarettes when he resumed his work. After a month-long period of worry and rest, Alma lost patience: Franz was keeping her from her life and making her exist under uncomfortable conditions.

When the Werfels went to their watchtower in the south, Alma gave Franz the big room on top surrounded by windows, while she spent her time in the damp, airless parlor downstairs playing Bach on the piano. Although he still thought he was going to die, he eventually turned to a new novel, one of his most charming, *Embezzled Heaven*. Franz's work gave their days both vitality and a needed routine, but as summer waned Alma looked out over the cold gray water and felt homeless, consigned to wander with the Jews and share a fate that should not have been hers.

In spite of his weakness Franz again adapted to new surroundings more quickly than Alma, and he seemed to revel in the challenge of speaking French and exploring the new neighborhood. Soon he met a group of political journalists and tried his hand at essays in that field. Alma wished that he hadn't. She thought he should be devoting himself to his other work, and she feared repercussions. "Werfel and I have both come to grief," she confided to her diary. "He believed in world revolution through bolshevism, and he could not know what would come of it. I believed that fascism would solve all of the problems of the world, but I, too, could not have known what the eventualities would be." [7]

Anna Moll was dying. Alma wanted to go to her mother in Vienna; she wanted deeply to share more hours with the woman who had been so important to her, her husbands, her children, and her friends. The trip was impossible; if Alma had been able to reach Vienna, she probably would not have been allowed to leave there again. She telephoned, and only found out that her mother was still breathing. She felt helpless and alienated. Late in November 1938, Anna died. Carl put a picture of Alma on his wife's bosom as she lay in her coffin; he then had to be put under constant guard, lest he commit suicide.

◖

In the last weeks of 1938, when Franz accepted an invitation to speak in Zurich, Alma went to visit Anna in London. Alone with her daughter, still experiencing the pains of her own mother's death, Alma did not mind the city or the strange country as much as she had before, but she resented the cold and damp. Instead of returning to their watchtower by the sea, Alma and Franz met in Paris to spend the winter there. Alma reacquired one of her most treasured possessions, the manuscript score of Anton Bruckner's Third Symphony. This had last been seen when she took it from the special case in the marble room in her house on the Hohe Warte and left it, with so many of the other treasures that had been part of Gustav's legacy to her, in the care of her estranged half sister Maria and her husband. Hitler, who was quite as enamored of Bruckner's music as of Wagner's, had tried to buy it, using Eberstaller as his emissary. That subservient member of the Party had tried to secure the manuscript for *der Fuehrer*. The good Sister Ida had outsmarted them all: she had wrapped the music in plain brown paper, and without revealing what was in the mysterious package had given it to the wife of a Viennese music critic who was leaving for Paris. Only when they were safely in Paris did the critic and his wife open the wrapper. Seeing the contents, they had the score delivered immediately to its rightful owner with best wishes. When Hitler realized the score was not to be his property, Moll and the Eberstallers were punished by being disallowed the privileges they had expected to receive within the Reich.

Just holding the manuscript in her hands made Alma feel comforted and linked to her past. She remembered events and thoughts of earlier years and thought she recognized her own identity. That recognition seemed to set Franz apart. After a night of partying, when both Alma and Franz had drunk too much, she wrote in her diary, "It is unbelievable, how weak the Jewish race is. I am tipsy, but do not seem so. When *he* is tipsy, he is poisoned and ill."[8] Franz could no longer endure alcohol. Alma was proud of her own tolerance, which she credited to her Christian heritage.

She went to see her friend Margherita Sarfatti, who had lived as a queen as Mussolini's mistress but now lived almost as a beggar in exile. Alma had pity for the woman and enjoyed her company, so Margherita became a frequent guest at the impromptu salons Alma staged in her small Paris hotel room. Other guests included such friends as Franz Lehar and his wife, Bruno Walter and his wife, and Fritz von Unruh, all of whom had either ended up settling in Paris or concentrating their time in the city.

Alma was also delighted to be reunited with the composer of *Louise*. "When Charpentier came," she wrote, "I was waiting by the elevator. We embraced each other, as if we were both completely used to doing so. Then we stood back from one another and we both had tears in our eyes. My small room in the Hotel Royal Madeleine has been changed into a bank of flowers worthy of a palace since he sent a huge basket full of them just before his arrival. When I told him that I had written a book about Mahler in which he and the whole era were considered, he jumped up and said enthusiastically that it would be wonderful, because then we would all look very good and important." [9]

The Baroness Bendstetten invited Alma to join her at the Mainbocher salon one day after lunch. When she arrived, Alma found that this was not a place where she could be comfortable, especially when she saw that her hostess expected her lap dog, Pipi, would be allowed to run and jump on the exquisitely covered chairs and couches. While the Baroness tried on six or eight "creations," Alma attempted to control the dog. She couldn't help hearing voices of the women in the adjacent rooms and noting purchases of dresses that cost 5000 francs, sometimes even more. Spending such a sum on a gown was anathema to her. She looked down at her own dress, one of several she had managed to carry out of Vienna in her suitcases, and felt shabby.

She left the salon, hailed a taxi, and gave the driver the address of a pastry chef whom she knew by reputation. The driver was reluctant to take her there. What business could a lady who had just come from Mainbocher's salon have in that other part of Paris? Alma persisted, and in the midst of poverty-stricken refugees she found the man for whom she was searching, a Jew from Dresden who had been driven from his homeland because he was living with an Aryan woman. Alma talked to them in German; they seemed to want to discourage her from buying their cakes and rolls, so out of place did she seem in their tiny hidden shop. She insisted on giving them a large order, and when the date-filled pastries and coffeecakes arrived in their rooms, Franz and Alma ate what seemed to them to be an emperor's feast.

Hitler was about to move into Czechoslovakia. Alma telephoned Franz's sister Hanna to warn her as strongly and clearly as she could that the Werfels should leave their country at once. Hanna understood Alma's cryptic message, but Rudolf Werfel was still too weak to travel. As the last of the children in Prague, Hanna had to stay with her father. Alma and Franz went back to the Riviera feeling powerless. There they found that the political climate had worsened and they were in danger. Alma suggested leaving immediately. Franz talked her out of it — he wanted to go on working and was tired of moving — so they agreed to stay until fall.

In September 1939 England entered the war. From that point on, Alma and Franz could not leave their little house without being searched and questioned. They learned how to pay off the patrols who knocked on their door; the police on the streets were sterner and more ominous. Residents of the village had taken to taunting and attacking people they had seen being questioned. Several times when Franz ventured away from his desk and out of the house to get lunch or coffee, he returned with his clothes soiled and torn from skirmishes with the local posses. The Werfels told themselves they had nothing to fear — their papers were in order, and they were entirely within their rights. Franz was driven into a state of exhaustion, however, and seemed to lose energy and his hope. Alma insisted that they move on to another town, another country. "Maybe America can again give me some strength," she wrote in her diary. "I need it." [10]

The patriarch of the Werfel family recuperated to some extent, and, after months of waiting, managed to escape to Vichy with Hanna and her family. It was difficult to obtain the permission needed even to go the short distance from Sanary-sur-Mer to Vichy, but Franz urgently needed to see his ailing father. When he and Alma were finally able to travel, there was barely room for them to squeeze onto the train. At every stop their papers were checked by pompous officials who left them short-tempered. They arrived in Vichy only to find that Rudolf Werfel had suffered another stroke and was severely impaired, though not in any imminent danger of his life. The couple visited briefly, then reboarded the train to go to what they called their home, still wondering what might happen next. In the watchtower Alma kept a small gun for protection. There was now such a strong decree against firearms that she buried the gun in the garden, considering that in this she was saving herself in one way and giving herself up in another.

Again they delayed making definite plans to move on, and decided to return to Paris at the end of the year. More and more friends and acquaintances had taken refuge there. As 1940 began, Alma was not feeling strong, but she tried to mask her malaise in order to act as a support to Franz. Winter broke, and they decided it was safe to return to Sanary-sur-Mer. On Easter, Alma went to Mass and thought of Johannes. "Is salvation supposed to come from this poor, harried old priest in his stained cassock, sad and grave, the victim of a poor, unholy existence?" she questioned. She thought about music. "Most Jewish melodies begin with a dissonance, such as the Wedding March from [Mendelssohn's] *A Midsummer Night's Dream* and the Barcarolle from [Offenbach's] *The Tales of Hoffmann*. That's because they have not yet found their Messiah and they thus still strive toward the ultimate promise! *We* start with the C-Major chord, as in the Prelude to *Die Meistersinger,* face up to the conflicts and end in Christ, who was and is . . . ! Is he real?" [11]

Rumors of impending danger sent Alma and Franz back to Paris almost immediately. They were again in the Hotel Royal Madeleine when the war erupted in France. Searches became more and more frequent. On May 10, 1940, the first air-raid sirens blared and they fled to the hotel basement in the middle of the night to await the all-clear signal. Alma was more annoyed than frightened. She yearned for oil, butter, soap, and any number of items that had previously been taken for granted, even during World War I. Once more, they retreated to their watchtower, visiting the senior Werfels in Vichy on the way. Alma continued trying to convince Franz to leave France, feeling that they could not continue this troublesome, aimless back-and-forth motion. He resisted, but when Alma heard that the Belgians had surrendered, she packed everything, including her Bruckner manuscript and the several of Gustav's scores still in her possession. They left for Marseille, intending to go directly on to America.

Daily they went to the consulate to request visas to let them leave France and travel across the Atlantic to the United States. They received no encouragement, no help, no papers. Premier Paul Reynaud took to the radio waves to appeal for help, saying the situation was grave but not desperate. Alma and Franz thought at once of the expression so similar and so representative of Viennese resignation: "The situation is hopeless but not serious."

This time the situation was hopeless. When the Werfels heard that Hitler had marched into Paris, they went from Marseille to Bordeaux, temporary seat of the French government, where they thought they might be better able to secure the necessary papers to get to Biarritz, drive across the long bridge at Hendaye, and escape to Spain. For an exorbitant fee, a driver agreed to try to take them to Bordeaux by way of Avignon and Toulouse. They had to spend the night in a run-down inn in Narbonne. On the second day roadblocks and inspections kept them from going beyond Carcassonne. The driver was delighted to give up, but Franz found that a train would be leaving for Bordeaux at two the next morning. Determined to reach his destination, he checked all of their luggage into the baggage cars except their overnight bags and they waited through the long hours

of darkness until the train arrived. The cars were so filled
with people that Alma and Franz could barely squeeze into
the wavering spaces between the doors. They didn't know if
their luggage was with them on the train. When they stopped
at the station in Bordeaux, so many people were mobbing
the platform and piles of suitcases, it was impossible for them
to retrieve their possessions.

Alma would be deserting everything she owned, including
her Bruckner score, but Bordeaux seemed to be their last
hope. They had to apply themselves to finding a place for
sleep and then begin the official procedures to obtain papers
the next day. While she waited for Franz to make a final
attempt to find their bags, Alma started talking to a brightly
painted young woman who was standing near her with
nothing more than a small makeup case. Encouraged by
the offer of money, the young woman said she might know
of a place where they could sleep, and gave them a card
with the address of a deserted whorehouse whose rooms were
oddly equipped but comfortable. Franz and Alma settled in,
then went out in search of supper, only to find all the inns
and restaurants either filled beyond capacity or closed.
Eventually they found bread, eggs, and a little wine. The
picnic they spread out in their room in the whorehouse
seemed more than adequate.

Quickly they realized there was nothing to be accomplished in Bordeaux, so, again paying an outrageous sum,
they found a driver who would take them on to Biarritz.
They anticipated the worst, but the ride passed almost without incident. In the crowded streets of Biarritz they ran into
old friends who offered help and advice. Franz began daily
trips to Bayonne, where they had been advised to try for
their visas. Before he could advance in the long waiting line
he heard that the Germans were waiting to claim the town
and would be there within a few hours. The Portuguese con-

sul in Hendaye was said to be both efficient and sympathetic, so Alma and Franz headed there, only to find that the
man they sought had been moved to St. Jean-de-Luz. On
they went again, to be met by further bad news: the good-
natured consul had lost his mind, thrown all the passports
that had been handed to him into the sea, and taken flight.
Franz, once so determined and even hopeful, took to his bed
in tears.

The next rumors sent them on to Pau, where there was
again no help to be found. Without a bed or a reasonable
meal, they went on to Lourdes, where they arrived on June
27, 1940, more tired and desolate than ever before. Again
they had to face the routine of searching for a roof, a bed,
and food. When it began to appear that their quest would
not yield even the most primitive rewards, an innkeeper's
wife took pity on them and moved a young couple out of
one room so the older exiles might rest. The accommoda-
tion was cell-like, but adequate, almost comfortable. They
lay down on the narrow bed longing only for sleep; it seemed
years since they had had a change of clothes, a bath, or the
chance to indulge in any of the vanities previously viewed
as simple necessities of existence.

Well rested, they went out the next morning — Franz for
a shave and Alma to see the bookstalls. She picked up pam-
phlets and devotional tracts telling the story of Bernadette
Soubirous, Saint Bernadette, which she read more as a tour-
ist than as a devotee. She showed the material to Franz, then
put it in her bag.

They continued their quest. Every morning, long lines
formed at the police station not far from the house where
Bernadette was said to have lived, and every afternoon the
refugees were sent back to their hotels with nothing to show
for their patience. As the days dragged on, Alma and Franz
took time to visit the grotto outside the village, at Massa-

bielle; there Alma attended services at the shrine where little Bernadette envisioned the Virgin Mary. The miracle of Lourdes intrigued them, though they knew they were living in hope of another miracle. As they watched the Nazi threat approach, they began to feel that their quest was futile.

After two long weeks, Alma and Franz were able to move into a larger room with separate beds. Separate sleeping quarters had been their custom. Their daily ritual did not change, however, for another fortnight — until late July. Then Alma received a message that a package awaited her at the post office. She went to retrieve it and found not the case containing her prized manuscripts but, rather, bags giving her and Franz a change of clothes and other small luxuries. The couple gaily put on the outfits, which now seemed quite new to them, and felt as if they could face their challenge with new stamina. On August 3, they were awarded the good-conduct passes that would allow them to return to Marseille.

In Marseille at dawn, they walked directly to the Hotel de Louvre et de la Paix, which they remembered fondly from better days. As they approached the entrance they saw a line of big new automobiles standing by the door. At once they knew that the inn had been taken over by the occupying German forces. The manager, an old acquaintance upon whom they could depend, confirmed their suspicions and rushed his new guests up the rear elevator and into empty rooms with whispered assurance that the occupants would be gone soon. The high officials did leave but the lower German officers remained in residence in the hotel. Alma, Franz, and the other civilian guests had to isolate themselves in their chambers and sneak through corridors and freight elevators in order to avoid delays or detention.

Marseille, like every other city on their route, was overcrowded, with food scarce and expensive. Many of the refugees could have afforded neither room nor board, had such been available; they were without passports and papers, and they had no idea of where they might go or what might become of them. Alma and Franz could at least take assurance in the fact that they had their rooms and their papers. Franz set out once more on his daily trips to the Czech consulate, where the lines never seemed to move.

The refugees who spent their days standing in the stagnant lines got to know one another, and rumors were rampant. Franz could not remain anonymous; as the most illustrious member of this small, tense community, he often heard his presence heralded up and down the queues, and he could no longer pretend he was not frightened. As the weeks passed without apparent progress, he and Alma occasionally allowed themselves a day on the beach, where the political threats seemed less real and imminent. In the evenings, after the offices had closed, the refugees wove elaborate schemes for escape, all of which seemed insane on the morning. The Werfels felt like people hanged, waiting to die.

One day, with no apparent cause, a trunk arrived bringing Alma her treasures — the manuscripts. It had been forwarded by their former host in Lourdes; the network of refugees was mysterious but efficient. Shortly thereafter — again for no apparent reason — a telegram arrived from New York advising the Werfels that their American visas had been sent by cable to the consulate in Marseille. They went at once to the office, only to be faced with another long line. Eventually they were told that the consul knew nothing of either cable or purported visas. Alma and Franz persisted and, after much paper shuffling and many messages, the papers were produced. Another hurdle had been crossed.

They took a taxi back to their hotel with the kind of optimism that comes not from the final victory but from tangible progress toward a goal. Sitting down, wanting to celebrate and relax, they realized they could not get a ship out of a French port, and would therefore need both Spanish and Portuguese visas before they could sail from Lisbon. At least they were out of serious trouble; the American visas now clipped inside their Czech passports would act as protection. But they still had to go through the procedures of procuring papers from not one but two more countries. So they started with Spain.

America-Grateful and Unhappy

LUCK CHANGED. The sun was blistering and the waiting
was almost too much for Franz to withstand in his tired and
desolate state, so Alma gave their calling card and a tip to
the doorman at the Spanish consulate. He disappeared, then
returned almost immediately to lead them directly to the
consul, where they were handed visas and wished the best.

They went to the Portuguese offices. Alma tried the same
ploy again, but was only sent to the back of another long,
unmoving line. For hours they waited, perspiring and feeling
weak as the sun approached its zenith. Suddenly a young
author who had written for Paul Zsolnay in Vienna, Hertha
Pauli, approached them. Alma and Franz had seen her in
both Paris and Lourdes, but she had no passport, and could
not hope to procure a visa. She had noticed Franz's suffering. After an exchange of greetings, Hertha excused herself,
then returned to invite the Werfels to accompany her for tea
or champagne. She had arranged to have the consul himself

see Alma and Franz at promptly four in the afternoon. By telephoning and identifying herself as Madame Werfel, the young woman had convinced the official that so distinguished a citizen as Franz should not be made to stand in long lines in stifling heat. Eager to meet a writer whom he admired, the consul consented to the appointment. By evening, Alma and Franz had their papers entirely in order.

Only then did the American who had reportedly been sent to help the refugees present himself in Marseille. Varian Fry, a representative of the Emergency Rescue Committee, found Alma and Franz registered in the hotel under the name of Mahler. Fry did not impress Alma at first glance, but his calmness and authority soon proved reassuring. He promised to reserve space for the Werfels on a ship as soon as possible. While they waited for further instructions, the rest of their luggage arrived, again directed by the network of fellow refugees. Fry could finally report that their departure would take place on the morning of September 12. Alma packed what had grown into a tremendous pile of bags and suitcases while Franz burned his unprinted manuscripts and drafts in a hotel ashtray, page by page. At dawn of the appointed morning, Franz and Alma assembled with Thomas Mann's son Golo, Thomas's brother Heinrich, and his wife Nelle.

Fry appeared with another American, a young man who was to serve as the refugees' escort under the more trying and difficult circumstances. All took a train to Perpignan, then changed for Cerbère, their last border stop. There had been some hope that the American visas might get them through Spain, but the Czech passports were not valid there, so the expedition was halted in a deserted hotel on a hill overlooking Cerbère. Early in the morning they decided over a breakfast of tea that if they could not go into Spain on the regulated roads or rails, they would proceed by foot. The solution was not ideal, especially in light of Franz's weak heart and Heinrich's advanced years. The younger American would be their guide and helper while Fry went ahead by train with all of their bags. The walk was not long, but it was trying, especially treacherous in the midday sun. They prepared to leave as soon as possible. Golo was nowhere to be found. With uncharacteristic carelessness, he had gone for an unannounced swim in the ocean. The Werfels and the Manns waited for two hours until he returned. The sun was already high in the sky when they left.

As they walked from their hotel through the village, Nelle realized it was Friday the thirteenth, a bad day, and she proposed that all turn back and wait for a more propitious time. Her companions talked her out of the superstition, but only after another delay. Then their escort proposed separating into two groups for the early, most difficult part of the climb. Franz and Alma went first, following the guide with the same resignation they had cultivated so well during their months of wandering. They no longer feared the worst, or even tried to predict what might happen to them. Alma wore sandals and an old, comfortable dress and carried a large pocket-book, into which she had stuffed a few of her jewels, the Bruckner manuscript, and what cash remained to them. Their homelessness had cost them dearly. They had no idea of when or where they might next be able to get funds. For more than two hours, they pushed on upward, sometimes along well-trodden paths though usually through rocky underbrush that seemed to lead them nowhere.

At the top of the mountain, the guide left Alma and Franz to go back and fetch the Manns. Panting and sweating, they looked out and realized that they could see the Spanish border station. When they had caught their breaths and been cooled by the breeze, they began their descent to the white hut. The door of the building was opened by a soldier who spoke no language that Alma could recognize. She and Franz tried to explain their plight with what words they guessed they might have in common, and with sign language. All the guard could understand was the gift of cigarettes pushed into his pocket. He gestured that the newcomers should follow him out of the hut, around a path, and back to another French border post — precisely the spot where they could not present themselves. Disgusted and tired, Alma offered more money. That got them through to the officer-in-charge, who warily waved them past. Alma and Franz climbed over rusty chains and walked toward the customhouse on Spanish land with great relief.

The guards who had seemed so difficult telephoned ahead, so the Spanish officers were expecting the visitors, and Alma and Franz were greeted with wine and good wishes. The keepers of the customs post appeared to be glad to have new ears upon which to sound their curses on Franco and Mussolini, and offered the wanderers seats in the waiting room while they awaited the arrival of the others in their party. Hours seemed to pass. The Werfels worried not only because the walk was arduous, but also because Heinrich was traveling under an assumed name. Golo was endangered because he was Thomas's son. When the Manns walked through the door of the small sterile room, Alma and Franz wanted to run and kiss them all, but they could not reveal that they were any more than casual acquaintances whose paths had happened to cross in the journey. A few of their remaining francs spread among the officers found them pleasant rooms in an inn not far from the customhouse.

They slept and waited to be summoned for the next passage. Although Alma and Franz thought they had nothing to worry about — all their papers were in order — they had learned to expect the worst. They were particularly apprehensive as they approached the end of their long journey in the company of the controversial Manns. When called to show their passports and visas, they filed one by one into a dingy room and sat down on hard narrow benches, staring at the floor and not daring even to glance at one another. Golo, in his youthful defiance, had taken a book and seemed to relax; Alma envied him. After what might have been hours, the officer handed back their papers with the proper stamps affixed. The refugees walked freely into Port Bau on the northeast coast of Spain. Fry was waiting with their luggage and led them to hotel rooms. In the aftermath of civil war, Spain was desolate, but they slept gratefully until it was time to catch the train to Barcelona.

From Barcelona they had to arrange to get to Lisbon; seats on direct airplane flights were almost impossible to secure. When two became available after a couple of days, Nelle and Heinrich took them and flew to safety. Alma, Franz, and Golo boarded a rickety train for Madrid, where they hoped there would be a better chance to book a flight. They longed for Fry's continued assistance, but his mission had only been to deliver them from France. The trio proceeded to the airport and quickly got onto a plane. When they walked onto Portuguese land, they allowed themselves to feel happy and relieved.

There were more long lines at the passport control in Lisbon, and when Franz reached the desk he came face to face with another scowling official. He handed over the papers along with a letter identifying him as the well-known author. The controller read every page attentively, looked up, and said, "I see you are of Jewish descent." [1] Franz did not respond, but turned slightly toward Alma, whose heart was pounding in fear. The officer stared at them, looked at the passports and visas, sneered, and gave them the stamps of approval that allowed them to walk on into Portugal.

In Lisbon they were not constantly exposed to the signs of war, so they quite enjoyed the two weeks of waiting before boarding the *Nea Hellas*, the last regularly scheduled

ship to sail from Lisbon to New York. To Alma's annoyance, passage on the Greek vessel was costing them as much
as they would have had to pay to travel on the *Queen Elizabeth*, but they had no choice. When they boarded the ship,
settled into their cabins, heard the whistles sound and the
engines start, and looked back to the retreating shoreline of
Europe, they felt for the first time in a year that they could
be themselves without threat of danger.

◆

Wartime radio in New York and London had announced
that Franz Werfel, the famous author, and his wife, Alma
Mahler, widow of the composer, were missing and pre-
sumed dead. When the New York press listed the same couple as well as Heinrich, Nelle, and Golo Mann among the
passengers who would be arriving on the *Nea Hellas* on October 13, 1940, a crowd of friends, acquaintances, journalists, and curious onlookers waited for them on the pier. The
Manns left the ship slowly, since Heinrich had been seasick
throughout the trip; Alma wanted to run off and kiss the
soil, so happy and invigorated did she feel. Perhaps she had
always been meant to live in America. Alma still had money
in the bank in New York, so she and Franz could plan their
future without having to practice strict economies. They arrived at the St. Moritz Hotel, where their rooms were of the
quality they had expected, and where they could again sleep
comfortably, eat and drink to their satisfaction, treat themselves to a few luxuries, and see friends.

During the first few weeks they allowed themselves to
catch up with the life they had left while on the escape; it
was almost as if they had lived on a submarine, out of time,
and had to surface and reestablish their contacts with people, places, and things. For Franz this meant starting to work
in a new country. For Alma, happy as she was to be back
in New York, it was difficult. At sixty-one, she hardly rec-

ognized the places she had seen and visited during her winters in Manhattan with Gustav. She spoke almost no English, and her friends from earlier visits were either dead or gone. As soon as Franz sat down at his desk to write, she felt lonely and unneeded, lost from any world she might have been able to call her own.

One of the first communications Alma received was a note telling her that her daughter remained safe and well in London. The message came from Kathe Berl, a young artist who had met Anna and shared her workspace a year or two earlier, then moved on to New York. Through Anna, Kathe had met Oskar and other members of that artistic circle. Alma summoned the note's sender, assuming her to be a woman of maturity. When Kathe arrived, Alma took one look, exclaimed, "My God, I called you Madam!" and welcomed the young woman as a daughter. For years Alma would think of Kathe as friend and surrogate daughter, though the ways in which the older woman played Kathe against Anna resulted in lasting animosity between the younger women.

Alma felt that she was of an age where she had every right to be set in her ways, even dogmatic. Those who did not approve could be damned. She believed that people should achieve according to her standards: a conductor had to be a composer (though modern standards in the concert world made this a rarity); an architect could not waste his time being a decorator. Alma told Kathe that she pitied both her and Franz because, as Jews, they had been humiliated. Kathe explained that she didn't feel humiliated at all and didn't see why she should be. The matriarch ended the conversation with a stubborn look of disdain, as if to say that humiliation alone would bring forgiveness.

Alma continued to dress in a uniform of black dresses, bedjackets, and wedgies, though she increased the amount of jewelry she wore, adding long necklaces and dangling earrings, and lightened her makeup to pink and white, accented by red lipstick. Her yellow hair was swept up on top of her head into a bed of curls. One could hardly miss noticing her as she walked on the streets of Manhattan. She was drinking Benedictine steadily, but not usually beyond her level of tolerance. The persons who say she was drunk do not seem to have known about her impaired hearing. Those who knew about this affliction, and realized that it became worse with the years, say she might occasionally have been tipsy, never drunk.

A few days after their first meeting, Kathe happened to run into Alma and Franz in Brentano's, the large bookstore. Franz was having a fine time exploring the city and dealing in English, and he led Kathe back to the small section that held German-language books. There he picked up a volume of his own poems, bought it, signed it, and gave it to their new friend as a present, saying, "This is the best thing that I have ever done."

Two days after Christmas, Alma and Franz packed again and boarded the train to California, where they thought they might like to settle permanently. Alma had found her memories of New York tinged with sadness — so many were the places and things reminding her of Gustav's time there and his death. Besides, she hated the cold, and the climate in Southern California was said to be ideal. The presence of the film industry in Hollywood opened a variety of new possibilities for Franz. Though neither of them had been to the western region of the United States — indeed, they had no idea of the country's expanse — they knew that friends had gone there before them, and they were on their way to join the Manns, the Schoenbergs, and other friends. Those who arrived in Los Angeles were ready to help those who were on the way. Friends found Alma and Franz a little house at 6900 Los Tilos Road, off Highland Avenue and within earshot of the reverberations from the summer concerts at the Hollywood Bowl. The house had been fully outfitted with the necessities, even a butler, when the Werfels arrived there on December 30.

As she and Franz toasted 1941 in their new house, Alma's reactions were mixed. She missed the city; in some ways, she would rather have been in New York. For the time being, however, she was glad to be settled in a place where Franz could work and she would not be cold. Her husband was charmed by the trees, the birds, the yard, and the freedom. Alma found people with whom she could converse in her own language, go into town, and attend an occasional concert. She came to admit that the new environs had advantages over a city hotel room or apartment.

Only four days after their arrival in the Hollywood Hills Franz returned to work, intent on fulfilling a vow he had made while they were living under trying conditions in Lourdes: if the Lord helped them safely to freedom, he would write a tribute to the child whose faith had prompted the miracle in that French town. The book was *The Song of Bernadette,* still his best known. As Franz began writing and rewriting the book in longhand, in the first of what would turn into several piles of blue notebooks, Alma was reassured.

Their days were quiet, arranged according to Franz's working schedule in the tradition Alma had learned during her years with Gustav. Alma wanted to savor the peace that was engulfing her with only a few friends, including Max Reinhardt and the Schoenbergs. The Werfels purchased an old car, but they did not venture out frequently; one does not stroll to a café in Los Angeles in the same way one walks down the street in Vienna, Paris, or Sanary-sur-Mer. Most of their acquaintances were Jewish, but that bothered Alma less than it used to. The "Jewish problem" seemed remote.

A letter from Austria revealed that Johannes Hollnsteiner had left the Church to join the Nazis and subsequently married. Alma tried to explain these events to her diary, saying that she had always known he was insecure and unreliable. What confused her was that this man who had been "the essence of a priest" had moved away from both her and his God, and she felt responsible. Franz, too, was disturbed. As a Jew writing a tribute to a Catholic saint, he saw in Hollnsteiner's defection an undermining of his own convictions.

The letters Alma received from friends and relatives in Europe were rare, and greatly anticipated. In July 1941, Hanna Fuchs-Robettin wrote, in English, "Our parents are in Marseilles waiting for Portuguese visas . . . Poor old Papa is very weak . . . and wants to join the children in the States."[2] Hanna and her family planned to travel on to America. Rudolf Werfel died soon after her letter was written. Through Fry's intervention, he had escaped the worst of the persecution and spent his last weeks in freedom. Franz was grateful and aligned himself with Fry's Emergency Rescue Committee, donating both time and funds. Meanwhile, during their stay in London, Hanna and her husband Herbert saw Anna, and Herbert began representing Franz's work in the English-speaking parts of the Continent.

By the summer of 1941, Franz finished *The Song of Bernadette*. Film rights sold almost at once for the then large sum of $50,000, and the Book-of-the-Month Club expressed serious interest. Alma and Franz felt optimistic about the future as they left for New York in September, planning to see old friends and meet with Franz's publishers. In the Eastern society, however, the conversation seemed to be limited to Hitler's conquests, and some people went on to speculate that the dictator might go so far as to try to take over America.

Franz increased his commitment to the many relief and refugee efforts. Through these organizations, he came into contact with a number of other activists and old friends, and felt he had been able to do something for his persecuted countrymen. Alma was not interested. She decided she was happier in California, far away from the war. After a few weeks in New York, the Werfels returned to Los Angeles and began the proceedings to make them citizens of the United States.

They considered California to be their home, but no sooner did they get there than they discovered that the man who had wanted to produce the film of *Bernadette* was on the verge of bankruptcy, and the Book-of-the-Month Club was concerned that the novel was too Roman Catholic to appeal to a mass American audience. Alma was distressed. She loved the book and thought it to be only a simple affirmation of faith. She couldn't understand how anyone could view the book as parochial; she respected her husband for having written it. Contrary to the conclusions of many readers and churchmen, *Bernadette* did not signal Franz's conversion to Roman Catholicism. Alma knew that it wouldn't and, remembering the negligible effect of Gustav's conversion to Christianity on those who had wanted to punish him for having been born a Jew, she didn't try to convince Franz to change his religion. She found herself envying her husband, since he had accomplished so much and she was doing so little.

Alma's own hopes were fading away: "We have built up our life in high style, but we have almost no money, and absolutely no capital. We sold our old car and have no prospect of getting a new one. Even if we were to battle for a new one, that would cost us a fortune, or rather, *the* fortune . . . Nature is empty and monotonous. Nature *creates* people. They have been here for two hundred years, and all they have created is a bit of Indian culture, and even that they deny. Add to that the gas stations and beauty parlors, they build those on the streets where it would be better for cars to be allowed to speed. Italy is really our home. Austria was only a poor preface, or so it has become since the war. Italy is homogeneous and has allowed mankind to rest for millennia on the blessed land. Those people who have brought forth such a blend of culture and nature are the only ones who have been really fulfilled since the time of the ancient Greeks."[3]

In March 1942, the Book-of-the-Month-Club accepted *Bernadette*. Franz was in the slump that invariably accompanies completion of a major work. Alma felt her husband "needs a new love, or a loving relationship. But that would mean great pain for me, since I live completely in and with him, and want nothing more — nor *can* want anything more."[4]

With *Bernadette*'s success they were invited into the Hollywood film community. At a party attended by Luise Rainer, who wanted to play the title role in the film of Franz's novel, and her husband Clifford Odets, the playwright, Alma met Erich Maria Remarque and developed a warm friendship with him. Here was a man with whom she could talk and drink; he was happy to keep his bottle of vodka while she poured from her Benedictine. Remarque addressed her as "Queen of the D.O.M. Benedictine," adding that a "toy without alcohol is artificial."[5]

In June 1942, Alma and Franz went to New York to visit his family. Alma had little patience left for any of the Werfels. Her widowed mother-in-law seemed worthy only of pity, something Alma did not easily give. Franz's sister Mizzi acted hatefully. Perhaps, Alma decided, it was just another trait of the family to make everyone's life miserable. She thought her whole trip had been ruined by Franz's relatives, but not much later she bought a house next door to her own in which "Mama" Werfel could spend her winters in the California sun.

Alma felt invigorated when she again began finding herself in the center of problems and gossip reminiscent of her life in Viennese society. One day she was having lunch with Golo Mann in the Beverly Wilshire Hotel; she felt compassion for this young man and wanted to help him out of the shell that seemed to separate him from his large, illustrious, and difficult family. Remarque happened to be sitting at a table near them, and as soon as he spotted Alma he ordered a bottle of fine old cognac to be brought from his room. Sitting down with Alma and her guest, Remarque monopolized the conversation and thwarted the hostess's purpose of giving Golo a dose of self-confidence.

The conversation turned to Hauptmann. When the younger man made a disparaging remark about her friend, Alma could not restrain herself. Golo had apparently decided Remarque and she were Nazi sympathizers because they were together in defending such men as Hauptmann and Richard Strauss. Alma was not arguing from politics but from practicalities. She thanked God that Hauptmann had not come to America to find himself living on charity at the age of eighty. She contended that Strauss had no choice but to remain in Germany, so dependent was he on German-speaking audiences for recognition. Golo, like many emigrés of the younger generation, saw leaving the Reich as a moral necessity. Alma believed a person left if it was imperative and possible. She would not condemn those who had stayed to live out their lives in their homeland.

Alma marked her sixty-third birthday remembering the words of the poet Annette Kolb, who, asked how she felt to be a refugee in America, said, "Grateful and unhappy." [6] Shortly afterward, in September 1942, Alma and Franz moved into their house at 610 North Bedford Drive in Beverly Hills, on a rather unpretentious block in a neighborhood both elegant and convenient. They no longer had to be slaves to their automobile: they could walk only a few blocks to shops and restaurants. In the house Alma put a new Steinway piano and a radio to replace the one the Zsolnays had provided for the house in Semmering. There was plenty of space for herself, Franz, and the butler, but there was no room at all for guests — precisely what Alma wanted. The house had been built for the actress May Robson and needed a few repairs but no major renovation. The move was fast and simple.

Knowing that they were going to stay in America, and wanting some reminders of her own country, friends, and family, Alma made efforts to have some of her possessions brought from Vienna, a task accomplished by prevailing either upon friends or, more often, American military personnel. Alma obtained quite a sizable number of the smaller items she had owned in Vienna and Semmering; they included books, papers, dishes, serving pieces, and other objects that would fit into suitcases. Each time something arrived in Beverly Hills, she rejoiced in reestablishing a tie with the past. She didn't know what she still owned, what might have been destroyed, stolen, or otherwise removed from the large numbers of things she had left behind.

Franz was working with their friend Friedrich Torberg on a script for a film about the life of Zora Pasha, a woman whose flagrant adventures had been recounted to him and Alma as legend during their journey to Egypt. The project had seemed filled with promise, and it had taken a great deal of Franz's energy. It came to naught, however, and he was at loose ends, wasting time and wandering about the house in ways that made Alma irritable. They took in a Siamese kitten, but it was accidentally killed. While Franz mourned, Alma thought again that everything beautiful and lovable in her life was taken from her.

The post brought a long-awaited communication from Anna in London, where, approaching her fortieth birthday, she was thriving, working harder and with more success on her sculptures. She had ended her affair with an architect whose business deals had been of a questionable nature, and she had married her fourth husband, the conductor Anatole Fistoulari. It amused Alma that her daughter had returned to musical circles, but she would have no respect for her new son-in-law — "Anyone can shake a stick." [7]

When Franz began work on a new play, *Jacobowsky & the Colonel,* optimism flooded the house. He was not feeling entirely well but he was prodded by Alma and Reinhardt to continue working on what seemed to be a very promising idea. Reinhardt had appointed himself godfather of the new project. The farce concerned the plight of a high-ranking Polish officer and a slight Polish Jew at the time of the fall of France. By March of 1943 Franz had made enough progress on the play to want to take a brief trip to New York, where there was always business to be attended to with publishers and agents, and where the couple would immerse themselves in a social and cultural milieu so different from the one in which they lived in California. On the way back to the West Coast, when the train stopped in Chicago, Franz and Alma took a taxi to the aquarium, where Alma was discomforted by the sight of fish swimming aimlessly in glass tanks.

In Beverly Hills, Alma attended to some of Franz's business matters to save him the tiresome paperwork and correspondence. She could handle basic tasks and represent her husband's interests, though occasionally she managed to get badly confused. Once, when she had drunk some Benedictine and couldn't hear clearly in the long-distance telephone connection, she ended up unwittingly agreeing to sell one set of rights to *Bernadette* several times over. Alma never admitted that she missed anything and never confessed to her hearing impairment. One evening when she, Franz, and Kathe Berl were sitting outside their house in the Hollywood

Hills listening to the distant sound of music from the Bowl, the wind changed and swept the sounds away from even the keenest ears. Franz and Kathe, sensing what had happened, commented quickly and casually that it was as if God had turned down the volume. Their remarks put Alma at ease and she confessed, "I thought I was the only one who couldn't hear."

The mix-up regarding the rights to *Bernadette* had to be resolved by friends and associates. Prominent among these were Gustave and Gusti Arlt, he a member of the faculty at the University of California at Los Angeles, and Adolph and Isolde Klarmann, he of the University of Pennsylvania. Problems of a higher order arose regarding the new *Jacobowsky*, however. Franz went on writing and rewriting in his blue notebooks while Reinhardt proceeded with plans for a New York production of the play. Sam Behrman began the adaptation; Odets soon took over the job. Ultimately, Franz did most of the adapting, with great irritation since working for the American stage was by no means his forte, and his mind was filled with ideas for a utopian "travelogue" later to be *The Star of the Unborn*.

As weeks of tiresome work passed, the author learned the hard way that the copyright laws of the United States differed significantly from those under which he had worked in Austria. Unlike Goethe in *The Sorrows of Young Werther*, he had no right to expand on the experiences or tales told to him by others and to call them fictional works of his own. Reinhardt's son was one of several people who made it known that various incidents and characters portrayed in Franz's new play had been the creation of others and were based on stories told to the author by them. When the situation exploded, Franz felt as if he had been caught writing unauthorized autobiographies of people whom he had merely passed on his path of exile. He hired an attorney and faced

Alma and Franz Werfel in Semmering

Bruno Walter, the conductor

Anna Schindler Moll, Alma's mother

Thornton Wilder, American author and playwright

Erich Maria Remarque, author of *All Quiet on the Western Front,* who called Alma "the Queen of the D.O.M. Benedictine"

Alma and Franz Werfel in their California home

OPPOSITE

Top: Franz Werfel in 1945, shortly before his death

Bottom: Anna Mahler, Los Angeles, 1954

"The Power of Words," a room in Alma's New York apartment

"The Power of Music," a room in Alma's New York apartment

Alma Mahler Werfel, about 1960

Alma with Anna Mahler in New York, about 1960

A portrait of Alma by her friend Kathe Berl

an accumulation of suits and settlements that cost him more money than he felt Jacobowsky and his damned Colonel deserved. Worse, all of the litigations took time away from the revisions of the play, and it was scheduled to go into rehearsal in the fall.

Alma was worried and tried to protect Franz from pressure as best she could, setting up a schedule that would give him quiet time in which to work and provide a pattern for their days. Essentially, she felt that Franz should work whenever he felt the urge to do so. If he wanted to rest, the whole household rested; if he wanted to eat, a meal was served. Alma rarely invited friends to visit when Franz was productive, but if he wanted to spend a social evening she would at once summon the Schoenbergs, Reinhardt, the Manns, Erich Korngold and his wife, the artist Fritzi Massary, the author Bruno Frank and his wife (Massary's daughter), the novelist Alfred Neumann, and, almost always, the Arlts. There were also a number of friends from the East Coast who were frequently visiting California, like Marlene Dietrich and her husband Hermann Kesser, also a writer. Ganna Walska, Alma's old acquaintance who had long ago married Joseph Fraenkel, turned up in Beverly Hills. After her husband's death she had secretly wed an Indianologist who slept on bare wood boards and who, after their divorce, moved to Tibet.

In the summer of 1943, the heat descended and Franz was not accomplishing much on *Jacobowsky*. Alma convinced him that he ought to escape to the cooler and greener town of Santa Barbara. Lotte Lehmann, the great singer, helped arrange for rooms there at the Biltmore and provided the name of a doctor who would be available should Franz need him. Alma was the trip's chief engineer, but her tactics had been so subtle that Franz apologized to her constantly for having deserted her for such a lovely, quiet spot, where he

was working quickly and living comfortably in his own private cottage. Alma was having a fine time on her own,
though she was surprised when Franz wrote that the play
had changed its complexion and no longer seemed to be a
farce, but, rather, a piece of serious theater. He sent the
manuscript to Alma for her comments. She sent words of
praise before Franz went on to his next task, then she passed
the pages to her husband's new secretary, Albrecht Joseph,
whose job was to transcribe the text from scratchy work-
books into presentable form. That young man was invalu-
able, a good worker as well as an interesting, articulate
companion. Joseph had performed the same duties for
Thomas Mann while he wrote *Doctor Faustus*.

Franz prolonged his stay in Santa Barbara. In August Alma
joined him, glad to be away from the heat of Beverly Hills
and from the society there, which began to seem to turn and
feed on itself. Shortly before she visited Franz, she went to
the Schoenbergs' to hear Eduard Steuermann play Arnold's
new Piano Concerto. Leopold Stokowski was to give the
work its first performance, and the composer was insisting
on at least forty-five rehearsals. Alma had championed
Schoenberg for more than three decades, but she was dum-
founded by his demands. "I don't believe that Beethoven
needed even one rehearsal in order to get to know his own
work," she wrote in her diary. "This kind of mathematical
method is very far from what we know as music, and leads
only into strange and distant areas. Oskar Kokoschka's genius was a thousand times greater, and his magic was
unique." [8] Alma's training with Zemlinsky had led her only
through Schoenberg's earliest works, not into the style he
called his method of composing with twelve equal tones. She
could be forgiven her lack of understanding of her friend's
late music, but her comparison between Schoenberg and Kokoschka was clearly founded in emotion, not in reason.

When one of Alma's acquaintances was arranging her daughter's wedding, Alma watched the procedures with horror. "America is dreadful. It takes every bit of poetry out of the world!"[9] Whenever she longed for Vienna, she remembered what the seer had predicted: she would return home after six years, would not want to stay, and would not have Franz. They stayed in Santa Barbara through Alma's sixty-fourth birthday, then returned to Beverly Hills.

One evening when Alma was particularly dissatisfied, the composer Korngold listed for her all the important events they had had the privilege of witnessing during their lifetimes: Strauss's *Elektra,* Gustav's *Das Lied von der Erde,* Stravinsky's *Petrouchka* and *Sacre du printemps,* Schoenberg's *Pierrot Lunaire* — all these were landmarks of their era. To this list Alma added Pfitzner's *Palestrina* and Charpentier's *Louise.* As they enumerated these accomplishments, Alma felt better. These were what mattered, not the wars or the turmoil of the decades.

They marked Franz's fifty-third birthday and the completion of *Jacobowsky* with a modest celebration on the evening of September 12. Late at night, after too many cigarettes and too much wine, Franz suffered a serious heart attack. Alma, terrified, summoned Dr. Wolff, who came and administered digitalis. The doctor confirmed Alma's opinion that Franz had to stop smoking. When told that he had poisoned himself with nicotine, Franz merely laughed. Torberg and Remarque came to visit, but neither Alma nor Franz could summon much interest in seeing people. Dr. Wolff suggested that they return to Santa Barbara. They had been there at the Biltmore for barely two days when Franz began feeling ill again, and they reached Bedford Drive only a matter of hours before he experienced a second seizure. The doctor returned, this time with consultants. They administered morphine and oxygen, but it took three full days to calm the patient and ease his pain. Franz lay despondent. To make things worse, word came of the deaths of Max Reinhardt and Paul Stefan. Alma felt that death itself was a contagious disease; that was the reason she would never put a photograph of a living person next to one of someone who was dead. She all but gave up hope. Franz did not seem to be gaining strength or will, and she wrote, "Emigration is a severe illness . . . and the fact that all of our friends come to ill is not a surprise." [10]

The doctors waited until the third week of November for Franz to be strong enough to have x-rays. During the procedure he had another attack, one that frightened even the physicians. Alma felt she couldn't go on living without him. She was his only source of loving care and companionship, but, she wrote, "in the evening he is tired, and in the morning he smells, as a wife should never have to sense." [11] Franz was ashamed of his incontinence and could not help himself; his condition was not improving. On December 14 he was stricken again. Father Cyril Fischer, a Viennese priest whom they had met in Santa Barbara, wrote to ask Alma if she would be "the angel who leads Franz Werfel to Christendom." [12] Alma felt like no angel. She said in her diary, "Marriage is really like an egg, in which two people are surrounded and separated from the world." [13]

The December twenty-third premiere of the filmed version of *The Song of Bernadette* was marked by all of the glitter and fanfare characterizing Hollywood in the early 1940s. Franz and Alma saw to it that their friends and associates, including the stagestruck butler and chauffeur August Hess, went to the gala. The Werfels stayed home together. Franz was stronger; he could talk and laugh, and he was interested in music and the outside world. Alma, too, felt better since friends such as Torberg and the Arlts had come into the house to help her tend Franz and give her some free hours.

When the Arlts visited on New Year's Eve, they tried to keep spirits high. None of them saw much to celebrate.

On January 1, 1944, Anna sent Alma a cable wishing her happiness and saying that she wanted very much to be able to visit in this new year with her baby daughter Marina Fistoulari. The message and the accompanying flood of memories sent Alma into fits of weeping. That, she knew, would do no good. At least Franz seemed finally to be on the way to recovery, with a desire to live. By February he was back to worrying about the clashes still surrounding *Jacobowsky*. Alma tried to keep signs of trouble from him, but his mind was so agile and curious that she could not deny him the truth, and sometimes the complications of the publication and production seemed even to amuse him.

Spring came, and Franz no longer required constant attention. Once she could do away with the fear that he was about to die, Alma made herself recall the other times in her life when she had thought she would not be able to go on living in the absence of another. She played Bach on the piano and began to dress and groom herself more carefully. She was in good health. She would almost certainly outlive Franz, as she had outlived so many others.

14

Years of Uncertainty

EARLY IN 1944, while Franz was recuperating, Marlene Dietrich and her husband had prevailed upon Carroll Righter to construct Franz Werfel's horoscope. The astrologer knew only that the person about whom he was writing had been born on September 10, 1890, in Prague. This person, Righter wrote, needed to take special care of his health from August 1943 through November 1944, and particularly in January 1944. That month had already passed by the time Franz read the chart.

For you practically have the chart of a genius which expresses itself through your idealism which is the strongest part of your nature. It is not the idealism of a light and frothy kind at all, but rather one that accomplishes your greatest amount of effectiveness through being aware of "the sins of the world" and through being so heartbroken by unfortunate world conditions that you are impelled to . . . whether

through lecturing, writing or other intellectual media is unimportant . . . place such facts before the general public
. . . The writer has never had a chart like this to delineate.
It is at once and the same time a chart of idealism, magnan-
imous and generous, with a lordly and lofty approach to all
problems and thoughts that come into your mind and before
you — sort of a combination of Florence Nightingale and Sir
Lancelot!! — and then in some ways and in practically the
same breath you are a "fussbudget" of the first water, being
most exacting where all details are concerned and almost
losing sight of "the woods for the individual trees"!! This
apparent contradiction can be used to advantage IF you use
the meticulousness indicated to work out carefully every word
uttered . . . but you need to have almost greater discrimi-
nation than a human can have to balance the two . . . You
would be wise to have someone about you — whether a secretary or one in a more intimate capacity — who retains for
a long period of time the inspiration that is yours and that
can attach themselves to your ideas and who can apply them
to Life itself and give you steadiness and a picture of how
your thoughts can be utilized in a practical manner.[1]

The analysis went on to cover another two years, well into
the future.

Franz was fascinated, especially when he read that he had
already managed to live through a period of ominous aspects. Alma was intrigued but not convinced. Franz's illness
had taken a toll on her own well-being, and she felt that her
husband did not appreciate the attention she had bestowed
upon him. Earlier, he had diligently courted her, trying to
rewin her affection every day. Now, as he recovered, he remembered little of the days and weeks she had spent at his
bedside with little hope or companionship.

Alma regretted even more than Franz did Torberg's decision to move from Los Angeles to New York in the summer

of 1944. Just before he was to depart, the friend brought Alma a photograph of Oskar. She stared at the face that was so familiar yet so strange and distant. She never thought of Oskar without experiencing a sense of regret, but that, too, had receded in her emotions. Looking at this picture, she had the feeling that both of their lives had progressed in the best ways.

She prided herself in being interested in the future, having little use for the past, especially now that she had a home in America. Franz encouraged her to see her new friend the humorist Ludwig Bemelmans, who tended to visit in the company of a string of different mistresses. Franz saw Alma's disapproval of Ludwig's style and life, but even that disapproval brought out her spunk, and her new friend could always make her laugh.

Good news arrived from Vienna. After seven years of proscription, a symphony by Gustav was to be performed there; in honor of the occasion, a memorial plaque would be unveiled in the Concert Hall. Both Alma and Franz felt a renewed hope. She looked forward to a possible increase in the royalties she received from Mahler's publishers. Franz moved slowly back to his desk and the notebooks holding sketches for *The Star of the Unborn,* his greatest work.

Late in August, Kathe Berl visited from New York. Alma wanted to be able to make noise around the house and entertain friends, but she could not talk Franz into going to Santa Barbara to work until they had all celebrated Alma's sixty-fifth birthday together in Beverly Hills. He left fearing that he would be separated from his wife on his own birthday, September 10, and bade Kathe a tearful farewell in the belief that he would not live to see her again. His fears were unfounded. On Franz's birthday Alma and Kathe piled into the car, with August at the wheel, to drive to Santa Barbara with a stylish feast of prune dumplings baked with the typical Czech noodle dough Franz had loved since boyhood.

At home in the autumn, the Werfels led quiet lives for reasons going beyond Franz's illness and Alma's concern: their friends were aging and slowing down. Franz worked with his secretary for four or five hours each day, dictating from his notebooks until Alma entered the study to announce lunch. Sometimes in the afternoon, when Franz was resting, Alma invited Al Joseph to join her for a drink. He declined — he did not drink in the afternoon. "Oh, yes, of course, you are a Jew," Alma answered. That led the clever man of letters to list the Jews who did indeed drink in the afternoons, evenings, even the mornings. At this friendly protestation, Alma would laugh. She felt that *her* remarks about the Jews were different from others'. She was speaking, after all, about a large group, not about individuals.

Alma enjoyed the company of Franz's young coworker, but she didn't need to wait for him to join her before pouring a drink. She was consuming as much as a bottle of Benedictine every day. She continued to order her favorite sweet libation by the case. The clerks at the neighborhood liquor store were well acquainted with both Alma and her butler August. Now and then, even they were surprised that so many bottles were being delivered to 610 North Bedford Drive.

Anna and Anatole cabled Alma for money, but she refused to send the Fistoularis any more than they already had received from her. Alma had been billed for nearly 3000 Austrian schillings for electrical work allegedly done on the house on the Hohe Warte, and she was feeling victimized by unseen sources. She tried to sell Gustav's manuscript of *Das Lied von der Erde,* but could not find a buyer who would pay her $7500 price. In the face of financial pressures, Alma and Franz thought that they needed to go to New York. In April 1945, Alma wrote to the manager of the St. Moritz requesting him to reserve rooms 1516 through 1519 for a period in the fall. He replied that he thought the suite she was ordering would be a bit extravagant for only two people, and suggested taking only three rooms. Alma delayed making a decision.

In the summer, Franz went to work in the quiet of Santa Barbara with his physician as both attendant and companion. *The Star of the Unborn* was nearly finished, and though Franz was still skeptical about the value of the work, his strength had returned and he seemed optimistic. Alma was not well. She had been running a low-grade fever for some weeks and, apart from her being exhausted and depressed, the doctors could not determine the cause. Twice she was put on a penicillin treatment. Alma had to wonder what would have happened had this new "miracle drug" been available when Gustav was dying; still, it did not cure her own disease. One of the physicians guessed that her teeth were at fault, so Alma had seven of them pulled; actually they were fine, and might otherwise have lasted her for the rest of her life.

Eventually, time provided the cure. Alma felt better as she spent the summer weeks alone knowing that Franz was working and was well tended. He wrote to her frequently to say how much he missed her and how guilty he felt about having left her by herself in Beverly Hills. He aimed to write twenty pages each day on his novel, and he was having a good time, going to the movies almost every evening with his friend. Alma didn't like films; she had trouble with English, and could not always hear or understand the soundtracks. Worse, when she did understand, she became totally involved in the plots, fretting over the fate of her favorite Erroll Flynn as if he would not survive the scene or the reel.

Alma visited Santa Barbara on August 10 and was satisfied to find herself unnecessary, almost a hindrance to the men's good times. August had driven her up the coast, and when she went back home on the thirteenth she was reassured by how happy and healthy Franz had seemed in the private bungalow on the corner of the hotel's spacious grounds. The morning after she reached home, the mail brought a special-delivery envelope with the poem "To Alma (After Parting)":

> *How very much I love you,*
> *I had not known,*
> *Before I was struck by*
> *These sudden separations.*
> *I am let of blood*
> *From so much suffering.*
> *Why do we realize things*
> *Only after they have been taken from us?*
>
> *That which you touched yesterday*
> *Now stares radiantly.*
> *Things seemed to be suffering sorely,*
> *Like animals.*
> *Not my life, but yours, was theirs,*
> *And now they live no more.*
>
> *I wander around*
> *Introspective and shy,*
> *Overflowing with fear in my heart.*
> *At home I try to make myself blind*
> *Because time is fickle,*
> *But space is true.*
>
> *In the nearby room, your life went on,*
> *You breathed there, called me, laughed, spoke.*
> *Oh!*
> *And I, and I — my heart is broken.*
> *Accept it, take it and don't be afraid for me.*
> *Accept it, take it and don't be afraid for me.*[2]

The poem did frighten Alma, but it was best for both of them that Franz stay in Santa Barbara. When he telephoned on August 17 to announce the completion of *The Star of the Unborn,* she was pleased by his accomplishment as well by the prospect of his return home in a happy and strong state. Alma tried to convince her husband to find someone to drive him back to Beverly Hills immediately, during the evening's cool. He insisted that August drive up to fetch him on the next day. When the car returned to Bedford Drive late in the hot afternoon, Franz's face was ash-white, and he took directly to his bed.

Alma was distraught. Her husband had seemed to be so much better in Santa Barbara, and she dreaded the thought of having to go through another siege of illness. Dr. Wolff came at once and administered morphine, therewith confirming Alma's worst fears. She stayed by the bed while Franz slept fitfully, then watched him break into a cold sweat and lose sensation in his extremities. Dr. Wolff was not to be found, but Alma finally located one of his affiliates, Julius Bauer, who answered her summons along with several consulting physicians. One of the doctors stayed with the patient throughout the night, allowing Alma to take some rest. By morning Franz's fever had risen again, and the congress of consultants reconvened. Bed rest was ordered, and during that Franz regained enough strength to rework some of his poems.

On August 25, he went out to dinner with Alma, Bruno Walter, and his daughter Lotte. The Walters had bought the house next door to the Werfels on Bedford Drive, and they rang the bell at 610 a few minutes before they were expected. As was his habit, Bruno sat down at the piano. This time he played bits of Smetana's opera *The Bartered Bride.* The lighthearted tunes inspired Franz to emerge from his room doing a gigue. His dance set the tone for an evening full of gossip and gaiety.

All went home tired and happy. On Sunday morning, the twenty-sixth, Franz and Alma lounged in the sun until lunch, after which Franz had a short nap, dressed, and went eagerly to work. Alma retired to the parlor with her books and music. After a few hours, as was her habit, she went to look in on her husband, to see whether he had made any progress and ascertain whether he wanted tea or company. She tapped on the door, called his name, knocked more loudly, called again, and entered. Franz was lying beside his desk, dead.[3]

The Arlts arrived within minutes. Alma massaged her husband's body and administered the oxygen routinely stored by his bed, but there was nothing to be done. She had lost her sweet man-child. She held his wallet, a tatty compilation of medals of the Virgin Mary, souvenirs of Bernadette, letters from his mother and Alma. The doctor gave Alma a sedative, and the hearse took the corpse away.

Franz's funeral took place on the morning of August 29 in the Pierce Brothers Mortuary in Beverly Hills. He had not wanted a religious service. Alma arranged that he was interred just as he had described the burial of the hero F.W. in *The Star of the Unborn* — in a tuxedo and silk shirt, with glasses in his breast pocket, a spare shirt, and several extra handkerchiefs. The eulogy was delivered by their friend Georg Moenius of the Franciscan Fathers.

On the morning of the funeral, Al Joseph, who was one of the pallbearers, stopped at Alma's house to check on her and take her on to the mortuary if necessary. Noting the late hour and aware that the mourners were already in their places, Joseph prodded the widow to leave her house. "I never go," she said.

She was busy rewriting Father Moenius's eulogy, which did not please her. Joseph tried to explain that another corpse was waiting to be blessed after Franz's and they could not postpone the service. Alma went on editing. At the mortuary, Bruno Walter rose to play a short piano piece by Franz Schubert. The assemblage included Igor Stravinsky and his wife, the Schoenbergs, Otto Preminger, the Mann family, and the Otto Klemperers. They continued to wait for the service to begin. Nothing happened. Several of the more knowing mourners suggested that someone else might play some music, but even the finest musicians in the group would not get up to perform after Maestro Walter. Moments passed, and the silence became oppressive. Walter returned to the piano to play the same Schubert piece again. Another round of grim, appreciative glances passed among the guests. The next group of mourners was waiting impatiently outside the door of the small chapel. Twenty more minutes passed. Walter played the same piece for a third time. Finally, Father Moenius entered, without Alma, to perform the ritual. By then, the reaction of the gathered crowd was more one of relief than of sadness. The eulogy began: "While we are sitting here on earth, Franz Werfel and Karl Kraus are shaking hands in Heaven." It was highly inappropriate. Kraus had supported Franz during his youth, but Alma had always detested the journalist. And Heaven was not part of her domain.

The day after the service in the mortuary, the Arlts drove Alma to Franz's grave in the Rosedale Cemetery. Father Moenius met them there to bless the remains in the presence of the widow.

15

The Last Years

ALMA TOOK SEDATIVES and slept in the hospital bed that had been brought in for Franz during the last months of his life. The Arlts stayed with her much of the time, tending to whatever business was urgent and directing August in his chores. In late October 1945, the friends succeeded in convincing Alma that she would benefit from a change of scenery. The three went together to New York, where Alma was lonelier still and frightened as she had not been before. Black people provoked her anxiety; so, in those weeks, did the impersonality of Manhattan's streets. She was glad to go home.

In Beverly Hills, she was comforted to have Bruno Walter living next door and the Arlts on call for help and companionship. Surrounded by memories of Franz, she was comfortable. Suddenly Hedda Hopper proclaimed over the radio that Alma would soon marry Bruno. The alleged bride was furious, and told the press that it was the most absurd and tasteless thing she had ever heard. Bruno walked across the lawn to visit, and Alma railed and fumed. "But would that be so terrible?" he asked.

Another shock came in a letter from Vienna. Sister Ida, Alma's trusted servant, had married a former Nazi named Wagner. Ida wrote that bombs had destroyed much of Alma's property; among the losses were the desks once belonging to Gustav and Franz and the papers and manuscripts stored with them.

It was not until she returned to New York in January 1946 to hear Bruno conduct Gustav's Fourth Symphony that Alma realized the extent of her loneliness. In front of Carnegie Hall after the performance she walked alone trying to find a taxi to take her through the ice and snow to her lonely hotel room. There she sat in the dark to think. She decided she had not really liked Gustav's music, had not been very interested in Franz's writing, but had been — and still was — impressed by Oskar's work. He was the one who mattered, and she wanted to find him and go to him. She felt better, but did nothing to put herself in touch with the artist beyond the occasional letters and telegrams they had been exchanging for more than thirty years.

At the age of sixty-seven, Alma had to face the prospect of living alone, without parents, children, husbands, or much likelihood of a lover. Newspapers and radio stations around the world had announced Franz's death, and Alma received many letters and telegrams — even more than she had received when Gustav had died — but these did not make any difference to her when she went to bed without anyone to whom she could so much as say "goodnight." Her most constant companion was the servant August, known as "the beautiful August" because of his good looks, fey charm, and theatrical pretensions. He billed himself as a poet and composer, and appeared in several operettas with a German-speaking troupe in Los Angeles. His lack of culture appalled Alma. "How could you not know that?" she would scream at him. What he did know was how to deal with and handle her. In spite of spats that resembled lovers' quarrels and occasionally led to a temporary "divorce," Alma always asked August to return to her service. She paid him well, and when they finally separated he bought a house in Los Angeles and lived off his savings.

Willi Haas, Franz's childhood friend who had been portrayed as the guide and companion of the hero in *The Star of the Unborn,* wrote to invite Alma to join him in India, where he could offer her a room in a paradisical villa on the Malabar coast.[1] She was tempted, but there were too many business matters needing attention. Adolf Klarmann was serving as executor of Franz's estate. The will had declared that everything would go to Alma and then, after her death, to Anna. The war had complicated this relatively simple scheme. The American rights to Franz's work belonged to Alma, but the foreign rights were under dispute. Franz's older sister, Hanna Fuchs-Robettin, decreed it was unjust for Franz to be allowed to have overlooked members of his immediate family. She wanted to sue Alma and secure the foreign rights to Werfel's work for herself, her sister Mizzi Rieser, and Mama Werfel. Hanna pursued legal action until it became evident that Zsolnay had cleverly put everything to which he held authority into Alma's name, where it was secure even under Austria's changing governments. The unpleasant battles, through which Alma was represented by the New York attorney Rudolf Montner, were resolved entirely to her satisfaction. She would never again have to worry about funds.[2]

For help and friendship in the practical areas of everyday life Alma continued to rely on the Arlts. Gustav Arlt was negotiating for the disposition of Franz's papers in the library of the University of California at Los Angeles, and Alma was working with a secretary to arrange the many randomly piled notebooks and sheets, as well as to decipher her dead husband's scrawl. She devoted herself to this project and felt that it kept her close to Franz. Contrary to some of her later claims, however, Alma did not complete or significantly edit any of Werfel's work.

In June 1946, Alma became a citizen of the United States. The occasion was duly marked with champagne and a small party. She was beginning to be restless again. Franz's papers were almost in order. Alma had been hurt and annoyed when *The Star of the Unborn* was badly received; the critics had expected something quite different from the author whom they identified with *Bernadette*. For the first time, Alma wanted to get away from the memory of Franz. She turned to the piano, and when she injured her right hand, her friend Kathe sent Scriabin's Etudes for the left hand alone, which she played with fascination and delight. She also played Chopin, and improvised on opera scores, including *Manon Lescaut*. But she did not have enough to do.

Alma booked a berth on the train to New York, where she spoke briefly on the radio about Werfel, and realized that even when she was hearing *Tristan* at the Metropolitan Opera her thoughts were still with him. She went home, concluded that Beverly Hills was not a place where she could live happily by herself, and thought seriously of moving back to Vienna. There was reason to believe that her Viennese business affairs were seriously entangled and her possessions lost, so she set about planning a trip to Europe.

A letter to Walter Gropius told him she was about to leave for an indefinite period, perhaps for good. He responded in September 1946 from his home in Cambridge, Massachusetts, apologizing for not having written to her when her husband had died. He and his wife were in Mexico and the

Rocky Mountains at the time, and the first thing he had heard was that Alma was about to marry Bruno Walter. "No," he wrote, "we couldn't be angry with you; a much too important part of my life was bound up with you . . . and Mutzi remains as something that we had (even though we've spent the later parts of our lives apart)."

In December, Alma received a request from London to help Mengelberg sell his manuscripts of Gustav's Fourth Symphony and the final movement of *Das Lied von der Erde.* She objected strongly, feeling that the conductor could not really need the money enough to justify selling the scores. Her trip was delayed repeatedly as she worked to resolve her American affairs. She refused to allow Franz's early poems to be published, saying that the release of these "very immature" works would damage his reputation. In deciding to bequeath some of Gustav's papers and photographs to the library in Vienna, she well knew it would be much more difficult for that library to procure the material than it was for her to proffer it. She had no idea what was actually remaining in her estate in Vienna.

Late in the summer of 1947, Alma left for Europe.[4] From the start, everything seemed to go wrong. Her plane from New York had to make an unscheduled stop in Newfoundland, where a pocket edition of Plato's *Republic* and a flask of Benedictine helped her withstand the day-long wait for the next plane. When she arrived in London, she was greeted by Anna, Anatole, and young Marina. Alma was shocked by how tired her forty-three-year-old daughter looked, and didn't think her new granddaughter at all pretty. She left quickly, satisfied only in the knowledge that Anna was comfortable, working well, and apparently content with her family.

After arriving in Vienna by another plane and checking into a modest room in the Hotel Krantz, Alma walked

around the city. She had heard tales of the destruction but
was shocked to see the Opera, the Burgtheater, and the cathedral in ruins. Next she sought her old friends. Sister Ida
seemed resigned to an unhappy future as Mrs. Wagner. Most
of the people Alma had known were either dead or gone;
those whom she could find seemed haggard and downtrod-
den. The only old friend whose life seemed almost un-
changed was the widowed Helene Berg, who had lived out
the war years in the country, faced Gestapo questioning
about Alban and his work, and retreated into her own private world of the occult. As Alma talked with the woman
whose world had once been so similar to her own, she realized that Helene had slipped away from reality, something
Alma did not want to do.

Then began the tedious and frustrating task of trying to
trace her possessions. The more she followed and wove together the various threads, the more she knew she could not
think of trying to settle again in Vienna. Bitterness and anti-
Semitism had not ended with the war, and she was still
damned because she had married two Jews. In numerous
offices, in conversations with countless sneering bureaucrats,
Alma confirmed that after her mother's death Carl Moll had
taken control of the entire estate and had given away or sold
the works of art that were under his trust for her. His plan
had been to get the cash needed to escape with his daughter
and son-in-law. These three were among the many suicides
on the day the Russians marched into Vienna.

Alma felt as if she were walking through a desert expanse
with only corpses in view. Her house in Semmering had been
sold to the Russians and "redecorated"; Oskar's mural over
the fireplace had been whitewashed. Her old house on the
Hohe Warte had been all but destroyed by American bombs.
The Molls' house in the same neighborhood had escaped
almost unscathed. It should have gone to Alma, but her half

sister had burned their mother's will, and now Alma was given the chance to buy the house for the equivalent of only a few hundred dollars. She knew the value of the striking building Hoffmann had designed, and she could still imagine Gustav's bounding up to the front door and into the hallway, so happy to see his young bride. Alma stared at the house, turned, and walked away from it for ever.

She was most infuriated by the fact that Moll had sold the Munch painting Walter had bought for her on the occasion of Manon's birth. If she could retrieve nothing else, she would crusade for the return of *The Midnight Sun*. She knew by then, however, that there were going to be no easy or immediate victories for her in Vienna. She returned to America by way of London with the conviction she would never see her homeland again.

Alma hired American lawyers to work on her behalf, but she had virtually no chance of winning her case. In the process of giving Moll and her stepsister the powers of attorney over her possessions, including the house in Semmering and various works of art, Alma had let herself believe the arrangements were only *pro forma* — she would soon be back in Vienna to resume her life. By writing down what she thought was a friendly agreement, she had relinquished all claims, and Carl's actions had been within legal boundaries. Alma tried to argue on moral grounds, but in the eyes of many Viennese officials what she had done by marrying Mahler and Werfel was much more despicable than what Carl Moll had done when he sold objects she thought still belonged to her. Bitterness engulfed Alma, and did not abate. Her family and her country had dunned her out of what was rightfully hers. She was being blamed for the shame and the sins of men whom she had married, men who had died and left her alone. She sat alone in the house in Beverly Hills. Soon she would be seventy.

Needlessly, Alma worried about money. She perpetrated a scheme reminiscent of her multiple sales of the rights to *Bernadette* when she offered her manuscript of Bruckner's Third Symphony to several different dealers simultaneously, asking a minimum of $5000 for it, getting nothing. A few months later, she tried to sell Franz's manuscript of *Musa Dagh* to the Armenian Evangelical Church in New York, where he had been honored and feted, but the institution did not have the money Alma asked. As had been the case in Vienna, property and possessions seemed to bring her trouble and frustrations.

In the early part of 1948, Anna spent a month with her mother in Beverly Hills. The two reestablished the relationship that had waned through separations and dissatisfactions. Having her daughter around helped Alma regain interest in what was going on around her. When Anna went back to London, Alma decided to stay active. She looked for some controversy, and found it easily.

Thomas Mann's novel *Doctor Faustus* had been published, a work of great genius and import with some dubious provenance. In creating the fictional composer Adrian Leverkuehn, Mann had drawn on the technique of composing with twelve tones, each equal to the others as espoused and taught by Schoenberg. By the time the novel appeared, the method had spread far beyond the small circle of Schoenberg students and disciples. But to many, Mann's hero was clearly Schoenberg. Though the author had named many real and living people in his text, he had neither mentioned nor credited the composer upon whom Adrian had evidently been modeled. Alma, a friend of Schoenberg and Mann, was happy to find herself in the middle.

There are many recountings of what was to turn into a legendary literary battle. One of the clearest descriptions of Alma's role appeared in the "Letters to the Editor" column of *The Saturday Review* at the start of 1949. Schoenberg wrote:

> Thomas Mann has taken advantage of my literary property . . . He did this without my permission and even without my knowledge . . . The supposition of one reviewer, that he obtained information about his technique from Bruno Walter and Stravinsky, is probably wrong; because Walter does not know anything of composition with twelve tones, and Stravinsky does not take any interest in it . . .
>
> I learned about this abuse by chance: I received a magazine containing a review of "Doctor Faustus"; wherein the twelve-notes composition was mentioned. Thereafter Mrs. Alma Mahler-Werfel told me that she had read the book and was very upset about his using my "theory" without naming me as author . . . When Mrs. Mahler-Werfel discovered this misuse of my property, she told Mann that this was my theory, whereupon he said, "Oh, does one notice that? Then perhaps Mr. Schoenberg will be angry!" . . . It was very difficult for Mrs. Mahler-Werfel to convince him that he must do something to correct this wrong.
>
> Finally I sent him a letter and showed him the possible consequences of ascribing my creation to another person . . . Much pressure from Mrs. Mahler-Werfel had still to be exerted to make Mann promise that every forthcoming copy of "Doctor Faustus" will carry a note giving me credit for the twelve-notes composition.[5]

Mann, in his response to Schoenberg's lengthy letter, said that he had been "astonished and grieved" by the whole affair. Schoenberg's ire, the author said, had been aroused by "meddling scandal mongers,"[6] and no pressure at all had been required to convince Mann to give the living composer his due credit. Whether Alma was the principal "meddling scandal monger"[7] made no difference. She had found herself involved in intrigue of Viennese proportions, and it made her adrenalin flow.

That summer, Eugene Ormandy conducted Gustav's Eighth Symphony at the Hollywood Bowl. He invited Alma to the rehearsals as well as the performance. She loved being recognized once more as the Widow Mahler, and offered her advice and comments freely. On her sixty-ninth birthday, August 31, 1948, well-wishers stopped at 610 North Bedford Drive throughout the morning, then a small midday party at the Arlts' was followed by a surprise buffet for sixty in Alma's own living room. Gifts included Erich Korngold's Violin Sonata, dedicated to her, and a book from Thomas Mann inscribed "To Alma, the personality . . . from her old friend and admirer."[8]

Alma felt more content than she had in a long while. She spent much time going through the letters and the papers accumulated over the years, trying to arrange them and make out the many different scripts. Her intention was to write or compile a book about her life. When she came across music, she went to the piano to play it, even though the doctor had warned her not to spend too much time at the keyboard, since she played with so much energy that it could become a strain on her body. Working with a secretary, she spent five months copying the letters Franz had sent her during their three decades together. She continued her practice of burning the letters written to her husbands and lovers. Some of her personal papers had been destroyed in the wars, but Alma still had boxes, drawers, and suitcases filled with the memorabilia of her life. In particular, she had saved everything she came across involving Oskar. As she was working, she received the news that Pfitzner had died; his widow sent pictures taken during his last days and a photograph of his death mask. Franz's death mask was somewhere stored in a shoebox. Alma was not sure where. This was one of the items remaining to be organized. Like the furniture and books from Franz's study, it was going to the library of the University of California at Los Angeles.

She did not have many visitors. Remarque stopped by, and Alma invited the composer-pianist Benjamin Britten and the tenor Jan Peerce to supper after a performance. The black cook, John, parted from his racing forms and produced a meal that would have taken anyone else days to prepare. He was a hero in the eyes of Alma's guests.

Anna visited her mother in the summer of 1949, and they talked about Anna's moving to California. She had separated from Fistoulari. Both the climate and the living conditions around Los Angeles were better suited than London to Anna's work on her large-scale sculptures. Mother and daughter found that they had more and more in common; they were, in fact, uncannily similar.

On her seventieth birthday, Alma received a letter from Oskar.

My dear Alma,
You're still a wild brat, just as when you were first carried away by *Tristan und Isolde* and used a quill to scrawl your comments on Nietzsche in your diary, in the same flying, illegible hand that I can make out only because I know your rhythm. Ask your friends, who are preparing to celebrate your birthday, not to tie you down to a silly, accidental, ephemeral calendar year. Tell them instead to give you a living, imperishable monument, by discovering a real American poet with a sixth sense for language, implication, rhythm and timbre — one who knows the emotional scale from tenderness to the most vicious sensuality, can extract it from my *Orpheus and Eurydice,* and will translate it into American (not modern English) — so that we may tell the world what

the two of us have done with and to each other, and may pass the living message of our love on to posterity. There has been nothing like it since the Middle Ages, for no couple has ever breathed into each other so passionately. So, there's a fine prospect for you, and as it will take time, you may as well forget calendar time. I don't even know when I was born, and I don't want to be reminded. I look forward to staging the translated *Orpheus* and at the same time kindling the lives of young generations with the fire that we two have set. We'll always be on the stage of life, we two, when disgusting banality, the trivial vestige of the contemporary world, will yield to a passion-born splendor. Look at the dull and prosaic faces about you — not one has known the thrill of playing with life, of relishing even death, of smiling at the bullet in your skull, the knife in your lungs. Not one — except your lover whom you once initiated into your mysteries. Remember that this love play is the only child we have. Take care of yourself, and spend your birthday without a hangover.

Your Oskar.[9]

In 1950, Anna left London with Marina and moved into a small house Alma had bought for her in Beverly Glen, near the university, where she would be teaching. The situation seemed ideal, but it was not long until Anna learned the liabilities of living so near her mother. For three decades, she had been away, visiting Alma, for the most part, only on her birthdays. Circumstances had not always permitted even that. In Los Angeles, Anna found herself in Alma's service, responding to the summonses of an old woman who appeared to fear being alone, and who seemed to be jealous of everyone and everything. Alma demanded from Anna the kind of attention she had expected from her husbands and lovers. She would telephone her daughter at any hour, pleading isolation and insisting on companionship. Since

Alma did not offer to send John or August with the car, Anna was left to dress Marina and take the bus connecting her house with her mother's by way of Sunset and Santa Monica boulevards. More often than not, by the time Anna hurried up to 610 North Bedford Drive, Alma was already in the company of two or three other people, all of whom she had summoned with the same urgency.

Anna was a great help to Alma in business matters, and she talked her mother into allowing the publication of Gustav's incomplete Tenth Symphony. In April 1950, the same month the agreement for issuing the Tenth was signed with Associated Music Publishers, Alma made another trip to New York. She was almost sure Manhattan was where she should live. There was more for her to do there, and the automobiles and patios of Southern California no longer suited her. She went back to Beverly Hills with the intention to move East as soon as possible.

On the night of July 13, 1951, Schoenberg died. Alma and Anna went at once to the family's Brentwood home to stay with the widow and children. The Mahler women could be of great help to others as well as to one another, but tension was growing between them once again. Romance had blossomed between Anna and Franz's former secretary, Albrecht Joseph. Alma did everything she could think of to put an end to the friendship: the young man was Jewish, and she had further convinced herself he was after Anna's money. She told each of them the worst she could think of about the other, horrid tales with only the smallest roots in fact. Anna and Al both knew Alma well enough not to take these seriously. In 1983 they remain happily married.

Anna didn't discourage her mother from moving to New York. When Alma found out that she would be able to realize a sizable profit from the sale of her house in Beverly Hills, she bought a building at 120 East 73rd Street with two apartments she could rent out, and a third for herself. Months passed before Alma was firmly established in Manhattan, where she felt more at home than she had since leaving Vienna.

Two rooms of her new apartment, which had a kitchen and bath down the hallway, were arranged to represent two powers of her life: the Power of Words, and the Power of Music. She called her parlor the Power of Words; it held books from floor to ceiling, and included the classics she had first learned through Max Burckhard, all of Franz's works, and volumes ranging from Plato to George Bernard Shaw. Most of the paintings in the parlor were Oskar's, among them his portrait of her that hung over an elaborate old secretary. There were so many works of art for such a small amount of wall space that Alma had to spread the objects over the backs of closed doors and perch the frames on filled shelves. Her furniture was minimal, and of mixed quality. There was a couch upon which one guest could sleep if absolutely necessary. In her bedroom — the Power of Music — there were another desk, a bed, a Bluethner piano, the cradle that Markart had made for her when she was born, baroque figures she had brought back from Vienna in 1947, a scene sketched by Ludwig Bemelmans for his novel *Now I Lay Me Down to Sleep,* and a safe holding her most valuable possessions. There were also the several paintings by her father that she had been able to find or retrieve, and photographs of her family — the dead always kept separate from the living. Gustav's picture was on the piano, in the place of honor. In moving Alma had disposed of much, including her two paintings by Paul Klee. For the better one she had been offered only eighty dollars, so she gave it to Stravinsky as a gift. She sent the other to a friend who was a priest.

In the autumn of 1952, settled in New York, Alma decided to make another trip to Europe. She would not go back to Vienna. The last two months of the year were spent in Paris and the first two months of 1953 in Rome, after which she traveled home by ship. On shipboard she met Thornton Wilder, with whom she built a lasting friendship. By post from his home in Hamden, Connecticut, and in person whenever he could visit her in New York, he expressed his devotion. "It is a great pleasure to exchange a jest with Alma Mahler-Werfel," he wrote. He called her "the soul of affirmation and self-reliance and courage." [10]

Alma had not abandoned the idea of a book about her own life, but the project had fallen into the hands of others. Precisely how much influence Alma herself had on the so-called autobiographies appearing in German and English is impossible to say. At the end of the English text there appears a quote from Wilder: "There is a land of the living and a land of the dead, and the bridge is love." The last five words became the title of the volume. Alma originally had planned another title, *Mein Leben: Der Schimmernde Weg* ("My Life: The Glittering Way"). The German version, which appeared shortly after the English one, is simply *Mein Leben*.

One of the happiest things Alma managed to accomplish when she moved to New York was to lure Sister Ida, "Schuli," to join her. Alma and her servant August had become so close that he had sent her poems on Mother's Day, but New York was not the place for him. Schuli could serve as cook, housekeeper, nurse, and also as daughter and friend. Alma depended on her completely.

In the vital musical circles of the East, people had begun to care a great deal about the name Mahler. Alma was invited to rehearsals, concerts, and receptions in New York, Boston, Philadelphia, and wherever one of the composer's works was being performed. She went out a good deal. When there was no opportunity to hear music or to be with people, she went on trying to retrieve her possessions from Vienna and challenging the forest of royalty statements from Franz's numerous publishers. She routinely invited people out to lunch — the time was more comfortable for her than the late hours that New Yorkers seemed to prefer for supper. Besides, the midday meal cost less. Alma always paid. She went from restaurant to restaurant until she found a few favorites. One of these was Chambourg, where she had bouillabaisse on Fridays. She liked Italian food at Gino's and lunch at the Plaza, but she never ate heartily. She picked small pieces from her plate and took only the tiniest cookies for dessert. Her calories came from the Benedictine.

On rare occasions, Alma saw one or another of Franz's relatives. Walter Gropius visited her whenever he came to New York. When word arrived that her granddaughter Alma, now an adult, would visit her, Alma was taken aback. This lanky young woman's presence in the apartment turned out, however, to be a pleasure. Both Almas enjoyed each other's company until the younger fainted. The doctor, summoned to tend a medical emergency, smiled when he announced that the patient was healthy and pregnant. Alma Mahler was stunned. The father, it turned out, was a prominent Viennese politician who was married and with whom the younger Alma had had an extended affair. Alma shipped her granddaughter off to Anna in California, where the baby girl was born. Great-grandmother Alma paid no attention to the child.

In the autumn of 1954, Alma went to Rome. It fell to her daughter Anna to take care of business in Vienna. This included seeing that Rodin's bust of her father was properly restored to its rightful place at the Opera. Alma later claimed it had been put on a spurious and lesser pedestal that should have held the bust of Strauss, but the chore was nevertheless accomplished in reasonable measure. Anna also went to the cemetery to inspect the graves of Gustav and Manon, about

which Alma and Walter were both concerned. From Linz, Alma received a letter from Hollnsteiner, who was teaching at the university in the town most closely associated with Bruckner. "Through you, by your hand, I became another person," he wrote.[11] Alma wanted nothing to do with him.

With terrierlike tenacity, Alma carried on negotiations with the bureaucrats in New York who could permit her to raise the rents she charged. She filled many days in communication with attorneys, state agencies, and tenants. When she wanted visitors, she telephoned friends and commanded their presence peremptorily, generally naming an hour in the late afternoon. Alma's tea meant cocktails; if she knew a friend's preference, it was always on hand. She hardly ever served a meal in her rooms, largely because there was so little space for tables and chairs, but also because her hearing had deteriorated to the point at which she needed to sit directly beside the person with whom she was conversing. Her seventy-fifth birthday passed with little fanfare. Her energy was limited.

Jean and Walter Kerr's adaptation of *Bernadette* ran for several weeks at the Xavier Theater on West 16th Street. The version for young theater troupes had received Franz's blessing. Alma was interested, but not impressed. She was enjoying being Alma Mahler more than Alma Mahler-Werfel. Gustav's music was back in fashion; Franz's reputation was on the wane.

Alma did more work on what would appear as her autobiography, culling through hotel stationery and matchbooks to recall places and people from her past. What she offered to her collaborators was a German typescript combining bits of narrative with excerpts from her diaries. She paid little attention to dates. Alma did not type, and had no concept of what was necessary to put together a book. At one point she considered naming the volume *Jeder Mensch weisst Alles,* but this idea was not pursued.

E. B. Ashton prepared the book for publication in English as *And the Bridge Is Love.* On the last day the text could have been halted or altered in any major way, Anna was in New York. Kathe Berl was concerned, knowing Alma neither could nor would give the book serious attention and fearing that it might misrepresent her or cause trouble with some of the many persons who had figured in her life. Anna and Kathe met on the corner of Lexington Avenue and 73rd Street at an appointed hour so that they could talk in peace, without constant interruptions from Alma. Anna had read the book and assured Kathe it was harmless. It was, to be sure, more harmless than it might have been, since Mrs. Scherman, Kathy's mother, had read what had been submitted and expressed her shock to her husband. They had insisted on behalf of simple decency that the publishers have the volume reworked. The English edition had very little to do with Alma's original work.

The German edition, called *Mein Leben,* came closer to the truth, thanks to the sensitive editing of Willi Haas. The text still contained a number of misrepresentations, however, and Alma, able to read the German version, threatened to sue the publishers, completely without grounds. The response to both books was heartening, and Anna encouraged Alma to write more. She never did.

Alma enjoyed her life in the musical community. In 1959, Benjamin Britten wrote asking for permission to dedicate to her "one of my best and most personal works," the Nocturne for tenor and small orchestra.[12] Alma assented with pleasure. Leonard Bernstein wrote to her every time he conducted a symphony by Mahler. He led the resurgence of interest in the music that, in turn, led to the growth of the royalty checks going to Alma. She attended rehearsals whenever she could, and almost always went to performances, where she was the honored guest. Once, at dinner at the Bernsteins', she was shocked by the vast size of their dwelling, evidently forgetting the twenty-eight rooms she had once commanded in Vienna.

In December 1960, when Georg Solti was making his first appearances at the Metropolitan Opera conducting Wagner's *Tannhaeuser,* Alma invited him and his wife Hedi to tea. The Soltis accepted and had to be a bit late because of his rehearsal schedule. Alma didn't tolerate lateness, and would usually accuse guests of being inconsiderate when they arrived after the appointed hour by saying, threateningly, "I have waited." She accepted the Soltis' excuse. When they arrived at her apartment, they found their hostess in her parlor with several other women. Alma directed Mrs. Solti to a chair among the females and put the conductor in the seat next to her, paying attention only to him through the dusk and into the evening. Her blue eyes were still commanding, and she had her old way of making the one person with whom she had established contact feel as if he (rarely a woman) were the only person in the world.

Alma was confused and dissatisfied by the rumors she heard about the reconstruction by Derryck Cooke of Mahler's Tenth Symphony. In February 1961, she wrote to the British Broadcasting Corporation ordering that there be no more broadcasts of performances of the symphony in its lengthened version. In the same month, Dr. Arthur Bookman wrote to Alma to refer her to the League for the Hard of Hearing. She never sought contact with these people who might have been of help. She was failing, and she did not like it. On her eightieth birthday, August 31, 1959, she scrawled on her calendar page a brief note saying she wished she were home in Vienna. She came to believe she was there, in the house of her childhood in Plankenburg, with her mother and father. In September 1962 Leonard Bernstein invited her to his rehearsals of Gustav's Eighth Symphony with the New York Philharmonic. Her interest in such events diminished when Oskar turned up in New York, the "evil demon," and asked for permission to visit her. Alma agonized over the opportunity, then decided to say no. She didn't want him to see her as an old and feeble woman. He sent her a cable: "Dear Alma, In my *Windsbraut* in Basel we are eternally united."

On August 31, 1964, Alma celebrated her eighty-fifth birthday. She had low blood pressure and something that might have been a form of diabetes. She thought the latter a "Jewish disease" and would not admit even to the possibility that she was suffering from it. Although a sore on her tongue would not heal, she refused to see a doctor. She did not like doctors, and believed that to be ill was an imperfection. Physicians had convinced her to switch from Benedictine, and when she went out to lunch she tried to drink martinis, but they tasted like turpentine. She invited friends to visit her on Sunday afternoons, but there were fewer and fewer individuals whom she could summon, so she lost enthusiasm for these salons. Nevertheless, she rose every morning and put on her pancake makeup and lipstick, a black dress, a jacket, a pink silk slip with pink silk flowers embroidered over the tatters, and never any panties.

Alma's strength failed and Anna was summoned from California late in 1964. Her mother had come to believe she had met the Crown Prince Rudolf of Austria on a mountaintop and he wanted to have a child with her. She thought she still lived in Plankenburg. Pneumonia set in. Alma died in her bed on Friday, December 11, 1964.

•POSTLUDE•

WITH THE RESURGENCE of public interest in Gustav's music, and with her own encouragement, Alma's legend had grown to a point where her own death commanded as much media attention as Franz's — and Gustav's. Much of the information for the obituaries was provided by Anna Mahler.

From the *New York Times* of December 12, 1964:

ALMA M. WERFEL,
WIDOW OF WRITER
She was also married to Mahler and Gropius.
Mrs. Werfel, who was once described as "the most beautiful girl in Vienna," recalled in her autobiography that she had always been attracted to genius. She noted that she had once confided to her first husband, Mahler, that what she really loved in a man were his achievements . . . Her intellect, which was nurtured by her brilliant father, complemented her beauty.

The *New York Telegram* announced the death thus:

ALMA WERFEL, 85,
WIDOW OF MAHLER
Mrs. Alma Mahler Werfel, 85, "the most beautiful woman in Vienna" at the turn of the century and the widow of the

composer Gustav Mahler, died yesterday at her home . . . Mrs. Werfel, who was born Alma Schindler, daughter of the Austrian landscape painter Emil J. Schindler, also was married to Walter Gropius the architect, and to Franz Werfel, the writer and poet . . . Mahler died in 1911 and his widow said she chose the expressionist painter, Oskar Kokoschka, as the next "feather for her nest."

By 1915, she had renewed acquaintance with Gropius and their marriage followed. Their daughter, Manon, died in her teens. While married to the architect, she met and fell in love with Werfel.

Gropius agreed to a divorce and his ex-wife went to live with her new lover. They were finally married in 1929. Werfel died in 1945 at the age of 54. His wife was 65.

During those years, there were other men in her life.

Among them, according to Werfel, were Gerhart Hauptmann, the German dramatist and poet; Dr. Paul Kammerer, the biologist; and Ossip Gabrilowitsch, the Russian pianist and conductor.

One literary critic commenting on her autobiography noted that "she missed Thomas Mann and, so far as the reader can make out, there was nothing between her and Richard Strauss."

Five years ago, Mrs. Werfel was asked how she kept busy at the age of 80.

"All night long," she said, "I read the Greek philosophers. Sometimes, I go during the day to a rehearsal or a concert. Never do I go out at night. And friends come in the afternoon to visit."

Geniuses? "Ah, no, it is sad. There are so few. Leonard Bernstein, Thornton Wilder. I cannot think of any others. It is not as it used to be."

A less tactful and high-minded writer in Los Angeles had asked Alma how she had managed to attract so many famous men to be her lovers. Ah, she answered, they were not great lovers, none of them was even particularly well endowed. But she flattered them. This, she said, had made them all feel very important.

The legend of the octogenarian Alma turned absurd.

On January 9, 1965, the *Dallas Morning News* printed a story by John Rosenfield:

ALMA WERFEL DIES:
GENIUS GALLERY

By simple logic, artistic creativity is emotional. Healthy emotionalism is of heterosexual origin and romantic voltage. Sex and/or love is arcanic even in this candid day. Its votal secrets are known fully to the participants only; they remain a closed book behind closed doors.

"All were geniuses, geniuses," once rhapsodized Alma Werfel about her official husbands . . . Her late [*sic*] autobiography . . . adds other "geniuses" without benefit of clergy. By her own statement, her loves included Oskar Kokoschka, the painter; Gerhart Hauptmann, the dramatist; Paul Kammerer, the biologist, and Ossip Gabrilowitsch, the pianist, conductor, and later husband of Clara Clemens . . . daughter of Mark Twain . . .

The late Mrs. Werfel was a monument to extraordinary facts of life. One was the puissance of romantic love, even in this century. Another was the basic utility of romantic love in the sublimations of artistic expression.

Another was, of course, that womanhood itself is a primordial career.

There never has been justification, in our opinion, for the claims through successive generations that Alma was merely a headhunter, a collector of geniuses. She was a vital part of their geniuses. She was involuntarily a part of a star-smitten life-force.

As a cynical American mother once advised her daughter, "Only marry for love, but make sure you go around only with rich men." The cosmos of the arts was the only envi-

ronment of "the most beautiful girl in Vienna." She knew
only geniuses.

Alma's funeral was held at the Frank E. Campbell Funeral
Home on Madison Avenue in Manhattan. One of her father's drawings was hung on the wall behind the coffin, and
tuber roses filled every empty space. The service itself was
almost as incongruous as the one that had been held for
Franz two decades earlier. The music was recorded; it was
not Gustav's. A priest addressed the small congregation —
only a few of the people who had wanted to attend could
be fitted into the little room. The eulogy was delivered by
Summa Morgenstern, a dear friend during Alma's later years
who spoke with the kind of thick Yiddish accent the de-
ceased had mocked and scorned.

After the service, the disposition of the body caused further friction. Some claimed Alma had wanted to be buried
in California with Franz. Others, those who prevailed, believed she would have wanted to be interred alongside
Manon, Gustav, and Maria. Alma's coffin began its trip back
to her native country while friends held a festive wake at
her old apartment in New York.

❧

Oskar Kokoschka lived on in Switzerland until 1979. His
obituary in the *New York Times* called him

> an intense participant in the literary, artistic, theatrical and
> political life of the 20th century . . . a painter, writer,
> graphic artist, illustrator, teacher and humanist. He is known
> especially for the penetrating portraits of his early years, in
> which he achieved psychological and emotional depth by
> means of a nervous, tense line and an "expressive" use of
> distortion, and for his later paintings of cities, done in a

mystical, imaginative vein that expressed the largeness of the metropolis and its power.

As a rebellious young man caught up in the cultural ferment of pre–World War I Vienna, Mr. Kokoschka became a cause célèbre, known for both the "decadent" quality of his art and for his authorship of two plays dealing with sex and violence . . . In 1912, he began an ardent love affair that was to last three years with Alma Mahler, the widow of the composer Gustav Mahler. The two lived and traveled together, and in 1913 the artist produced an allegorical representation of their liaison that is considered one of his greatest works, an intense, Baroque canvas that depicts the two lovers lying together in a cockleshell whirling through space . . .

On Sunday, Valentine's Day 1982, the *Washington Post* printed the following item in its newsy column called "Limelight":

ALMA MATER [*sic*]

When song-and-snipe man Tom Lehrer was in town at the end of December to oversee the production of Arena Stage's production of "Tomfoolery," he was asked why the song "Alma" was not included in the show.

"Oh," he said, "there does seem to be an Alma cult, but for most people it would take too much explaining . . ."

So much, you might think, for Alma.

But there, lo and behold, at the base of the railroad trestle at the foot of Arizona Avenue and Canal Road, someone has spray-painted against the background of endless years of mostly unintelligible graffiti . . .

GUSTAV MAHLER

ALMA

Oh, Gustav Mahler loved her all right, but so did Walter

Gropius, Franz Werfel and, as Lehrer says, "practically all the top creative men in Central Europe." Alma Schindler Mahler Gropius Werfel was, you might say, the Liz Taylor of the Bauhaus.

Lehrer wrote the famous, or infamous, song shortly after Alma's death, when he was a professor of mathematics at Harvard. In the belief that Alma would have been amused, and in the sure knowledge that ducks do envy swans, the lyric is reprinted here:

The loveliest girl in Vienna
Was Alma, the smartest as well.
Once you picked her up on your antenna
You'd never be free of her spell.

Her lovers were many and varied
from the day she began her . . . beguine.
There were three famous ones whom she married
And God knows how many between.

Alma, tell us,
All modern women are jealous,
Which of your magical wands
Got you Gustav and Walter and Franz?

The first one she married was Mahler,
Whose buddies all knew him as Gustav.
And each time he saw her he'd holler,
"Ach, that is the Fraeulein I must haff!"

Their marriage however was murder.
He'd scream to the heavens above,
"I'm writing Das Lied von der Erde,
And she only wants to make love."

Alma, tell us,
All modern women are jealous,
You should have a statue in bronze
For bagging Gustav and Walter and Franz.

While married to Gus she met Gropius,
And soon she was swinging with Walter.
Gus died and her teardrops were copious.
She cried all the way to the altar.

But he would work late at the Bauhaus,
And only came home now and then.
She said, "Vat am I running, a chowhouse?"
It's time to change partners again.

Alma, tell us,
All modern women are jealous.
Though you didn't even use Ponds,
You got Gustav and Walter and Franz.

While married to Walt she'd met Werfel,
And he, too, was caught in her net.
He married her, but he was careful,
'Cause Alma was no Bernadette.

And that is the story of Alma,
Who knew how to receive and to give.
The body that reached her embalma
Was one that had known how to live.

Alma, tell us,
How can they help being jealous?
Ducks always envy the swans
Who get Gustav and Walter — you never did falter —
With Gustav and Walter and Franz.

Notes
Select Bibliography
Index
❧

•NOTES•

REFERENCES to published works cited throughout the notes are abbreviated. For full documentation, consult the Select Bibliography following the notes. Unpublished material is documented at the beginning of the bibliography.
AM-W refers to Alma, and GM to Gustav Mahler.
All translations are by the author except where otherwise credited.

Chapter 1. Alma Maria Schindler (pages 1–21)

Details of Alma's youth have been taken from the two so-called autobiographies, *And the Bridge Is Love* and *Mein Leben,* as well as from the author's interviews with Anna Mahler (September 1981), Kathe Berl (1979–1980), and Anna Marie Maier-Graefe (November 1979).

1. Extensive information on Jakob Emil Schindler and his work is available in the archives of the City of Vienna, Austria.
2. For further information on Gustav Klimt and the cultural climate of Vienna at the turn of the century, see Strobl, *Gustav Klimt: Drawings and Paintings;* Janik and Toulmin, *Wittgenstein's Vienna;* Metropolitan Museum of Art, *The Imperial Style: Fashions of the Hapsburg Era;* and Schorske, *Fin-de-Siècle Vienna: Politics and Culture.*
3. Information on Alma's studies and relation with Alexander von Zemlinsky is primarily from her diaries and his letters to her.
4. AM-W, *And the Bridge Is Love,* p. 14.
5. Ibid.
6. Undated letter from Zemlinsky to Alma.
7. Ibid.
8. Undated letter (1900), ibid.
9. Undated letter (1901?), ibid.
10. Ibid.
11. Ibid.

12. Ibid.
13. Letter (probably 1901) from Zemlinsky to Alma, quoting her remark to him.

Chapter 2. The Most Beautiful Girl in Vienna (pages 22–44)

Background material in this chapter has been taken from AM-W, *Mein Leben* and *And the Bridge Is Love,* and from La Grange, *Mahler,* vol. 1. For further information on the life of Gustav Mahler, see also Blaukopf, *Mahler: A Documentary Study;* Gartenberg, *Mahler: The Man and His Music;* and Wiesmann, *Gustav Mahler in Vienna.*

1. La Grange, *Mahler,* vol. 1, p. 668.
2. AM-W, *Gustav Mahler: Memories and Letters,* p. 15.
3. Author's translation of the poem. Ibid., p. 16.
4. Ibid., p. 18.
5. Ibid.
6. Ibid., p. 19.
7. Ibid., p. 207.
8. La Grange, *Mahler,* p. 675.
9. AM-W, *Gustav Mahler: Memories and Letters,* p. 207.
10. Ibid., p. 208.
11. Ibid., p. 209.
12. Ibid.
13. La Grange, *Mahler,* p. 678.
14. Ibid., pp. 678–79.
15. AM-W, *Gustav Mahler: Memories and Letters,* pp. 210–11.
16. Ibid., pp. 211–12.
17. Ibid., p. 214.
18. Ibid., p. 216.
19. Ibid., p. 218.
20. La Grange, *Mahler,* pp. 684–90.

Chapter 3. Alma Schindler Mahler (pages 45–72)

Reminiscences in this chapter taken from AM-W, *Mein Leben* and *And the Bridge Is Love,* and AM-W diaries.

1. AM-W, *Gustav Mahler: Memories and Letters*, pp. 218–19.
2. AM-W diaries, January 5, 1901.
3. Ibid., early 1901.
4. Ibid.
5. AM-W, *Gustav Mahler: Memories and Letters*, p. 55.
6. See ibid., pp. 77 ff.
7. AM-W diaries.
8. Ibid., July 1904.
9. Ibid.
10. AM-W, *Gustav Mahler: Memories and Letters*, p. 244.
11. Ibid., p. 243.
12. Ibid.
13. AM-W diaries, January 1905.

Chapter 4. *New York — The Metropolitan Opera (pages 73–99)*

1. See AM-W, *Gustav Mahler: Memories and Letters*, p. 282.
2. Ibid., p. 289.
3. The diagram, ibid., p. 290.
4. GM, *Gustav Mahler: Selected Letters*, p. 301.
5. Ibid.
6. AM-W, *Gustav Mahler: Memories and Letters*, p. 303.
7. GM, *Gustav Mahler: Selected Letters*, p. 311.
8. Ibid., p. 319.
9. Ibid., p. 321.
10. Ibid., pp. 321–22.
11. Ibid., pp. 322–23.
12. AM-W, *Gustav Mahler: Memories and Letters*, p. 306.
13. See GM, *Gustav Mahler: Selected Letters*, p. 328.
14. Ibid., pp. 329–30.
15. Ibid., p. 331.
16. Ibid., p. 333.
17. AM-W, *Gustav Mahler: Memories and Letters*, p. 151.
18. GM, *Gustav Mahler: Selected Letters*, p. 339.
19. AM-W, *Gustav Mahler: Memories and Letters*, pp. 319–20.
20. Ibid., pp. 322–23.
21. Ibid., p. 323.
22. Ibid., p. 324.
23. GM, *Gustav Mahler: Selected Letters*, p. 346.

Chapter 5. *Crisis — Walter Gropius (pages 100–118)*

Reminiscences in this chapter have been taken from AM-W, *Mein Leben* and *And the Bridge Is Love,* and from conversations with Kathe Berl and Anna Mahler.

1. GM, *Gustav Mahler: Selected Letters,* pp. 348–49.
2. Ibid., p. 350.
3. Ibid., p. 353.
4. AM-W, *Gustav Mahler: Memories and Letters,* p. 172.
5. Ibid., pp. 328–29.
6. Ibid., p. 329.
7. GM, *Gustav Mahler: Selected Letters,* p. 359.
8. Ibid., pp. 362–63.
9. Ibid., p. 363.
10. AM-W, *Gustav Mahler: Memories and Letters,* p. 175.
11. Ibid., p. 333.
12. Ibid., pp. 333–34.
13. Ibid., p. 335.
14. Translation of Rueckert's poem is by the author.
15. AM-W, *Gustav Mahler: Memories and Letters,* p. 335.
16. Ibid., p. 336.
17. Ibid., pp. 337–38.
18. Ibid., p. 178.
19. Ibid., p. 342.

Chapter 6. *Gustav's Death (pages 119–132)*

1. Information about Mahler's continuing negotiations with the Vienna Opera and similar details are from Blaukopf, *Mahler: A Documentary Study,* pp. 268 ff.
2. GM, *Gustav Mahler: Selected Letters,* p. 368.
3. From *New-Yorker Staats-Zeitung,* May 21, 1911.
4. Blaukopf, *Mahler: A Documentary Study,* p. 270.
5. AM-W, *Gustav Mahler: Memories and Letters,* p. 186.
6. GM, *Gustav Mahler: Selected Letters,* p. 371.
7. This quotation and information on Mahler's last concert are from Blaukopf, *Mahler: A Documentary Study,* pp. 271–72.
8. AM-W, *Gustav Mahler: Memories and Letters,* p. 192.

9. *Neue Freie Presse* quoted in Blaukopf, *Mahler: A Documentary Study,* p. 272.
10. *Neue Freie Presse,* May 12, 1911, as quoted ibid.
11. *Neues Wiener Tagblatt* (Vienna), May 13, 1911, as quoted ibid., p. 273.
12. Information on Mahler's financial status is from conversations with Anna Mahler and from Blaukopf, *Mahler: A Documentary Study,* pp. 273–74.

Chapter 7. *The Widow with a New Genius* *(pages 133–162)*

Much of the information concerning Alma's reaction to Mahler's death is from conversations with Anna Mahler; see also AM-W, *And the Bridge Is Love* and *Mein Leben.*

1. AM-W, *And the Bridge Is Love,* p. 68.
2. Ibid.
3. Undated letters (mid-1911 to early 1912) of Paul Kammerer to Alma.
4. Ibid.
5. Ibid.
6. Ibid.
7. Ibid.
8. For further information on the life of Oskar Kokoschka see: Gatl, *Kokoschka;* Hodin, *Kokoschka: The Artist and His Time;* and Kokoschka, *My Life.*
9. Kokoschka, *My Life,* p. 25.
10. Ibid., pp. 26–27.
11. Ibid., p. 27.
12. Ibid., pp. 72–73.
13. Letter from Kokoschka to Alma, April 15, 1912.
14. Ibid., undated.
15. Ibid.
16. Ibid.
17. Ibid., April 30, 1912.
18. AM-W diaries.
19. Ibid.
20. Letter from Kokoschka to Alma, summer 1912.
21. Ibid.
22. Ibid.

23. AM-W diaries, 1913.
24. Ibid., early 1913.
25. Ibid.
26. Ibid., August 1913.
27. Ibid., fall 1913.
28. Letter from Kokoschka to Alma, autumn 1913.
29. Ibid.
30. Ibid., early 1914.
31. Ibid.
32. Both poems are in the Mahler-Werfel Collection.
33. AM-W diaries, May 17, 1914.
34. Ibid., May 20, 1914.
35. Ibid.
36. Ibid.
37. Kokoschka, *My Life*, p. 84.
38. AM-W diaries.
39. The Violin Concerto Alban Berg composed in 1935 and dedicated "To the Memory of an Angel" (Alma's daughter Manon Gropius) employs material from the same cantata by J. S. Bach.

Chapter 8. Alma Schindler Mahler Gropius (pages 163–181)

Details and impressions of Alma's relationship with Walter Gropius and with her children have been taken from interviews with Kathe Berl and Anna Mahler.

1. AM-W diaries, early September, 1914.
2. Ibid., October 6, 1914.
3. Letter from Joseph Fraenkel to Alma, late 1914, Mahler-Werfel Collection.
4. AM-W diaries, late 1914.
5. Ibid., October 1914.
6. Ibid.
7. Letter from Kokoschka to Alma, late 1914.
8. AM-W diaries, December 23, 1914.
9. Letter from Kokoschka to Alma, undated (December 1914/January 1915?).
10. AM-W diaries, January 15, 1915.
11. Kokoschka, *My Life*, p. 84.

12. AM-W diaries, February 2, 1915.
13. Ibid., spring 1915.
14. Ibid.
15. Letter from Kokoschka to Alma, spring 1915.
16. AM-W diaries, spring 1915.
17. Ibid., August 19, 1915.
18. Ibid., September 16, 1915.
19. Letter from Kokoschka to Alma, November 7, 1915.
20. Kokoschka, *My Life*, p. 73.
21. AM-W diaries, January 1916.
22. Kokoschka, *My Life*, pp. 74–75.
23. Ibid., p. 96.
24. AM-W diaries, summer 1916.
25. Ibid., autumn 1916.
26. Ibid.
27. Ibid.
28. Ibid.
29. AM-W, *And the Bridge Is Love*, p. 91.

Chapter 9. Franzl — Poet and Revolutionary (pages 182–202)

Impressions and some details concerning Franz Werfel and his work have come from interviews with Anna Mahler, Kathe Berl, and Albrecht Joseph, as well as from letters in the Mahler-Werfel Collection, and AM-W, *Mein Leben* and *And the Bridge Is Love*.

1. AM-W diaries, autumn 1916.
2. AM-W, *And the Bridge Is Love*, p. 97.
3. AM-W diaries, January 1, 1918.
4. Ibid., January 5, 1918.
5. Ibid.
6. Letter from Werfel to Alma, January 18, 1918.
7. Ibid., January 1918.
8. AM-W diaries, February 6, 1918.
9. Details of the events surrounding Werfel's visit are attributed to the diary Franz was allegedly keeping at Alma's behest, and recounted in AM-W, *And the Bridge Is Love*, pp. 102 ff.
10. In the Mahler-Werfel Collection.
11. Ibid.

12. Werfel, *Star of the Unborn,* pp. 372–75.
13. Details on the discussion of names for the child are from letters of Franz to Alma.
14. Details of the confrontation with Gropius are from AM-W, *And the Bridge Is Love,* pp. 119–22.
15. AM-W diaries, August 1918.
16. Ibid., September 1918.
17. Ibid.
18. Ibid.
19. Letter from Franz to Alma, autumn 1918.
20. *Neues Wiener Journal,* November 21, 1918; also AM-W, *And the Bridge Is Love,* p. 127.

Chapter 10. The Complicated Family (pages 203–227)

Some of the details of family life have been taken from conversations with Anna Mahler, Albrecht Joseph, and Kathe Berl.

1. AM-W diaries, January 9, 1919.
2. Ibid., early 1919.
3. Ibid.
4. Ibid.
5. Ibid., February 2, 1919.
6. Ibid., February 1919.
7. Kokoschka, *My Life,* pp. 118 ff.
8. AM-W diaries, spring 1919.
9. Ibid.
10. Ibid.
11. Letter from Franz to Alma, spring 1919.
12. AM-W diaries, summer 1919.
13. Letter from Kokoschka to Alma, summer 1919.
14. AM-W diaries, summer 1919.
15. Letter from Franz to Alma, summer 1919.
16. AM-W diaries, July 1919.
17. Ibid.
18. AM-W, *Mein Leben,* p. 179.
19. AM-W diaries, late summer/early autumn 1919.
20. Ibid., November 1919.

21. Reminiscences of Alma's visit to Amsterdam are from AM-W, *And the Bridge Is Love, Mein Leben,* and AM-W diaries.
22. Manuscript of "To Alma" in the Mahler-Werfel Collection.
23. Reference in an undated letter from Franz to Alma.
24. Ibid., autumn 1920.
25. Ibid.
26. Reminiscences of Alma's meeting with Kokoschka are from AM-W diaries.
27. The saga of the electricity is recounted in AM-W diaries.
28. Ibid., December 1926.

Chapter 11. *The Essence of a Priest* (*pages 228–242*)

Much information in this chapter has been taken from interviews with Anna Mahler and Albrecht Joseph, from AM-W diaries, and, to a lesser extent, from AM-W, *Mein Leben* and *And the Bridge Is Love.*

1. AM-W diaries, early 1932.
2. Ibid., spring 1932.
3. Ibid.
4. Ibid.
5. Ibid.
6. Ibid.
7. Ibid.
8. Ibid.
9. Ibid., also AM-W, *And the Bridge Is Love,* p. 227.
10. AM-W diaries, May/June 1935.

Chapter 12. *Refugees* (*pages 243–268*)

Information in this chapter has been taken from conversations with Kathe Berl and Anna Mahler, from AM-W diaries, and, to a lesser extent, from AM-W, *Mein Leben* and *And the Bridge Is Love.*

1. AM-W diaries, April 1936.
2. Ibid., April/May 1936.
3. Ibid., June 2, 1936.
4. Ibid., summer 1936.

5. AM-W, *And the Bridge Is Love,* p. 233.
6. Ibid., pp. 233–34.
7. AM-W diaries, summer 1938.
8. Ibid., early 1939.
9. Ibid.
10. Ibid., spring 1939.
11. Ibid., April 1940.

Chapter 13. *America — Grateful and Unhappy (pages 269–289)*

Information in this chapter has been taken from Fry, *Surrender on Demand,* conversations with Kathe Berl and Luise Rainer, AM-W diaries, and AM-W, *Mein Leben* and *And the Bridge Is Love.*

1. AM-W, *And the Bridge Is Love,* p. 168.
2. Letter from Hanna Fuchs-Robettin to Franz, July 1941, Mahler-Werfel Collection.
3. AM-W diaries, autumn 1941.
4. Ibid., March 1942.
5. Ibid., May/June 1942.
6. Ibid., August 1942.
7. Interview with Kathe Berl.
8. AM-W diaries, August/September 1943.
9. Ibid.
10. Ibid., September 1943.
11. Ibid., November 1943.
12. Letter from Father Cyril Fischer to Alma, mid-December 1943, Mahler-Werfel Collection.
13. AM-W diaries, December 1943.

Chapter 14. *Years of Uncertainty (pages 290–298)*

Information in this chapter is taken from interviews with Albrecht Joseph, Anna Mahler, and Kathe Berl, and from AM-W diaries.

1. Horoscope and analysis by Carroll Righter, January 1944, Mahler-Werfel Collection.
2. Manuscript in the Mahler-Werfel Collection.

3. Details of Franz's death are from AM-W, *And the Bridge Is Love,* pp. 294 ff.

Chapter 15. *The Last Years (pages 299–318)*

Information in this chapter is taken from conversations with Kathe Berl, Anna Mahler, Albrecht Joseph, Anatole Fistoulari, Georg Solti, and Leonard Bernstein, and from AM-W's diaries and various letters and financial statements in the Mahler-Werfel Collection.

1. Letter from Willi Haas in the Mahler-Werfel Collection.
2. Letter from Hanna Fuchs-Robettin in the Mahler-Werfel Collection.
3. Letter from Gropius to Alma, September 1946.
4. For details of Alma's journey, see AM-W, *And the Bridge Is Love,* pp. 298 ff.
5. *The Saturday Review,* January 1949.
6. Ibid.
7. Ibid.
8. AM-W, *And the Bridge Is Love,* p. 303.
9. Ibid., pp. 304–5.
10. AM-W diaries, ca. 1953.
11. Ibid., autumn 1954.
12. Letter from Benjamin Britten to Alma, 1959, Mahler-Werfel Collection.

Postlude *(pages 319–326)*

Information not credited in these pages has been taken from the author's interviews.

•SELECT BIBLIOGRAPHY•

THE UNPUBLISHED MATERIAL referred to in this book is contained in the Mahler-Werfel Collection in the Charles Patterson Van Pelt Library of the University of Pennsylvania in Philadelphia. This extensive collection includes Alma's diary, memorabilia, and photographs, as well as letters sent to Alma by Alexander von Zemlinsky, Paul Kammerer, Oskar Kokoschka, Walter Gropius, Franz Werfel, Arnold Schoenberg, Alban and Helene Berg, Franz Schreker, her lawyers and counselors, and many others. Much of the written material in this archive has been typed in German by unidentified transcribers. The author's spot checks have revealed that these transcriptions were done faithfully, within the limitations of difficult handwriting, time's disintegration of paper, and the absence of Alma's own communications.

Bayer, Herbert, Walter Gropius, and Ise Gropius, eds. *Bauhaus, 1919–1928*. The Museum of Modern Art, New York, 1938.

Blaukopf, Kurt, comp. and ed. *Mahler: A Documentary Study*. Oxford University Press, New York, 1976.

Fry, Varian. *Surrender on Demand*. Random House, New York, 1944.

Gartenberg, Egon. *Mahler: The Man and His Music*. Schirmer Books, Macmillan Publishing Co., Inc., New York, 1978.

Gatl, Giuseppe. *Kokoschka*. Hamlyn Publishing Group Ltd., London, 1971.

Hodin, J. P. *Kokoschka: The Artist and His Time*. New York Graphic Society, Greenwich, Conn., 1966.

Janik, Allan, and Stephen Toulmin. *Wittgenstein's Vienna*. Touchstone/Simon & Schuster, New York, 1973.

Kokoschka, Oskar. *My Life,* trans. David Britt. Macmillan Publishing Company, New York, 1974.

La Grange, Henry-Louis de. *Mahler,* vol. 1. Doubleday & Company, Garden City, New York, 1973.

Mahler, Alma. *Gustav Mahler: Memories and Letters,* enlarged, revised edition, ed. Donald Mitchell, trans. Basil Creighton. The Viking Press, New York, 1969.

Mahler, Gustav. *Selected Letters,* ed. Knud Martner, trans. Eithne Wilkins, Ernst Kaiser, and Bill Hopkins. Farrar, Straus & Giroux, New York, 1979.

Mahler-Werfel, Alma. *Mein Leben.* S. Fischer Verlag, Frankfurt am Main, Germany, 1960.

Mahler-Werfel, Alma, in collaboration with E. B. Ashton. *And the Bridge Is Love.* Harcourt, Brace & Company, New York, 1958.

Metropolitan Museum of Art, The. *The Imperial Style: Fashions of the Hapsburg Era.* New York, 1980.

Monson, Karen. *Alban Berg.* Houghton Mifflin Company, Boston, 1979.

Schorske, Carl E. *Fin-de-Siècle Vienna: Politics and Culture.* Alfred A. Knopf, New York, 1980.

Strobl, Alice. *Gustav Klimt: Drawings and Paintings,* trans. Inga Hamilton. Rizzoli, New York, 1976.

Werfel, Franz. *The 40 Days of Musa Dagh,* trans. Geoffrey Dunlop. The Viking Press, New York, 1934.

Werfel, Franz. *Star of the Unborn,* trans. Gustav O. Arlt. The Viking Press, New York, 1946.

Wiesmann, Sigrid, ed. *Gustav Mahler in Vienna,* trans. Anne Shelley. Rizzoli International Publications, New York, 1976.

Wingler, Hans M. *The Bauhaus: Weimar, Dessau, Berlin, Chicago,* trans. Wolfgang Jabs and Basil Gilbert, ed. Joseph Stein. MIT Press, Cambridge, Massachusetts, 1978.

•INDEX•